Praise for

EVANGELICALISM AND THE POLITICS OF REFORM
IN NORTHERN BLACK THOUGHT, 1776–1863

"With a keen sense of historiography and vast research, Rita Roberts plumbs the American paradox of why black Americans, largely rejected by the white, founding generations of the republic, declared their allegiance to its ideals. Evangelical religion, she declares, gave black Americans faith in the imperfect republic. Her saga is a powerful corrective that black Americans lacked place in early American politics."

—GRAHAM HODGES
author of *David Ruggles: A Radical Black Abolitionist and the Underground Railroad in New York City*

"Rita Roberts's book shows why African American history is also American history, why neither can stand alone as a complete account of our past. Roberts introduces readers to several generations of influential black reformers for whom evangelical Protestantism provided a path to an American identity cleansed of its racial biases and truer to its own avowed commitment to fundamental human equality. This is a wise and learned book, but also a timely one."

—JAMES OAKES
author of *The Radical and the Republican: Frederick Douglass, Abraham Lincoln, and the Triumph of Antislavery Politics*

During the revolutionary age and in the early republic, when racial ideologies were evolving and slavery expanding, some northern blacks surprisingly came to identify very strongly with the American cause and to take pride in calling themselves American. In this intriguing study, Rita Roberts explores this phenomenon and offers an in-depth examination of the intellectual underpinnings of antebellum black activists. She shows how conversion to Christianity led a significant and influential population of northern blacks to view the developing American republic and their place in the new nation through the lens of evangelicalism. American identity, therefore, even the formation of an African ethnic community and later an African American identity, developed within the evangelical and republican ideals of the revolutionary age.

Evangelical values, Roberts contends, exerted a strong influence on the strategies of northern black reformist activities, specifically abolition, anti-racism, and black community development. The activists and reformers' commitment to the United States and firm determination to make the country live up to its national principles hinged on their continued faith in the possibility of the collective transformation of all Americans. The people of the United States—both black and white—they believed, would become a new citizenry, distinct from any population in the world because of their commitment to the tenets of the Christian republican faith.

Roberts explores the process by which a collective identity formed among northern free blacks and notes the ways in which ministers and other leaders established their African identity through an emphasis on shared oppression. She shows why, in spite of slavery's expansion in the 1820s and 1830s, northern blacks demonstrated more, not less, commitment to the nation. Roberts then examines the Christian influence on racial theories of some of the major abolitionist figures of the antebellum era, including Frederick Douglass, Martin Delany, and especially James McCune Smith, and reveals how activists' sense of their American identity waned with the intensity of American racism and the passage of laws that further protected slavery in the 1850s. But the Civil War and Emancipation Proclamation, she explains, renewed hope that America would soon become a free and equal nation.

Impeccably researched, *Evangelicalism and the Politics of Reform in Northern Black Thought, 1776–1863* offers an innovative look at slavery, abolition, and African American history.

RITA ROBERTS is a professor of history at Scripps College and the Intercollegiate Department of Africana Studies at Claremont in California.

EVANGELICALISM

AND THE POLITICS

OF REFORM

IN NORTHERN

BLACK THOUGHT

1776–1863

Antislavery, Abolition, and the Atlantic World

R. J. M. Blackett and James Brewer Stewart, SERIES EDITORS

Rita Roberts

EVANGELICALISM AND THE POLITICS OF REFORM IN NORTHERN BLACK THOUGHT 1776–1863

Louisiana State University Press Baton Rouge

Published by Louisiana State University Press
Copyright © 2010 by Louisiana State University Press
All rights reserved

Manufactured in the United States of America
First printing

DESIGNER: Mandy McDonald Scallan
TYPEFACES: Text, Whitman: Display, MrsEaves and No. 7 Type
PRINTER: McNaughton & Gunn, Inc.
BINDER: John Dekker and Sons, Inc.

Library of Congress Cataloging-in-Publication Data

Roberts, Rita.
  Evangelicalism and the politics of reform in northern Black thought, 1776–1863 / Rita Roberts.
     p. cm. — (Antislavery, abolition and the Atlantic world)
  Includes bibliographical references and index.
  ISBN 978-0-8071-3708-6 (cloth : alk. paper)
  1. African Americans—Race identity—Northeastern States. 2. African Americans—Religion—History. 3.
Evangelicalism—United States—History. 4. Republicanism—United States—History. 5. Free
African Americans—Northeastern States. 6. Antislavery movements—United States—History. I. Title.
  E185.9.R63 2010
  305.896'073--dc22

                                                                                    2010021248

The paper in this book meets the guidelines for permanence and durability of the Committee on Production
Guidelines for Book Longevity of the Council on Library Resources. ∞

to
Terry

CONTENTS

ACKNOWLEDGMENTS

This book could not have been written without the work of dedicated scholars who first compiled and edited for publication antebellum African American materials from obscure archival holdings. I am forever in Dorothy Porter's debt. Her compilation and editing of *Early Negro Writing, 1760–1837,* sparked my interest in exploring the values and ideas of free blacks in this period. Likewise, Howard Holman Bell's editing of the National Negro Convention records complemented Porter's work, allowing for a better understanding of northern black activism. Other editors of African American documents to whom I owe a great debt include Herbert Aptheker, John Blassingame, Philip Foner, George Walker, and C. Peter Ripley, who with his colleagues edited the invaluable *Black Abolitionist Papers.* I am also grateful for the many librarians who took special interest in this project. Librarians at the Schomburg Library in Harlem and the Boston Public Library were especially helpful, and I owe a special note of gratitude to Philip Lapsansky at the Library Company of Philadelphia, who never tired of my multiple requests for materials. The Huntington Library in San Marino, California, was my home away from campus for several years, providing the much needed space to think and write. I also benefited from the wisdom of several colleagues who read and commented in-depth on portions of this work, including Claremont colleagues Tony Crowley, Stuart McConnell, and David Yoo, and those outside Claremont: Spencer Crew, Eric Foner, Adam Green, Graham Hodges, James Horton, Emma Jones Lapsansky-Werner, and Gary Nash. To my friend and colleague James Oakes I owe a special debt of gratitude for his encouragement, thorough reading, precise editing, and incisive comments on almost all of the chapters. While Albert Raboteau was not directly involved in this project, I have benefited tremendously from his work and consistent support. I am especially grateful to Richard Blackett and James B. Stewart, the editors of the Louisiana State University Press series

"Antislavery, Abolition, and the Atlantic World," who included this study in their series and, along with the anonymous readers for LSU Press, helped me develop a more comprehensive interpretation of northern black thought. Special thanks, too, to Derik Shelor for his diligent editing and Rand Dotson of LSU Press for seeing the book through completion. Dedication of this book to Terrence Roberts does not begin to express my appreciation for being with me and for me.

EVANGELICALISM

AND THE POLITICS

OF REFORM

IN NORTHERN

BLACK THOUGHT

1776–1863

Introduction

Since the late 1980s, northern free black experience has come under increased scholarly scrutiny. The pathbreaking studies of W.E.B. DuBois's *The Philadelphia Negro* (1899), Leon Litwack's *North of Slavery* (1961), Benjamin Quarles's *Black Abolitionists* (1969), and James Horton and Lois Horton's *Black Bostonians* (1979) constituted most of the scholarship before the 1980s on African Americans living in the northern states before the Civil War.

Since then, studies of northern blacks have multiplied significantly. James Horton and Lois Horton have broadened their community study of Boston to include an examination of African American culture and communities in the entire northern region in several articles and essays and in their book *In Hope of Liberty* (1997). Patrick Rael's astute study *Black Identity and Black Protest in the Antebellum North* (2002), follows the Hortons' regional perspective but focuses more on the ideological foundations of northern black activism and the ways in which elite African Americans appropriated and appealed to the dominant society's ideals and values for gaining rights of citizenship. Studies of black activism in some major cities of the North such as Julie Winch's *Philadelphia's Black Elite* (1988), Gary Nash's *Forging Freedom* (1988), and especially Leslie Harris's *In the Shadow of Slavery* (2003) address not only community formation but also the significance of the development of a middle class that increasingly became distant from the northern black majority, who were generally illiterate and either poor or working class. These urban studies add to our understanding of not only growing, and perhaps inevitable, class conflict among northern blacks, but also distinct interests and means of protest.

A more specific yet intellectually broad recent study is Craig S. Wilder's book *In the Company of Black Men* (2001), in which the role of New York City African societies is examined for understanding the foundation of African American cultural development. At the same time, Erica Armstrong Dunbar has contributed to our understanding of the significant role women played in the formation of the Philadelphia free black community in her book, *A Fragile Freedom* (2008). Other important works, such as Mia Bay's *The White Image in the Black Mind* (2000) and Bruce Dain's *A Hideous Monster of the Mind* (2002), include Revolutionary and/or antebellum northern black ideas about racial ideology in their studies of African American racial ideas into the twentieth century or American ideas about race in the early republic.

Individual activists have also come under close scholarly scrutiny in David Blight's definitive book on Frederick Douglass, *Frederick Douglass' Civil War* (1989), in Julie Winch's recent comprehensive and insightful study of one of the wealthiest African Americans in pre–Civil War America, James Forten, *A Gentleman of Color* (2002), and in Richard S. Newman's important biography of African Methodist Episcopal founder Richard Allen, *Freedom's Prophet* (2008). The thoughts and values of some black abolitionists are also examined in contrast to certain white abolitionists in studies such as John Stauffer's *The Black Hearts of Men* (2002) and Richard S. Newman's *The Transformation of American Abolitionism* (2002). The above studies and others in the field enable close examination of specific aspects of the life, activism, and experience of the people of the "first emancipation."

This book expands historical understanding of the multiple dimensions of early American character through an exploration of the thoughts, ideas, and values of an influential population of northern free blacks living between the Revolution and the Civil War. It amplifies the above scholarship, particularly Rael's study of the ideological foundations of protest, through a further examination of the intellectual underpinnings of northern black activism and community development. With a stress on the voice of the subjects of the study, *Evangelicalism and the Politics of Reform* asks why a significant portion of the population of African descent identified strongly with the American cause during the Revolutionary age and took pride in calling themselves American at a time of evolving racial ideology and expanding slavery. The argument stated succinctly is that as a consequence of conversion to Christianity, a significant and influential population of northern blacks viewed the developing American republic and their place in the new nation through the lens of evangelicalism. Hence American identity, even the formation of an African ethnic community and later an African American identity, developed within the evangelical/ republican ideals of the Revolutionary age. From the late eighteenth century into the nineteenth century, evangelical values influenced the strategies of northern black reformist activities, specifically abolition, antiracism, and black community development. The activists'/reformers' commitment to the United States and firm determination to make the country live up to its national principles of liberty and equality hinged on their continued faith in the possibility of individual and collective transformation of all Americans. Americans, black and white, would become a new people, distinct from any population in the world, because of their Christian republican faith. Northern black reformers' faith in the United States wavered in the 1850s, but the coming of the Civil War renewed their hope that America would soon become a free and equal nation in which common citizenship would be based on allegiance to the Declaration of Independence and the Constitution, not on race.

More specifically, as a consequence of their evangelical faith, a significant number of African Americans living in the North reflected American political, social, and economic thought in critical ways. That is, black thought from the Revolution to the Civil War was framed within pervasive ideologies or belief systems that were evolving in the United States, but with distinct and important differences. Northern free blacks embraced Protestant evangelical republican principles and the new market economy based in capitalism, but at the same time they stressed the universality of republican ideals of freedom and equality in their vision of the new country. In this sense of what would become known as civic nationalism, those who took on leadership positions in the late eighteenth century established an evangelicalism distinct from the dominant society that persisted throughout the period of study.

Black evangelicalism was both sacred and political; it involved a firm commitment to the evangelical principles of a Bible-centered religion that stressed the conversion experience as central to the Christian life. At the same time, black evangelicalism centered on biblical precepts that asserted equality and freedom. The republican principles coming out of the Revolution asserting natural rights were, to the black evangelical's mind, founded in Scripture. To inculcate their understanding of Christian principles to the northern black majority, ministers, in particular, believed physical distance from whites was essential. They also thought it was necessary to establish a common black identity for ethnic solidarity as a means to achieve their vision of African Americans' place in the new nation. Their means became in the ensuing years a critical element of black evangelicalism, though it remained hotly contested then and perhaps now. Ultimately, leaders expected people of African ancestry to become full-fledged citizens of the new republic, a nation founded on the principles established in Christianity, the Declaration of Independence, and the Constitution. In other words, they broadened the notion of evangelical conversion to national proportions. Evangelical Christianity would provide the foundation for the new republic. With its transformative power it would enable Americans to practice their founding principles. Influenced by the multi-varied and inchoate millennial themes of the late eighteenth century, they envisioned a new nation that they hoped to shape in meaningful ways.

Even African American rejection of racial ideology, a central feature directing American laws and policy, relied on general and pervasive ideas, values, and belief systems of the larger society. Likewise, although this book does not develop this latter point, many northern blacks who emigrated outside the United States remained committed to early nineteenth-century American thoughts and ideals, namely evangelicalism. Most northern blacks who participated in conventions, edited and/or published newspapers, served as ministers, were active in the abolitionist and temperance movements, or wrote petitions, narratives, autobiographies, or letters viewed themselves and other blacks as thoroughgoing Americans engaged in directing the course of the new nation.

Emphasis in this book on the influence of religion and Anglo-American political ideology on northern black thought and activism complements and amplifies recent scholarship concerned with black religious thought. David W. Blight and John Stauffer, as two scholars mentioned above who have contributed significantly along with others to the historiography of northern black community and activism, are also important for their emphasis on the role of evangelicalism in contributing to our understanding of individual African American activists' thought. Blight examines how the Civil War impacted Frederick Douglass and how Douglass maintained faith in the nation at its most critical period, and Stauffer argues that an "interracial alliance" which formed among a few radical abolitionists, Frederick Douglass, James McCune Smith, John Brown, and Gerrit Smith, transcended the pervasive racism of their day. In several ways, my study complements, amplifies, and also broadens geographically and chronologically both Blight's and Stauffer's works. This study broadens even more John Saillant's important work on Lemuel Haynes, *Black Puritan, Black Republican* (2003), in which he demonstrates Haynes's reliance on evangelicalism and republicanism to understand his New England world and the broader American society. Likewise, my study of African American intellectual foundations enhances, broadens, and at the same time particularizes such studies as Graham Russell Hodges's books *Root and Branch*

(1999) and *Slavery and Freedom in the Rural North* (1997), in which evangelicalism is discussed extensively but not developed as the foundational element for
understanding black activism and black American identity.

In grounding the importance of evangelicalism and the influence of
American republican ideals among the majority of northern black activists,
this study asserts that individuals like David Walker, Henry Highland Garnet,
and Martin Delany were complex reformers who often and simultaneously
expressed pan-African, black nationalist, and evangelical themes in their
demands for change. Black nationalism and evangelicalism were not mutually exclusive, but at the same time this book does not support the notion of
"black nationalism," "black nationhood," or a "black nation" as fundamental
for understanding northern African American reform and/or Christianity in
this period.[1] The language of black nationalism remains, at least to this writer,
too amorphous, inchoate, and presentist as an explication of late eighteenth-
to mid-nineteenth-century northern black reformers' thought in this period,
though the language may very well apply to nonreformers. In examining the
thoughts, motives, and actions of most activists/reformers who served as
editors, ministers, teachers, and businessmen and women in the North from
the Revolution to the Civil War, this book centers our understanding of late
eighteenth- and early nineteenth-century northern black reform through an
in-depth study of its evangelical foundations.

Following the lead of Mark Noll, Albert J. Raboteau, and other historians of
American church history and theology, evangelicalism is defined in this book
as Protestantism that made the Bible the ultimate religious authority. Evangelicalism stressed conversionism (or the new birth), asserted strong belief in
activism (or the Christian's responsibility to influence family and society), and
argued that belief in Christ's redeeming work was at the center of Christianity.
As Noll notes, Protestant evangelicals dominated religious discourse between
the Revolution and the Civil War.[2] Within evangelicalism, millennialism, or
the belief that human history is divinely ordained and will lead to a period
of perfection on earth, became a prominent theme in late eighteenth- and
nineteenth-century American Christianity. Northern black reformers' embrace
of evangelical Christianity placed them within the mainstream, though with
some variation, of American religious thought. Raboteau's work on the central
importance of evangelicalism in black Christianity and how it diverged from
the dominant religion has greatly informed this work.[3]

Similarly, black reformers' embrace of the principles of the natural rights doctrine that developed in the Revolutionary era across both sides of the Atlantic as the ideology of the founding republic moved them into the dominant belief system of American political ideals. The problem for scholars who have recognized that African Americans shared basic political values with most Americans has been trying not to get mired in the hotly contested scholarly controversy concerning exactly what constituted American political ideology. After two decades of protracted and often vitriolic debate, historians, legal scholars, and political theorists have generally agreed that early American political thought drew upon multiple traditions—including liberalism and republicanism—during the Revolutionary War era and into the early republic. As historian Alan Gibson has summarized, because of the debate, scholars of the American founding have uncovered a confluence of ideas and political language previously ignored.[4] Although debate continues, most scholars now agree that America's founders developed a political philosophy in which they were committed to the Lockean notion of natural rights and social contract and "almost universally accepted the constellation of concepts that were embedded in the Declaration of Independence." They based their understanding about the origins and ends of governments upon the liberal assumption that all men were created equal "and thus all legitimate governments derived their just power from the consent of the governed."

Paradoxically, liberalism, as political theorist Rogers Smith and others have noted, included within it other ideologies, namely "inegalitarian" ideologies, that confounded and contradicted the very principles upon which liberalism purportedly was established. As discussed in chapter 5, racial ideology coincided with the development of American liberalism and intermingled with traditional gender ideology in new and different ways. In other words, the American founders not only borrowed from sources of the past in justifying the Revolution and creating the foundations of the new republic, but were also influenced by their present political economic interests and the interests of others like them as they envisioned the new nation.

Founders assumed men might, or would most likely, pursue self-interest over public interest and that checks and balances were necessary for controlling concentrated power. They privatized social concerns, such as religious belief, that ancient and medieval powers generally placed within the purview of government. Few founders believed government was responsible for the beliefs and opinions of citizens or that government should interest itself in creating a common character.

This latter issue, the question of whether Revolutionaries believed government should direct the thoughts and beliefs of citizens, has been, and continues to be in some circles, a point of scholarly contention, particularly among those stressing elements of America's founding within a classical republican tradition. The problem, political theorists and scholars of the classical era note, concerns language. American Revolutionaries (borrowing from eighteenth-century English oppositionists) used classical republican language such as "civic virtue" and "public good," but either (like the English oppositionists) meant quite different things, gave multiple meanings to these terms, or modified the classical understandings. While founders believed a primary purpose of government was the promotion of the public good and that virtue was critical for a republican government, their understanding of human nature was a mixture of believing man was naturally selfish and aggressive but also possessed "certain redeeming qualities." They assumed the multidimensionality of human motivations and thought that "constitutional structures and constraints had a profound effect upon whether men acted upon their best or worst inclinations." With regard to public or common good, the founders, Gibson explains, did not limit the meaning to an aggregation of individual interests, maintenance of public institutions, or the protection of individual rights; instead, they "seem to have understood the public good . . . as something like the collective articulation of self-interest properly understood."[5]

My study relies on recent scholarly language for understanding and explicating northern black political thought. Thus, in the following pages, I use republicanism, a word used by late eighteenth- and nineteenth-century Americans, to show how black evangelicals, like other evangelicals, combined various strains of political thought to situate themselves within American values and ideals. Their stress on freedom and equality and the necessity of civic virtue for the maintenance of a "true republic" was expressed by Americans of all types and served as the guiding force of black evangelicalism throughout the period of study. Christian republicanism would be the underpinning for the new republican nation. It gave northern blacks a sense of what the new government's ideals and responsibilities could be.

Just as scholars have debated American political theory, philosophers, political theorists, historians, sociologists, and others are engaged in controversy over the significance, meaning, and importance of individual and collective identity. The scholarly literature concerning this topic is vast and multiplying incrementally. My argument that the population forced into the Americas and

Caribbean to work for Europeans as their slaves moved individually and collectively from distinct ethnicities and ethnic communities to embrace more general terms of identification relies on the notion of theorists Charles Taylor, K. Anthony Appiah, and many others that "identity" is not somehow inherent in particular individuals or groups of people. Taylor's theory of the "dialogical" character of individual identity formation informs my assertion that the individuals of this study developed a sense of who they were in dialogue with the evolving dominant European American society, simultaneously resisting negative views that rendered them inferior and integrating, modifying, and at times embracing certain aspects of American culture that asserted principles of human equality and the natural right to freedom. The identity established by those in leadership roles, however, was not a racial identity. Racial identity came later, in the post-Reconstruction era. During the time of this study, individuals who engaged in the project of nomenclature and nomenclative discussions were concerned with distinguishing their experience and their histories from most Americans to inculcate values for individual and group esteem and for establishing a united front from which to demand inclusion into the body politic, full participation in American society. Thus, individual and collective identity for those in this study concerns an identity that is more definitive of an ethnic identity rather than a racial identity. In the late eighteenth and very early nineteenth centuries, black men who held leadership positions hoped that the African identification they adopted would help shape the present and the future.

Definitions of nation, nationality, and nationalism in this book are borrowed mainly from Benedict Anderson, Ernst Gellner, and Eric Hobsbawm, who locate the idea of nationality and nationalism in modernity. Anthony D. Smith, who sees nationality as originating in pre-modern forms, informs my understanding of ethnicity and ethnic community to explain the ways in which individuals and groups come to call themselves "African" and/or African and American in the northern part of the United States.[6]

At the same time, this study does not ignore the complexity and diversity of the entire northern black population. While a more common identity develops among the emerging first generation freed population, complete solidarity is elusive. Recognizing historian Leslie Harris's discussion of a growing rift within New York City's black population in which an emerging black middle class forms through the development of an agenda of moral reform during and after the Revolutionary era, I argue for the necessity of separating out those mostly evangelical Christians who had a clear material and cultural stake in the new republic.

The individuals of this study often referred to as "elite" did not necessarily reflect all or even most northern blacks' values, beliefs, and actions. Indeed, as ministers, editors, intellectuals, teachers, businessmen, and other professionals, they were in the minority of a population lacking access to literacy and property ownership. But this minority population possessed tremendous influence within the emerging urban free black communities, often acting as spokespersons for all northern blacks, sometimes all people of African descent, within the larger society. They were individuals who were often leaders of community institutions, such as schools and churches, but sometimes not. In general they talked to one another and white allies and enemies about their place in the new nation. When they did talk to the poor black northern majority they were often didactic if not condescending, like most reformers of whatever color or ideology, in their attempts to inculcate their evangelical morality. Thus the subjects of this book were activists/reformers in their determination to transform the dominant society while simultaneously urging the northern poor black majority toward collective moral, political, and economic advancement.

Some black reformers, as Harris notes, repeated white abolitionists' and humanitarians' admonition of moral reform before citizenship.[7] In doing so, these reformers anticipated the "uplift ideology" of the late nineteenth century, which became what historian Kevin Gaines argues was a means of authenticating the existence of an elite "as evidence of what they called race progress."[8] In the antebellum period, those who took on leadership positions lacked a middle-class ideology. Most of those who would constitute an emerging black middle class were far too connected to slavery and/or their artisan roots to form a clear and distinct social level. Still, much of the ingredients for the black middle class existed in the antebellum era, and the language of some reformers, including those who denigrated manual work, suggested that black middle-class consciousness was in formation. Other elements were also evident in the antebellum period: education, nonmanual work, a degree of financial stability often reflected in income, and concern for respectability, self-restraint, and decorum, ingredients already existing in white middle-class culture by the 1850s and especially after the Civil War.

For antebellum black Americans, race and racism would interfere with the ability of most to generate the homes, incomes, and patterns of consumption to parallel their white counterparts. Yet there is no question that, along with the above accouterments, black middle-class consciousness and ideology began to form in the antebellum era, and interest in establishing clearer social levels would seem inevitable once an even larger uneducated and poor black majority appeared after the war. Of course, class ideology is fluid, continually transforming, and multivalent in any era. Gaines has not only captured the primary elements constituting the values of the late nineteenth-century black middle class, but he also reminds us that the uplift ideology of that period was formed within the constraints of "power relations structured by race and racism."

The importance of examining the ideas, values, and activities of the northern antebellum black minority who engaged in a reform movement lies not only in expanding an understanding of the early American experience and more specifically African American antebellum thought, but also of how an emerging antebellum northern black middle-class morality set the stage for African American politics from the post-emancipation era into the early twentieth century.

The term middle class is difficult to define, particularly when one tries to define it within the sole parameters of occupation, income, and education. Race intervenes in any discussion of class in the United States, meaning that blacks' aspirations and educational attainments rarely match their occupational status in this country's history. More recently, several scholars have argued for a more inclusive definition that recognizes the importance of social values, not simply an individual's occupation or income.[9] For my purposes, middle class is defined by a combination of social values and educational, economic, and occupational aspirations and attainments. The individuals of this study were evangelicals who were mostly educated, or at least literate, and with incomes that generally allowed for property ownership, often a home. There were also a few wealthy reformers, some of whom had incomes to match wealthy white Americans.

Additionally, this study tends toward a dominant male voice. This is not to say women are absent in the foregoing pages, but that they were generally excluded, until the latter part of the antebellum era, from national and state conventions and editorial and ministerial positions. Yet several women did make themselves heard, as is shown in the ensuing chapters. The language of those who left records has not been altered; spelling and grammar are quoted directly to preclude further distortion of writers' ideas.

Chapter 1 of *Evangelicalism and the Politics of Reform* explores the process of collective identity among northern free blacks from the colonial period to the Revolutionary era. It notes the ways in which ministers and other leaders established their African identity through emphasis on shared oppression and creation of a common past for political and social reasons. Connected to the creation of a common identity, chapter 1 discusses how black leaders viewed the importance of evangelical Christianity in the development of viable African institutions within emerging free black urban communities during and immediately after the Revolutionary War.

Chapter 2 shows how black Americans' acceptance of Christianity informed their understanding of political thought during the Revolutionary era. I argue that the grounding of Christianity and accompanying national commitment to republican ideals of equality and freedom led blacks irrevocably down the road toward American identity. In his treatise "Liberty Further Extended . . . ," Lemuel Haynes, a black Revolutionary soldier, illustrates the path blacks took from embracing Christianity to understanding American Revolutionary ideals biblically.

Chapter 3 examines why, in-spite of slavery expansion in the 1820s and 1830s, northern blacks demonstrated more, not less, commitment to the nation. Rather than accept the idea that they should leave the United States, as many politically influential American leaders advised, most northern black editors, ministers, teachers, and others decided that they must play a greater role in developing the America they believed was divinely ordained. David Walker, the southern-born passionate activist living in Boston, exemplified northern free black evangelicals who, heavily influenced by the series of religious revivals sweeping the nation, transitioned from believing that divine intervention would end slavery to the belief that it was God's plan that blacks play a critical role in reforming, or recreating, American society. Thus, they expanded and intensified efforts to move America toward universal freedom and equality.

Chapter 4 follows the previous chapter in further examining the various plans and programs black evangelicals created to abolish slavery and end racism. Focusing mainly on African American involvement in the abolition movement, the chapter reveals the degree to which conversations about abolition indicated their belief in themselves, their God, and the political process. Terms of identity and separate black organizations created serious debate among black evangelicals about whether they were contributing to the problem of racism and denial of citizenship or helping resolve it.

Chapter 5 explores how northern blacks responded to the evolving racial theories in antebellum America. Christianity influenced not only their response but also the development of their own theorizing about race. Racial theories of major abolitionist figures of the antebellum era, including Frederick Douglass, Martin Delany, and especially James McCune Smith are examined in detail.

Finally, chapter 6 reveals how activists' American identity waned with the intensity of American racism and the passage of laws that further protected slavery. The decade ended, however, with renewed faith and hope as reformers viewed the Civil War in an increasingly millennial fashion, as God's means of abolishing slavery and cleansing the nation in preparation for its evangelical mission to the world.

When I started this study several years ago, I was surprised about the extent to which the subjects of my research identified themselves so fully as American. My primary question was why. Why such a strong identification with the United States, a nation that enslaved most people of African descent and limited those who were "free" so much so that one scholar has called their status "quasi-freedom"? This book explains the important role evangelicalism played in the development of American identity for a prominent northern black minority from the late eighteenth century to the Civil War and the ways in which black evangelicalism, in turn, informed their goals, values, methods of activism, and reformist understanding of the emerging racial ideology and the impending war.

CHAPTER 1

Becoming African, Becoming Christian

RELIGION AND THE EVOLUTION OF A COMMON IDENTITY

We the African Members, form ourselves into a Society, . . . for the mutual benefit of
each other . . . as true and faithful citizens of the Commonwealth in which we live.
— Quoted in Dorothy Porter, ed., *Early Negro Writing, 1760–1837*

Timing was almost everything. For a small and growing population of northern
free blacks, conversion to Christianity, beginning with the First Great Awakening, set the stage for the reception and appropriation of the Revolutionary
ideals pervasive in the last quarter of the eighteenth century. These two belief
systems, Christianity and late eighteenth-century Anglo-American ideology, or
what Revolutionaries called "republicanism," contributed to the evolution of
American national identity for many blacks living in the North. Moreover, the
latter could not have developed without the former: the development of black
American national identity depended on the reinterpretation and acceptance
of primary themes in American Protestantism. Consequently, conversion to
Christianity and personal and collective application of Revolutionary ideals of
freedom and equality provided the foundation for an emerging free northern
black Christian population that came to view themselves as "American."

But the forging of American identity among the small but influential elite
was the last stage of a three-step process. Tracing their origins to diverse West
and West Central African populations enslaved in the northern region of
British North America, northern blacks first established a distinct "African"
identity that overrode the cultural and regional differences so critical to the
identities of their ancestors. Though many ethnic groups shared cultural
elements with one another, enslaved Africans represented distinct cultures

from mostly small-scale societies based in kin networks. These various ethnic groups competed for resources, exchanged specific cultural elements, and engaged in an intricate interregional trade system.[1] The nature of the slave trade, the economic development of the British North American colonies, the political goals of European American colonists, and, importantly, the interests of the slaves themselves contributed to the creation of an African identity in the northern region of North America that eventually transcended ethnic distinctions among West and West Central Africans.

Wishing she were dead so that she could return to her country and friends, enslaved West African Chloe Spear resented her Boston master's insistence that she attend Sunday church services. The sermons, to the young girl enslaved in late eighteenth-century Revolutionary New England, were dry and incomprehensible; she "took no interest in it." Chloe could not hear the sermons very well anyway. She and other young slaves were assigned seats remote from the congregation's view. Isolated from the rest of the worshipers, Chloe and her compatriots played games in church. It was not until she was assigned the task of taking her master's children to school that she became interested in reading. She convinced a schoolteacher to teach her how to read after school closed. Her first and probably only primer was the Bible. Literacy opened a new spiritual world to Chloe. She now had hope in *this* world. The biblical passages she most loved and memorized were ones that spoke to her situation, scriptural verses that gave her comfort and solace. The verse Chloe Spear loved most: God was "no respecter of persons."[2]

Chloe Spear was just one of many slaves who converted to Christianity in the mid- to late eighteenth century. Although never the primary labor system in the northern colonies, slavery existed in every colony north of the Chesapeake. From the earliest decades of settlement many northern colonists, like their southern counterparts, used slave labor when white indentured servants were not available in sufficient numbers. In New England, the number of blacks increased by more than 50 percent each decade between 1680 and 1720. By 1750 they made up over 3 percent of the total population. In the middle colonies, blacks constituted over 10 percent of the population by 1720. They were especially numerous in the cities. From 1700 to 1750, the number of blacks in New York City increased from around 750 to 2,300; in 1720, the black population was almost one-quarter of the city's population.[3]

In southern New England, on Long Island, and in northern New Jersey, the vast majority of slaves were involved in tending stock and raising crops for export to the West Indies. Cereal farmers in northern New England, the Hudson Valley, and in Pennsylvania also depended on slave labor, albeit in smaller numbers. White indentured and free farm workers generally made up the bulk of the workforce in these regions, but increasingly enslaved Africans became a more significant part of the labor force on large farms. In the mid-eighteenth century, slave labor in southern New England constituted as much as one-third of the labor force, and at times over half of the workforce, especially in the area around Narragansett Bay, where large slaveholders behaved more like the colonial planter class of the low country. Some northern slaves also worked in the few rural industries, such as tanning, salt production, and smelting, but a large number worked in the urban areas. While before the mid-eighteenth century slave labor had been primarily domestic in Newport, New York City, Boston, and Philadelphia, after 1750 it quickly became a central element in trade. A growing number of bondsmen worked in the maritime industry as teamsters, wagoners, and stockmen on the docks and in the warehouses. And, as a consequence of the growing economy, a middling class could now afford, like the elite, to have slaves in their shops as well as at home. Indeed, bound labor became commonplace in the maritime trades and was integral to the productivity of numerous others. Throughout most of the colonial period, slaves arriving in northern colonies usually came from the Caribbean. But because of rising demand in the mid-eighteenth century, an increasing number came directly from Africa. For example, 70 percent of the slaves arriving in New York came from the Caribbean and other mainland colonies and the rest directly from Africa before 1741. After that year, the numbers reversed. In Philadelphia, over five hundred enslaved men, women, and children were imported from Africa in 1762 alone. With increased reliance on slavery and a significant population from Africa, northern slaveowners tightened control over those in bondage and the tiny free black population.

While not as barbarous as Caribbean or Carolina slavery, northern slavery was harsh and could be brutal. Taking their lead from West Indian slave statutes, northern colonists established slavery as a legal institution. Slaves could be bought and sold, inherited, auctioned, traded, mortgaged, and alienated as collateral for debts of their masters. Yet in New York slaves could own and transfer property, receive and bequeath legacies, and many were permitted to work for their own benefit during their free time. Until the mid- to late eighteenth century, slaveholders did not automatically own the property of slaves. Curiously, free blacks could not own property in New York and New

Jersey, and a Pennsylvania statute prescribed reenslavement of "any free Negro" physically capable of working but refusing to do so. And, as in the South, physical appearance determined status. Individuals of apparent African ancestry were presumed to be slaves unless they could prove otherwise. But increasingly physical appearance was deceptive, as sexual alliances produced a growing population of children of mixed ancestries, African, Native American, and European. As in the southern colonies, by statute or custom, northern colonies fixed slave status according to that of the mother.[4]

The northern colonial slave codes were similar to those of the southern colonies. They detailed the responsibilities of whites to keep all blacks under the supervision of whites. The codes revealed not only colonists' determination to create a stable labor force, but also their interest in maintaining white supremacy. For blacks, the lash was the main instrument of control, and when it failed or slaveholders wanted to set an example, the gun, rope, or burning were used seemingly without hesitation. Generally, those in bondage were forbidden to own weapons, denied physical mobility or the right to engage in trade of any kind, and not allowed to consume strong drink. A Pennsylvania statute forbade blacks from entering taverns under penalty of whipping and exacted a fine on the tavern owner who served black customers. The rights of blacks varied from colony to colony and might depend on their status as slave or free. The middle colonies established special courts for blacks, for example, but New England colonial law did not distinguish between the judicial rights of blacks and whites. Slaves could sue for freedom in New England courts, give court testimony, and had the right to a jury trial in criminal cases. Yet even in New England the law was harsher on blacks than whites.

The right to terrorize enslaved men, women, and children was built into the legal system of the northern colonies. Crimes against property, including running away, were severely punished. The most serious crime was the killing of a white person. New York, with the largest slave population and, not surprisingly, the harshest laws, meted out brutal punishments on those accused of killing whites.[5] For example, two slaves were sentenced to death by torture when found guilty of murdering a white family on Long Island in 1707. One witness to the executions explained that the men "were put to all manner of torment possible." One of the condemned criminals was hung alive in chains and partially impaled so that his death was prolonged for several hours. As historian Edgar McManus notes, though rare, "such terroristic displays demonstrate that New Yorkers had ample capacity for ferocity when the safety of the white community was threatened."[6] Considered the destruction of valuable property, slave murders of one another also led to barbarous punishment. When an enslaved man killed another slave in 1696, the court sentenced him "to be hanged by the neck till he shall be dead, and to be cut with a knife in his throat and after to be hanged in a chain for an example to others."[7]

Rejecting bondage, slave men, women, and children resisted in a number of ways. Like most slaves of whatever age, Chloe Spear engaged in day-to-day resistance. She refused to allow her slaveholders to define her. She learned to read secretly because her first master believed literacy made slaves "saucy." But running away, destroying property, and resisting punishment were also common in the colonial era. Because of the nature of unfree labor in New England, many slaves ran away with white servants. Born in Dukandarra, Guinea, around 1729, Broteer Furro was captured in 1735, enslaved, and eventually taken to Rhode Island. At twenty-two years old, Furro, renamed "Venture" because the steward of the slave ship purchased him with his own "private venture," fled slavery with three servants, one of whom was "Heddy," an Irishman who had hatched the scheme of escape. Heddy then betrayed his fugitive companions when he stole their clothing and boat and left them stranded at the east end of Long Island. After finding Heddy, Venture concocted a scheme of his own that he hoped "might afford some chance for my freedom, or at least be a palliation for my running away." He returned Heddy to their master and blamed the Irish servant for the escape plan. "I informed my master that Heddy was the ringleader of our revolt, and that he had used us ill." Heddy was imprisoned and Venture was sold, separated from his wife and one-month-old baby.[8] Another form of resistance involved self and family purchase. Many northern slaves worked at odd jobs during leisure hours to purchase their freedom and/or that of relatives. Absalom Jones, enslaved from birth in Delaware and Pennsylvania, purchased his wife's freedom before his master permitted him to purchase his own. Jones would soon become a leading figure in the development of Philadelphia's free black community.[9]

The ultimate form of resistance was insurrection, and a few northern slaves, like their southern counterparts, plotted and carried out rebellions against the system. For instance, between May 11 and August 29, 1741, thirteen black men were burned to death at the stake and seventeen were hung for an insurrection involving reported attempts to burn down the City of New York. Two white men and two white women were also hung in what was called the "New York Conspiracy," or the "Great Negro Plot."[10]

Within decades of the New York Conspiracy, however, slavery in the North had declined precipitously. The nature of the diversified economy and the interest in and availability of European laborers meant northern slave labor was a "stopgap measure." The influx of Europeans after 1715 ensured the further decline of reliance on slave labor. Also, free workers resented slave labor competition. Artisans particularly complained that slave artisans undercut their ability to earn decent wages. This resentment was revealed in the earliest years of British North American colonization. Free artisans in mid-seventeenth-century Boston tried to end slave labor in the skilled crafts, and later, in the 1730s, New York porters complained that slave competition impoverished them and their families. Although slaveholders at first ignored such complaints, they could not do so indefinitely. Free worker discontent multiplied with increased European immigration, so much so that by the Revolution John Adams believed white workers in Massachusetts would abolish slavery on their own if the courts and legislature did not act quickly. By the 1760s, the demand for slave labor in the northern colonies was diminishing.[11]

Northern slavery declined further during the Revolutionary War era, when slaves took advantage of wartime disruptions and simply fled bondage. A few were given permission to flee by loyalist slaveholders. For instance, an enslaved woman in Rhode Island received a pass by her hurriedly departing owner in 1777 to go wherever she could get a decent living. The number of runaways increased sharply after the 1775 machinery devised by the colonial legislatures for slave control broke down.[12]

Moreover, slave men participated in the Revolutionary War in exchange for freedom. Historian Benjamin Quarles has shown that when it became increasingly difficult to raise volunteer forces, northern patriots, and some in the Upper South, recruited black men. After 1777, New England employed more slaves in the armed forces than any other region. Except for South Carolina and Georgia, the new states made provisions for many men to gain their freedom in exchange for military service. Additionally, thousands fled to the British with the hope of gaining freedom; about five thousand left, taken first to Nova Scotia and eventually settling in England or Sierra Leone after the British evacuation in 1783.[13]

While patriots often used the trope of slavery to unite against Britain, Revolutionary ideals of freedom and equality also factored into the decline of northern slavery. Increasingly likening their subordinate status in the empire to that of slaves, patriots contended that Parliament would reduce them to slavery. "We won't be their Negroes," snarled John Adams in 1765; God "never intended us as slaves." As historian Timothy Breen has argued, the colonists' source of anger was less in parliamentary taxation without representation than "it was the sudden realization that the British actually regarded white colonial Americans as second-class beings, indeed, as persons so inferior . . . that they . . . deserved a lesser measure of freedom."[14] As patriots were engaged in distancing themselves from the degradation of enslavement, other colonists, a few long opposed to the system, seized on the more liberal climate to argue for the abolition of slavery. Abolitionists joined with slaves in urging legislators and other influential citizens to examine the inherent inconsistencies between demanding freedom for themselves while at the same time enslaving others. In the late 1770s and 1780s, many newspaper editors attacked the institution. Consequently, northern public opinion switched from a general apathy to a growing opposition.

Not surprisingly, states with insignificant or small slave populations were more open to abolitionists' pressure. Abolitionists succeeded almost immediately in Massachusetts. Judges there upheld several slave freedom suits and petitions with a broad interpretation of the 1780 constitution. Vermont, with only a few slaves (about twenty-five), expressly forbade slavery in its constitution. By 1790 there were no slaves in either state according to the census. The details of abolition in New Hampshire are obscure and ambiguous. State legislators did not pass a law specifically banning slavery until 1857, but several court decisions emancipated many slaves in 1783–1784. Enslaved men and women in New Hampshire, like those in other parts of New England, exploited Revolutionary rhetoric in petitioning and suing for their freedom. In a 1779 petition, slaves asserted their natural right to freedom and condemned American slaveholders for unjustly holding freeborn people in bondage. While the New Hampshire legislature ignored the slaves' petition, slavery was never a major factor in the colony's labor system. Out of New Hampshire's black population of around 800, about 150 remained in bondage in the 1790s; by 1800 the census reported eight slaves; in 1810 there were none.

New Hampshire's ambiguous policy of emancipation was probably similar to the gradual abolition laws enacted in the remaining northern states. Abolitionists' insistence on the expansion of libertarian principles competed with another Revolutionary principle: the sanctity of property. In short, abolition in the states with significant slave populations contended with economic, political, and ideological realities. As a result, legislatures in these states created a policy that essentially freed no one, at least not immediately. Gradual abolition freed only the children born to slave mothers after a specified date. Usually these "freed" children were then bound or "apprenticed" to the mother's slaveholder until adulthood. Pennsylvania, the first state to adopt a gradual abolition law, for example, emancipated children who were born after the passage of the March 1, 1780, law but bound children born after that date until twenty-eight years of age if they were male, and twenty-one years old if female. The status of those born before that date was unchanged. Rhode Island, Connecticut, New York, and New Jersey, states with large or significant slave populations, all passed laws similar to Pennsylvania's between 1784 and 1804. New York and New Jersey, the largest northern slaveholding states, had approximately 21,000 and 12,000 slaves, respectively, in 1800.[15]

The gradual abolition laws essentially subordinated natural rights doctrine to economic and political interests, specifically rights of property. Demanding compensation for their capital investment from a citizenry opposed to increased financial burdens, politicians devised a means that placed the burden on the most vulnerable in the society: those in bondage and their children. Work from the adults and children, in other words, ostensibly compensated slaveholders for their original investment.[16]

Gradual emancipation would have prolonged northern slavery to the 1860s had it not been for the persistence of the abolitionists, free blacks, and the slaves themselves as they joined together in pushing for total abolition. Abolitionists, alarmed that slaveholders were taking advantage of the many loopholes in the law and shipping their slaves to the West Indies and the South, ensured that state legislatures strengthened the gradual abolition law. They maintained a vigilant watch for violations and pushed for total abolition in those states with gradualist policies. The Pennsylvania legislature considered requests in 1792, 1799–1801, 1811–1812, 1820–1822, 1826, and 1840. By the latter date, there were only a few older slaves; the 1850 census listed none. The New York legislature, with its considerably larger slave population, went beyond its Pennsylvania counterpart by passing a law for the total abolition of slavery beginning July 4, 1827. Even so, as historian Nell Irvin Painter reminds us, indentured children of former slaves remained in servitude into the 1850s. New York slave Isabella, who would name herself Sojourner Truth, freed herself the year before the abolition law went into effect, but her children remained in servitude for nearly two decades.[17]

Many slaves and newly freed blacks helped speed up the emancipation process directly. Self-purchase, a system by which slaveholders "permitted" slaves to purchase their freedom, became a primary means of emancipation for many men and women. Once free, they then purchased family members. Like many other husbands, former runaway Venture Smith, taking the surname of his last slaveholder, bought himself, his wife, "Meg, the wife of my youth, whom I married for love and bought with my money," and two children from slavery. Smith performed almost any job, including fishing, lumbering, and farming, to gain freedom for himself and his family. Slaveholders also manumitted large numbers of slaves through their wills in the late eighteenth century.[18] Consequently, by the first quarter of the nineteenth century slavery represented an insignificant institution in the North.

As ethnic populations spanning significant regional and cultural differences, sub-Saharan West and West Central Africans viewed themselves as distinct peoples. Yet, more than 120 years of shared enslavement and shared resistance in northern colonies contributed to the complex phenomenon of an evolving common "African" identity. From the beginning of enslavement, diverse peoples of West Africa and other parts of sub-Saharan Africa united in resistance.[19] Planning slave insurrections depended partly on the ability of particular ethnic groups to form alliances of some sort. According to historian Michael Gomez, from the initial point of capture, "captives from more than one ethnicity may have found themselves hold up in the same barracoon, thus initiating the message that the one thing they all shared was their blackness, a message that became even clearer upon considering the contrast with their European captors." The experience of oppression on slave ships was, historian Sterling Stuckey asserts, "the first real incubators of slave unity across cultural lines, cruelly revealing irreducible links from one ethnic group to the other." For pragmatic reasons, most ethnically diverse African people in the Americas united against a system that exploited them almost uniformly. This common oppression evoked resistance among diverse Africans.[20]

Resistance to bondage remained a primary catalyst for West and West Central African unity throughout the period of American slavery. Records, though for obvious reasons scarce, show that some rebel leaders recognized the importance of developing solidarity among diverse Africans. Stuckey describes such a development in South Carolina when Denmark Vesey surrounded himself with leaders of several African ethnic groups in his plot to overthrow slavery in 1822.[21] A similar strategy occurred in colonial New York when "a group of enslaved Cormantines [Akan] and Pawpaws [Papaw-Nago] not long from Africa" joined forces, burned buildings, and killed or wounded several whites in a 1712 insurrection. And historian Leslie Harris notes that alliances were also formed among Akan, other West African, and possibly East African slaves in the 1741 conspiracy where slave rebels swore war oaths and relied on a shaman, probably Akan, to support them. New York City, the most diverse urban center of the thirteen colonies, not only had a large black population (one of every five persons was black and mainly enslaved) but also an extremely diverse one.[22]

But creating alliances with different African populations for successful rebellion was not a seamless process. Scholars of the Atlantic slave trade have specified major regions from which African slaves were drawn at different periods of the trade. In the seventeenth and eighteenth centuries, enslaved Africans generally were from Senegambia, the Gold Coast, the Bights of Benin and Biafra, and West and West Central Africa, meaning that enslaved men, women, and children taken to the southern British North American colonies were often living and working among those with whom they shared a language. According to current scholarship, the opportunity to maintain ethnic distinctions and in some instances remain to some degree separate from other ethnic groups was more possible, at least in the southern colonies, than many previous scholars realized.[23]

Yet, for northern slaves, time, distance, space, and the nature of northern slavery accelerated the process of combining particular West and West Central African cultural elements. As a society with slaves instead of a slave society, northern society with its smaller numbers had a greater diversity of West and West Central African populations. During much of the colonial period, Africans arrived in the North in small numbers more directly from the Caribbean. Although the majority of slaves were probably African born (in New England alone the figure was 75 percent), they generally lived, worked, and engaged in social activities with slaves whose ethnic group likely was different from their own. Also, because children were cheaper, significant numbers of those taken to North America were youths. In the eighteenth century at least 25 percent, possibly 33 percent, were children at the point of embarkation. In the northern colonies, the number was probably even higher. Not only did northern colonies receive so called "surplus" slaves but also large numbers of young children. In fact, many New England slaveholders requested children, and not only for financial reasons. They assumed children would have a greater degree of cultural malleability (including linguistic dexterity) and could therefore be trained for trades or domestic work with less resistance.[24]

Men, women, and children enslaved in the northern colonies from West and West Central Africa more readily ignored cultural differences not simply because of their smaller numbers and close contact with the evolving dominant European American culture, but also because of what some scholars have called generalized elements of shared West African cultures. Populations of the Akan or Gold Coast, the Bights of Benin and Biafra, Senegambia, Sierra Leone, the Grain and Windward Coasts, and West Central Africa shared important cultural traits, some more than others. Shared elements cannot, however, ignore distinctions. Gomez notes that "although there are striking similarities of culture and social and political organizations in various regions of Africa, there are also important differences. The key to understanding the process by which these diverse groups of immigrants attempted to fashion a sociocultural coherency is an appreciation of the nature of these differences."[25]

Scholars of West and West Central Africa have assiduously identified cultural traits shared in common and the distinctive elements in these regions. The common cultural traits shared among the Bambara, for example, involved similar social structures, including social stratification and religious beliefs. Religion was central in these various cultures that did not distinguish between the sacred and secular. Many of the cultures held a system of religious beliefs that featured a supreme transcendent god and lesser gods involved in the daily lives of the people. Priests and devotees often explained the will of the gods for the individual and society by means of spirit possession.

Besides the belief in a transcendent deity with divine associates, many West Africans embraced a world in which the "living dead" or the recently departed held powerful sway over the individual and the society. Ancestors played a prominent role in many cultures, making family, whether patrilineal or matrilineal, a fundamental unit and often the foundation of social, political, and economic life. Ancestral spirits were guardians of the society's customs. Consequently, burial rites were important means of honoring the recently departed; it was essential to maintain positive relations with ancestors, who held power over the fertility and health of the descendants.

Some scholars point to a degree of intercultural exchange among West and West Central Africans. Stuckey cites several examples of shared celebrations among diverse ethnic groups in West Africa. For example, women from various parts of sub-Saharan Africa performed dances common to several countries in interregional celebrations. Similar dance, music, and burial rituals were central in the lives of the many societies and were sometimes performed together.[26] In addition to intercultural exchange, an interregional trade had developed over the centuries, long before the Atlantic slave trade. Gomez notes that Senegambians engaged in trade between the coast and the interior, which enabled cultural exchange.

The generalized cultural similarities contributed to the potential for the development of a common identity among culturally diverse enslaved men, women, and children in the Americas and Caribbean. Africans in the British North American colonies, according to Albert Raboteau and Sterling Stuckey, found common ground in generalized belief systems and specific religious rituals celebrated in West Africa. Stuckey focuses on the "ring shout" as a means by which diverse ethnic groups came together in their new world. He argues that in the areas where most enslaved Africans originated, a sacred ring ceremony permeated the cultures. Linked to the burial ceremony, the dance was a means of achieving union with God as individuals slowly and discretely danced counterclockwise around a circle to the soft rhythm of drums. The dancing and singing that accompanied the drums were directed to the ancestors and gods. In time, the tempo and revolution of the circle quickened. According to Stuckey, the ring in which Africans danced and sang is the "key" to understanding the means by which diverse African peoples "achieved oneness in America."[27] While it seems the predominance of the ring shout convincingly demonstrates similar cultural practices among diverse African ethnic communities and provided a means toward uniting liturgical practices in North America when diverse ethnic populations encountered one another in bondage, the ring shout alone could not have united complex societies from much of sub-Saharan Africa. Still, evidence suggests that the ring shout remained prominent in some black American liturgical practices into the late nineteenth century, proving Stuckey's assertion of its importance.

But the idea that northern slaves, smaller in number, generally isolated from other slaves, and in constant interaction with European American society, were able to share cultural elements seems nearly impossible because of the nature of the New England and middle colonies' economic systems. Largely commercial and agriculturally diverse, these economies depended less on slave labor. Yet even in New England, where the majority of slaveholders owned only one or two slaves, many Africans often lived and worked in concentrated areas. According to historian William D. Piersen, blacks were "primarily concentrated in and around the coastal urban centers, along the river systems, and in the Narragansett region of Rhode Island."[28] In the middle colonies and states the "clustering" of enslaved Africans existed similarly. Historian Shane White has demonstrated not only that New York City had a large population of blacks, mostly slaves in the colonial era, but also that slaves were concentrated on the western end of Long Island and in parts of New Jersey. "In 1771, 20 percent of the population in Richmond and Queens Counties were slaves. Even more strikingly, one in every three residents of Kings County was a slave, a ratio that would not have been out of place in the South."[29]

Concentrated in specific areas of northern colonies, many Africans arrived with particular, though clearly not fixed, worldviews, values, ethics, and beliefs. Their interpretation of reality changed as a consequence of the enslavement process. Slowly, but for some more rapidly, Africans in North America engaged in intercultural exchange as they were confronted with a dominant and generally hostile European culture. Africans in the Americas and Caribbean were, after all, engaged in a political struggle. It no longer mattered (or mattered much) whether, as Gomez argues, specific cultural forms could be maintained over time. What mattered was "achieving a self-view in opposition to the one prescribed by power and authority." Africans were forced to rethink what constituted community.[30]

West and West Central Africans in the northern colonies adapted their beliefs and cultural practices to their new world. From New England to the middle colonies, many slaves incorporated elements of West African burial practices even into the nineteenth century, after large numbers of blacks converted to Christianity. Revealing their belief in the "living dead," some New England slaves requested burial sites near the house or where children played so they might hear children's voices. And, as in the South, amulets or charms functioned as means of protection and empowerment in the northern colonies and states, as they had in West Africa, particularly among the Bambara. One report in pre-Revolutionary Philadelphia noted that on Sundays, holidays, and fair days Africans were seen "dancing after the manner of their several nations in Africa, and speaking and singing in their native dialects."[31] In addition, when possible, many slaves in New England and elsewhere in the northern colonies followed West African building designs, art, dress, music, dance, modes and styles of communication, trade, work routines, culinary and labor skills, and herbal medicine practices. Particularly noteworthy is the fact that Massachusetts Puritan divine Cotton Mather learned the effective Akan method of smallpox inoculation from slaves.[32]

Two holidays, "Pinkster" and "Negro Election Day," revealed even more the extent to which West and West Central Africans in the northern colonies remembered elements of specific African cultural practices and blended it with their culturally diverse American present. Besides taking advantage of opportunities to meet together during New England elections, beginning in the mid-eighteenth century, blacks, slave and free, participated in an annual festival in which they, in part, honored individuals of African ancestry. Large numbers of slaves speaking various African languages elected black governors and kings and, borrowing from African forms, satirized white society while at the same time reinforcing particular African customs. Piersen explains how the election site and symbols of authority like canes reflected "African choices," and a large number of those elected had direct ties with African royalty or were African born. These officials often had real power among New England blacks and, as in Africa, they might also fill a judicial function. "Pinkster" also demonstrated a blend of African and European American cultural influences. Originally a holiday of the Dutch Reformed Church's celebration of Pentecost, Africans in New York joined in the celebration, though not as church members, and included some elements of West and West Central African musical and dance traditions. The Pinkster holiday among blacks lasted into the early nineteenth century in various parts of New York and took on, like for the New Englanders, a political dimension with the election of political leaders.[33]

Thus Africans, reduced to the common slave status or a denigrated "free" status and living and working in concentrated areas of the North, shared multiple cultural traditions that opened the possibility of moving toward a more unified identity. For many Africans enslaved in the northern colonies, the Caribbean served as a "way station." Venture Smith was taken first to Barbados, where the majority of slaves on the Rhode Island slaver disembarked. Like many captured children, he was not wanted for work on the sugar plantations and ended up in New England, where his Narragansett owner used him for domestic and farm work and where slaveholders imitated southern planters owning large farms worked by slaves. The largest plantation in Newport rivaled large plantations in the southern colonies, meaning the young slave had many opportunities to interact with other Africans of varying ages and ethnicities. Abraham Redwood of Newport owned 238 slaves who mostly worked in the fields.[34]

Though a child when captured, Smith reveals the degree to which children remembered something of their African past. He recounted elements of his society's customs and landscape and that of nearby regions. In his narrative, Smith stresses most of all family dynamics, the process of brutal capture of himself and others, and his experience as a slave and eventually as a free black in New England and Long Island. As importantly, he demonstrates the degree to which northern slaves interacted consistently with each other and white workers, slaveholders, and Indians in the community. Though concentrated in particular areas of the North, however, slaves were not isolated from dominant West European cultures. Thus, the evolving European American culture influenced and was influenced by the African population, and particular Native American populations.

Yet, while Smith worked alongside white indentured servants from the beginning of his enslavement, he identified with individuals of African ancestry. He, like other northern blacks in the mid- to late eighteenth century, called himself "African" and referred to others of African ancestry as his "own countrymen."[35] More likely isolated from those with whom they shared a specific cultural heritage, perhaps holding some similarities in critical belief systems, and, most importantly, experiencing common oppression in and out of slavery, it is not surprising that individuals and small groups developed (as did some indigenous American populations and other immigrant populations) a more encompassing identity.[36]

By the late eighteenth century, African identity simultaneously enabled an imagined "country" of common ancestry and solidarity. Northern blacks established their own myth for the present reality, an identity that was both political and social. It would help the growing numbers of newly emancipated men and women in the late eighteenth and early nineteenth centuries unite in their struggle against persistent inequalities in law and custom and at the same time contribute to the formation of a community that was distinct from yet part of the newly established American republic. Venture Smith's experience in New England shows how persistent inequalities toward former slaves contributed to the idea of a commonality among blacks. When treated unjustly by a prosperous white captain, Smith realized that the courts would not treat him fairly because "Captain Hart was a *white* gentleman, and I a *poor African, therefore it was all right and good enough for the black dog.*" Smith's addendum to his insightful pronouncement on the New England caste system not only underscores the existence of a collective African identity but also demonstrates that he maintained a distinct sub-Guinean identity. He claimed that such unfairness "in my native country," referring this time specifically to Guinea, would have been "branded as a crime equal to highway robbery."[37]

The battle ahead, many blacks decided, required solidified political action and at the same time demanded more than politics for a viable identity. For those who had been outright commodities, a collective identity enabled a sense of what it meant to be human. A clear identity distinct from the terms of enslavement, in other words, would provide what philosopher Charles Taylor calls a "framework."[38] Africans in America would have a base upon which to make judgments about their place in the universe, their existence in America, and their personal choices. While northern colonial records reveal that seventeenth-century West and West Central Africans in North America were sometimes identified by whites and by themselves as being members of particular ethnic groups, by the late eighteenth century many called themselves African. Individuals whose ancestors were Yoruba, Nupe, Susu, Ibo, Bambara, Fulani, Mende, Bakongo, Malimbo, Ndungo, Luba, and so on called themselves "African," referred to the African continent as their "native country," and to one another as their "countrymen."[39] Thus, in a political and social act, newly manumitted blacks and others who were either born free or had been free for some time referred to themselves as "of the African race" and "free Africans." Reflecting the broad meaning of nation, Phillis Wheatley, a famous New England poet, regarded Africa as "my nation." African identity existed also in the Upper South among other free blacks, including Benjamin Banneker, who, like northerners, defined race in the eighteenth-century sense of distinct nations or peoples, not as biological fact, when he stated: "I am of the African race."[40]

The white majority, of course, aided and profoundly influenced northern blacks in the process of establishing their collective African identity. First, diverse ethnic Europeans existed in a "plural landscape" in which they moved toward a common ethnic identity in the colonial period. African immigrants, relegated politically and socially outside European society, did the same. This new shared identity imbued blacks individually and collectively, as it did whites, with a sense of unity, coherence, and purpose.[41] The nature of the slave trade not only contributed to ethnic African diversity, but also meant that some slaves who were kidnapped as small children lacked sufficient cultural memory of their country of ancestral origin. Thus a common identity was probably inevitable given persistent common oppression. Second, most northern whites ignored the diversity among African populations living in their midst. They were an undifferentiated "african" people. With the nomenclature fairly well in place within American society by the late eighteenth century, individuals from Africa, or whose ancestral homes were in sub-Saharan Africa, easily embraced the idea of an African identity.[42]

First, leaders set about to establish "African" as the primary term of identity by including African in the names of their social institutions. The New York African Society, the Sons of Africans, the St. Thomas African Episcopal Church, the African Bethel Church, the African Marine Fund, the African Masonic Lodge, and many other churches, fraternal groups, and charitable organizations signified an identity distinct from that of European Americans to establish pride and sense of place. While "negro" or "people of colour" were other terms of identification, African became the official designation of black institutions in the late eighteenth and early nineteenth centuries. Almost every society and organization northern blacks created in the early new republic era included "African" in the title.[43] It seems the term "negro" may have been a designation used more by whites than blacks in this period and later.[44]

Second, for those engaged in the development of free northern urban communities, this identity had to signify more than the oppressive nature of their existence. They wanted blacks to view themselves as individuals with a shared history and culture. An African identity had to be one in which former slaves who had been dehumanized in law and custom asserted respect and dignity in freedom. Thus they created a romantic pre-European contact African past that transcended the geographical boundaries of the Americas and European oppression. In his 1814 speech celebrating the abolition of the Atlantic slave trade, Russell Parrott, assistant pastor at Philadelphia's St. Thomas African Episcopal Church, described an Edenic land in which familial relations existed undisturbed. "Fancy yourself on the fertile plains of Africa—see . . . a father, surrounded by a flock of innocents . . . bound . . . to paternal home . . . here is the land of his nativity—here dwells his father, his mother, the partner of his affection, and the friend of his heart."[45]

William Hamilton, a carpenter and New York City community leader, told the New York African Society for Mutual Relief in 1809 that the "country of our forefathers might truly be called a paradise." Parrott, Hamilton, and others, especially at celebrations of the abolition of the Atlantic slave trade, likewise described Africans as a "harmless" people "who had ever been strangers to the arts of deception, and unsuspicious of treachery in the bosoms of others."[46] The grain of truth in this paradisiacal story is that the more politically democratic Ibo, located in the Bight of Biafra area, accounted for nearly one-quarter of the total African importations to North America.[47]

While a romantic past enabled pride and sense of self, ministers and other speakers emphasized the experience of oppression, an experience that most individuals of African ancestry knew on multiple levels. Beginning with graphic portrayals of the capture, coffles, dungeons, middle passage, and finally enslavement in the Americas, the leaders' stress on shared oppression, past and present, became the basis of a history that would be the primary means for uniting in common purpose. Africans were distinct in American society, chroniclers implied, and needed solidarity to survive and challenge the oppressive powers. Hamilton's history of an idyllic African country continued with details of kidnapping and enslavement. Similarly, Parrott's portrayal emphasized European disruption of African life: "When in the midst of his domestic enjoyment, a fiend steals in and mars all his happiness; the slave merchant, whose steps are marked by desolation and dismay, at one stroke destroys all his sublunary joys; tears from the bosom of his family, the poor African! . . . He is hurried to the bark, prepared for his reception, where begins the career of his ignomy, and his sufferings."[48]

The slave trade, according to Parrott and others, was the essence of cruelty and barbarism. On the slave ship "enormities are committed that would make 'angels weep.' . . . The passage is one continued scene of suffering and barbarity." Africans packed on vessels were tortured, mutilated, lacerated, and infected with disease. Some, driven to desperation, refused to eat. Whether the captives resisted directly or indirectly, their captors reacted with "slaughter and death."[49] At the same time that chroniclers stressed common ancestry, they also stressed familial separation in their depiction of the brutal capture and finally the sale and purchase of West and West Central African men, women, and children. "With the purchaser, it is not whether he separates parents and children, or husband and wife; a thought of this kind never enters his cold, calculating soul; but if such or such a one, will suit him best."[50]

In the process of forming their collective identity, chroniclers equated shared enslavement in the United States with the brutality of the experience of the middle passage. Slaves lacked any legal recourse. They were "entirely at the mercy" of tyrants. The lash was used consistently, and if a slave survived severe beatings and other forms of inhuman treatment, "ceaseless toil" was the future. They might work with "heroic fortitude," but were considered more brute than human. In this system, slaveholders suppressed intellectual development and instead "inculcated . . . ignorance," then asserted slaves' incapacity for learning.[51]

If insurrectionists like Vesey and others recognized the utility of forming alliances among diverse Africans enslaved in America, so too did those whose plan to resist involved less violent means. Russell Parrott, William Hamilton, Richard Allen, Newport Gardner, Prince Hall, and others who assumed leadership in the evolving free black communities of the northern states joined southern insurrectionists in their endeavors to unite or reinforce a collective identity among diverse Africans. Because of their unique circumstances, these northern blacks simply took the formation of alliances to another level. They began constructing an ethnic community through a shared history framed largely by the Atlantic slave trade and American slavery, but one that also included a fictive national identity in which Africans illustrated true humanity in opposition to their captors. The intensity of this endeavor indicates that the creation and maintenance of a common African identity was critical to the development of the northern free black community.

At the same time, chroniclers of the shared African past turned the oft-repeated European rationalization for African enslavement on its head. They contrasted pre-European contact civilized Africa with European barbarism and savagery. Citing the depth of involvement of the major western European powers in the slave trade, Parrott noted, "man assumed the nature of the savage; plucked from his bosom every sentiment of pity; and, to gratify his accursed avarice, devoted to lasting bondage his equal man."[52]

Proving philosopher Charles Taylor's point that humans negotiate their identities through dialogue with others, early black leaders imagined a political and cultural identity that they then transferred back onto an African past while disregarding, or lacking any knowledge of, the specificities of many West and West Central African cultural practices.[53] It seems that men who assumed leadership roles established a more patriarchal African past than many of their ancestors actually experienced. In their historical interpretations, these chroniclers claimed that men held political, economic, and social power in contradistinction to the reality wherein women often played primary roles in trade while some held positions of power in certain West African societies.[54] Clearly, northern black men's history of an African "country" reflected not only that their present status informed their romantic history of an African past, but also the degree to which they had adopted specific western cultural norms.

Indeed, the establishment of a common and glorious African past with the articulation of an oppressive American present had more to do with the elite's agenda for the newly freed men, women, and children just coming out of slavery and settling in the burgeoning free black communities. Leaders lacked appreciation for specific West or West Central African cultural traits still evident among many northern blacks in the late eighteenth and nineteenth centuries. As importantly, community leaders strategically ignored the diversity among people of color, particularly in New England, in which a significant population of Narragansett and Wampanoag intermarried with Africans. Many of these New Englanders identified more, or as much, with their Native American past. Other populations of color, often of European and African ancestry or Native American, European, and African ancestry, had little interest in viewing themselves as "African." Ministers in particular were more concerned about bringing order to the burgeoning free black urban communities. For this they relied mainly on traditional western traditions, especially Christianity, rather than look to West and West Central Africa for values, customs, and beliefs.

The small but influential black minority accepted Christianity because it met individual and collective spiritual needs. But at first only a tiny minority became Christian. In New England, a slave woman was baptized in 1641, only three years after her arrival. And a 1661 petition for freedom in New Netherlands reveals that Reytory Pieterson, a "free Negro woman," had been a Christian since 1643 and probably earlier. In 1693, Puritan minister Cotton Mather established weekly prayer meetings for several Massachusetts slaves.[55] Slaveholders generally resisted slave conversions because they were unsure if the law permitted Christians to enslave other Christians. They were unwilling to lose labor for slaves' religious activities or were simply indifferent; slaveholders persistently complained about the potential deleterious effect of slave conversions. Skepticism about the law remained into the mid-eighteenth century in spite of colonial laws protecting slaveholders' investments and clerical assurances to masters that the "soul of the slave might be saved and the slaveholder left in possession of his property."

Anglican clergymen particularly complained of a general apathy and antagonism against the instruction of slaves in all the colonies. As missionaries for the Society for the Propagation for the Gospel in Foreign Parts (SPG), Anglican clerics were engaged in a program, organized in 1701, to have more direct supervision over the religious needs of the colonies. Almost immediately the society showed great interest in the Christianization of Africans and Native Americans. In 1703 the SPG opened a catechizing school for "Indians and negroes" in New York, and soon after in other colonies, north and south.

Yet the SPG had minimal success. Generally, missionaries reported that Native Americans were not interested and slaves were too often discouraged from attending.[56]

Despite the barriers to evangelism, a number of blacks converted to Christianity through the SPG. The organization's records demonstrate a gradual increase from the early to late eighteenth century. These efforts were particularly successful when the SPG combined efforts with the Associates of Dr. Bray, an Anglican organization devoted exclusively to converting "Negroes or Native Indians." Although these missionaries gave minimal attention to Native Americans, they catechized hundreds of blacks in their newly established schools. And through the distribution of Bibles, the Book of Common Prayer, and other literature between 1702–1785, many black men, women, and children gained a rudimentary education in the North because of the Protestant stress on individual responsibility through the understanding of Scripture.[57]

But Anglicans consistently complained of Dissenter competition for the souls of blacks. In Pennsylvania, according to Reverend Robert Jenney, rector of Christ Church in Philadelphia, "dissenters of all sects and sizes" were attracting black converts. In 1745 Jenney asked the secretary of the SPG in London for the assistance of a catechist partly because he wanted to compete successfully with other Christian denominations for black converts. He believed there was great potential for conversions among blacks in the city and added that he had already baptized several. Africans, Jenny explained, had a "disposition to Religion" but were running after "Vagrant Factious Preachers." They would stay in the faith if "properly instructed." Yet, black catechumens converted often for reasons unrelated to spiritual desire. It seems gaining literacy was a primary interest to many of those who attended SPG and Bray Associates schools. The missionary reports confirm that Anglicans educated many more blacks than they converted.[58]

Christianity had to undergo discrete changes before appealing spiritually, socially, and politically to a larger black population in the late eighteenth and early nineteenth centuries. By then, American Protestantism had combined evangelicalism, republican political ideology, and common sense moral reasoning to produce a Christianity distinct from that of the rest of the Western world. Evangelicalism, defined as stressing the conversion or new birth experience, the authority of the Bible, duty to self and society, and the centrality of Christ's redemptive act, became the dominant voice of American Protestantism from the 1790s to the 1860s.[59] As such, when more blacks converted, they embraced a religion more open to innovation, more democratic, and more experiential. At the same time, Christianity had secularized in areas critical to black religious and political interests. This revised Christianity provided a foundation upon which to envision the new nation as one of promise and inclusivity.

Evangelicalism met the spiritual needs of many British North American blacks. The process of northern black conversion sped up from the mid-eighteenth century onward. George Whitefield's evangelizing efforts in the colonies beginning in 1740 heralded the "Great Awakening," a series of revivals that contributed to a significant increase in the number of black baptisms. Whitefield, who made seven journeys to the colonies, arrived in New England in the fall of 1740 and united scattered revivals flaring up in Massachusetts, Connecticut, Pennsylvania, New Jersey, and elsewhere. In his trip to Boston, part of his first American tour, he showed disdain for the cherished Anglican formalism and denominational distinctions. He and other "awakeners" unwittingly established a "populist theology" that asserted "God's grace was no respecter of persons" and "encouraged," as religious historian Mark Noll explains, "ordinary men and women to treat their own religious experience with as much respect as the directives of traditional authorities." The Great Awakening marked a transition in Protestantism from a clerical to a lay religion in which the minister was no longer the inherited authority of the church and the church constituted the converted.[60]

Whitefield's challenge to Anglican doctrine coincided with other developments in western European Christendom that contributed to a stress on the conversion experience and an intimacy with divinity. These aspects of Christianity appealed to blacks. Embracing a less staid, more ecstatic religion, Whitefield confronted Anglicans in Boston with the doctrine of the ministry of grace and free will. He advised his fellow clergymen to "preach new birth, and the power of godliness and not insist so much on form." To the dismay of some Anglican clerics, Whitefield reached thousands in Boston, including many blacks. Matters had become so bad, an SPG missionary complained, that "Men, Women[,] children, Servants, & Nigros are now become (as they phrase it 'Exhorters')." He was shocked that the worship service consisted of "groans, cries, screams, & agonies . . . tears . . . ridiculous & frantic gestures . . . some leaping, some laughing, some singing, some clapping."[61]

The emergence and pervasiveness of evangelicalism, beginning with the revivals of the Great Awakening and lasting into the early nineteenth century, greatly affected many blacks' view of Christianity, especially during and after the Revolutionary War. Revivals sweeping up and down the eastern seashore expanded the number of northern black Christians. According to religious historian Mechal Sobel, revivals "opened common ground on which whites and blacks could share religious experience, and blacks immediately responded."[62]

With representation in almost all the British North American colonies from the early seventeenth century, Baptist preachers stressed the conversion experience. Conversion occurred at a specific moment in time as the Holy Spirit worked upon the soul of a "convicted sinner." White and black converts "felt" the Holy Spirit and often experienced trances or visions while under conviction. In the minds of the converted, conversion was a specific act in which they experienced the divine presence. God manifested himself to them in a salient way.[63]

After serving nearly eight years in the Continental Army, black New Hampshire Baptist convert Charles Bowles "began to feel that though he had escaped the dangers of the battle field" he could not escape the judgment of God. Under conviction, Bowles, like many white converts, simultaneously experienced "angry flashes" of God's countenance and "the hopeful invitations of Calvary offering peace and pardon to the penitent." This spiritual war was a "contest between the kingdoms of light and darkness." The repentant Bowles found peace only when he accepted "divine grace."[64] Besides stressing the importance of conversion, the Baptist doctrine required specific rites and rituals. Total immersion of adults symbolized the death of the old life and the beginning of the new life in Christ. For Bowles, baptism occurred soon after his public profession of faith.[65] Music, mainly singing, played an important role in Baptist liturgy. Baptists stressed community, and clergy and laymen in the late eighteenth century developed a rich communal life in which all members were regarded as "brothers and sisters." Eventually, Bowles became an evangelist who ministered primarily to whites in Vermont and New Hampshire for more than forty years. Although Bowles's skin color negatively intervened in encounters with some whites, his biographer stressed the preacher's positive experiences with a community of believers who openly expressed respect and admiration for the black clergyman's untiring evangelism.[66]

A sense of community and an emphasis on conversion was evident in early Methodism as well. Like Baptists, many viewed conversion as a particular moment in time. Delaware slave Richard Allen, who became one of the most prominent and influential ministers in the development of northern free black urban communities, believed conversion was the most salient experience of his life. In his autobiography, Allen traces his experience of conviction, repentance, assurance, and finally the desire to evangelize: "I was upwards of twenty years of age, during which time I was awakened and brought to see myself, poor, wretched and undone, and without the mercy of God [I] must be lost. Shortly after, I obtained mercy through the blood of Christ, and was constrained to exhort my old companions to seek the Lord. I went rejoicing for several days and was happy in the Lord, in conversing with many old, experienced Christians."[67]

Like Allen, black Methodist converts Jarena Lee, Zilpha Elaw, and Julia Foote experienced conversion and found in Methodism an answer to their spiritual longings. Tracing their spiritual journeys in their autobiographies, all three women felt the "calling" to preach and became itinerant preachers throughout the northern states.[68] Elaw also ventured into the South as a self-elected missionary to the slaves and finally to London in the decades before the Civil War. As a young teen, Elaw's sense of spiritual uneasiness was not lifted until her conversion, when she experienced God's presence, which eliminated all "doubt of the manifestation of his love to my soul."[69]

Within Methodism, the conversion experience was the foundation of a doctrine that stressed Arminianism, or God's grace available to all, and a kind of perfectionism in a highly organized and centralized church polity. American Methodists, like their Baptist counterparts, stressed spiritual growth and moral improvement after conversion. Richard Allen joined a Methodist society in the early 1780s, during the war.[70]

European American evangelicals confronted Africans in America with a religion that was more conducive to syncretism. Whereas the more traditional American denominations—Congregationalism, Anglicanism, and Presbyterianism—stressed doctrine and polity, the evangelicals, some of whom were representatives of these denominations, developed an often highly emotive, if not frenetic, liturgy that shared elements with traditional West and West Central African religious ecstasy. The conversion experience was palpable in evangelicalism. From the start of the First Great Awakening, revivals often included flamboyant and emotional preaching that might lead worshipers into moments of fainting, mourning, weeping, and shrieking. Many individuals under conviction of the Holy Spirit experienced trances and visions. Ministers stressed the work of the Holy Spirit, the third member of the Trinity, who resided in the heart and the mind. Praying for tangible evidence of conversion was an important aspect of many revivals. The transformative event or conversion was the beginning of the new life.[71] And while Christianity stressed the existence of guilt, a foreign idea in African religions, it also stressed concepts familiar to West and West Central Africans: individual commitment and purpose to know and do the will of the gods. Moreover, evangelicalism stressed community and music, especially song, so highly valued in West African cultures.[72]

Additionally, neither Baptist nor Methodist denominations required an educated clergy. Generally denied access to higher education, black men, slave and free, were able to hold positions of leadership, found churches, and preach, as were uneducated whites. Evidence of conversion and divine calling served as the basic qualifications for preaching. By the early nineteenth century, a significant number of black preachers in the North, mostly Baptist and Methodist, continued the evangelization efforts established by whites in the early eighteenth century. The evangelical focus on a "calling" rather than education reflected the egalitarianism implicit in evangelicalism. Slaves were included in the brotherhood of Christian communion. And in a kind of reverse social hierarchy, as exemplified by Charles Bowles and Richard Allen, slaves and free blacks preached to whites. In contrast to the distance and formality of the traditional denominations, Baptist and Methodist meetings "brought black and whites closer to equality."[73] Black membership in these denominations increased.

Biblicism within evangelicalism, or the belief that the Bible is the ultimate religious authority, enabled redefinition or emphasis on key scriptural texts that fit with northern black spiritual *and* political interests. Many black evangelicals, like white evangelicals, interpreted Scripture "intuitively." Not only preachers but individual converts believed in their ability to interpret Scripture on their own. They determined Christian morality based on their own reading. African-born Chloe Spear eventually found Christianity appealing because to her mind it stressed human equality and confirmed her sense of the injustice and inhumanity of bondage. In contrast to the dry, incomprehensible sermons her master forced her to attend, the Christian God Spear would come to worship was no "respecter of persons."[74] Spear, like most other black converts, quickly joined an evangelical denomination; she left the Congregational church of her master and became a Baptist after manumission. The Baptist rite of immersion may have reminded her of a West African religious ritual.[75]

Blacks accepted evangelical Christianity not only because it met spiritual interests, but also because it supported their political and social ends. Some prominent Baptists and Methodists took strong antislavery positions in the late eighteenth century, contributing significantly to black interest in Christianity. Methodist conferences in 1780, 1783, and 1784 strongly attacked slavery and attempted to eliminate it, first among the clergy and then the entire membership. And John Wesley, the founder of the sect, along with early leaders of American Methodism, vigorously opposed slavery. Baptists in Virginia, Kentucky, New York, Indiana, Illinois, and Ohio strongly condemned slavery as well. With its more autonomous church structure, individual Baptist churches and associations publicly opposed slavery. According to the General Committee of Virginia Baptists in 1789, slavery was a "violent deprivation of the rights of nature" and Baptists were to "make use of every legal measure to extirpate this horrid evil from the land." In the 1790s, the Shaftsbury Association of New York expressed its "sense of that freedom which every child of Adam is entitled to by nature; and of which they cannot be deprived but by hostile usurpation."[76] In spite of the opposition of some, however, most Methodists and Baptists quickly accepted slavery, finding justification for it in the Bible. Indeed, antislavery positions were constantly under attack from the beginning.[77]

Even so, for black Christians, the Bible articulated principles of freedom, equality, and justice that provided the ideological foundation for the abolition of slavery and for human equality. These political elements would join with the spiritual to constitute black evangelicalism. Christianity not only provided a "frame" from which to base moral judgments, but it also helped develop the ideal of a unified African identity.[78] Community leaders believed all blacks should become Christian. They wanted a common black religion that would become part of the shared ethnic identity based in common oppression and ancestral history to create the unity necessary for a viable black community that participated in American society. Perhaps because their ancestors came out of religion-centered cultures that influenced their political and economic lives, many blacks were open to the religious influence of the dominant society and viewed it as a means of black solidarity. Sufficiently distant from their ancestral cultural milieu and maintaining spiritual interest, those who were intensely involved in creating an African identity and establishing institutions filled their religious void with a belief system that for them explained their present predicament as enslaved or newly freed peoples. A close study of early black fraternal and mutual relief societies shows that the establishment of African identity was closely tied to Christian affiliation. A significant population of blacks in the North coalesced around their "African" institutions and their newfound faith. From its beginning, black Christianity had spiritual, social, and political dimensions.

Preachers like Richard Allen committed themselves to uniting newly freed northern blacks and bringing order to the developing communities through Christianization. For Allen, Christian morality, as he interpreted early Methodism, was the only means by which blacks could find purpose and dignity. Serving as an itinerant preacher to blacks and whites in the Delaware, New Jersey, Maryland, and Pennsylvania regions after purchasing his freedom, Allen decided that his mission was specifically to blacks in America. Accepting a call to Philadelphia, he "saw a large field open in seeking and instructing my African brethren, who had been a long forgotten people and few of them attended public worship." He established prayer meetings and created a "society" in 1786 for forty-two members.

Allen soon decided that black Christianization necessitated separation from white churches.[79] This political act of resistance involved physical distance from whites, especially white clergy, as well as control over concepts and values essential in black clerics' minds. Black Christianity, even among northern elite blacks, could not be a replica of white Christianity. Black preachers refined Christianity to meet the spiritual, social, and political interests and exigencies of a distinct and oppressed population in and out of slavery.

Black spirituality was integral to black identity: who and what they were, their individual self and collective sense of worth, purpose, and mission became part of the preachers' evangelizing programs. Ministers like Allen hoped to mold slaves and free blacks' conception of themselves through the inculcation of Christian values, particularly the belief in the worthiness of all humans. The existence of African enslavement, its origins, and its significance had to be explained within the same religion that supporters of slavery used to justify enslavement. Stressing some biblical principles over others, black ministers, engaged as much in a political agenda as a spiritual one, wanted control over the sermons and liturgy so that principles of human equality and justice were prominent and the oppression of Africans was reconciled with the growing idea of a benevolent and loving God. Those of African ancestry living in the United States needed a script, black clerics believed, a story, a means of resistance that countered white claims of black inferiority either because of enslavement or, increasingly, innate characteristics.

Thus, Allen led in the struggle for separate black churches. White clergymen reinforced a growing number of black ministers' and laymen's calls for separate black churches with policies of blatant discrimination, essentially continuing the colonial custom of treating blacks as inferior beings. In Philadelphia, Methodist officials significantly aided Allen's plan when they extended discriminatory church practices rather than establish greater equity in seating and the taking of sacraments. Allen and Absalom Jones immediately led blacks out of St. George Methodist Episcopal Church to establish two of the earliest black churches, Methodist and Episcopalian, in Philadelphia.[80]

Like Philadelphians, men and women in other northern towns and cities successfully established black Methodist, Baptist, and Presbyterian churches in the late eighteenth and early nineteenth centuries; by 1821 two black Methodist denominations had been established. Clearly, racism contributed disproportionately to black interest in religious separation. But just as evident is the fact that several northern blacks were committed to separate religious meetings, often before discriminatory policies were in place or enforced. In New York, black Methodists began meeting separately in the 1790s while still maintaining membership and attending services at the John Street Church. In 1786 the Methodist John Street Society had a membership of 178; of this number, nineteen were black women and six were black men. When the black membership increased, discriminatory policies were instituted. Black preachers were no longer allowed to preach to a racially mixed congregation and only occasionally to black members. New York was still a slave state and white ministers stressed obedience. In the fall of 1796, black New Yorkers established their own church and created their own denomination, the African Methodist Episcopal church, called the African Methodist Episcopal Zion church in 1821.[81]

Black Baptists experienced segregation and discrimination similar to that shown to black Methodists. In recounting his conversion in a white Hartford, Connecticut, Baptist congregation, Jeremiah Asher remembered experiencing little or no prejudice in the 1820s. The pastor encouraged his participation in church committees and even wanted him to preach periodically to the mostly white congregation. He was a recipient of their full "Christian affection." But as more blacks joined the church, white attitudes changed dramatically. The church instituted separate seating, with "negro pews" almost entirely concealed from the congregation and with their backs to the preacher. Asher led the protest against the new policy and finally left the church. His old church tried to get him and other members to return with the promise of transferring the "negro pews" to the gallery. Asher wanted to know why separate seating was necessary at all when so many pews were vacant. Eventually he and other black Baptists formed a separate Hartford church with Asher as pastor.[82] On the other hand, black Philadelphia Presbyterians separated, according to their early nineteenth-century black church historian, even though they could not point to any specific discrimination policy. The "prevailing opinion" was that blacks wanted their own minister and control over their own local church government.[83] Local church power included the power over ideas, ideas about individual and collective identity.

A 1792 broadside prepared by the "Representatives of the African Church of Philadelphia" summarized some of the prevailing northern black religious separatist sentiments of the late eighteenth and early nineteenth centuries. Besides the political problem that whites were incapable of understanding black experience in slavery and quasi-slavery and supported the notion that blacks should be controlled, black Christians were convinced that white clergymen and their congregations would not meet the spiritual, social, or psychological needs of the emerging free northern black population. The "line drawn by custom . . . between them and the white people all evince the necessity and propriety of their enjoying separate and exclusive means, and opportunities of worshipping God, of instructing their youth, and taking care of their poor."[84] The writers of the broadside expressed northern black sacred and secular interests, their concern for experiencing democracy and equality, qualities largely inaccessible to blacks in white institutions. They wanted voice, if not control, over black religious and secular instruction. Just as critical, the writers stressed the distinct experiences, not simply past but present, of whites and blacks in American society.

Thus, separatism was in part a response to racism. But racism was only one of the interrelated elements concerning distinct values, goals, and purposes that for many northern blacks necessitated distance from whites. Even some of the most supportive white Christians seemed incapable of envisioning black Christians as equal participants in evangelism, church activities, and particularly church structure and policy, never mind equality within American society. White Christianity did not stress the fundamental themes of black Christians: blacks' right to freedom, justice, and equality.

Within a spiritual/political interpretation, Black ministers believed that Judeo-Christianity provided the religion that addressed the needs and interests of Africans' experiences in their new world. Ministers stressed Jewish bondage and divine liberation as evidence of biblical opposition to slavery. Clerics, laymen, and laywomen drew almost exact parallels between Jewish bondage and African enslavement. The minister at Philadelphia's St. Thomas African Episcopal Church, Absalom Jones, for example, asserted that Israel's enslavement demonstrated that a people raised up for a divine purpose could fall victim to captivity and bondage. The Jews were slaves "compelled to work in the open air, in one of the hottest climates in the world; and probably without a covering from the burning rays of the sun." They worked long, hard hours "performed under the eye of vigilant and rigorous masters." They were punished with beatings, given food of the "cheapest kind" containing little nourishment, and their sons were dragged from their mothers' arms to prevent insurrection. Israelites, according to Jones, lived under these conditions for nearly four hundred years, but a loving God did not forget his people, nor was he insensitive to their cries of sorrow. Although for mysterious and "wise reasons," God allowed Jewish enslavement and recorded every injustice "in order to testify, at a future day, against the authors of their oppression."[85] "He has seen ships fitted out from different ports in Europe and America . . . for the bodies and souls of men. He has seen the anguish . . . when parents have been torn from their children, and children from their parents. . . . He has seen them thrust into holds of ships, where many have perished from want of air." And God saw the instruments of torture—"the whip, the screw, the pincers, and the red hot iron"—used by overseers, slaveholders, and slave mistresses to control their involuntary laborers.[86]

As interpreted by black ministers, Christianity not only condemned human bondage but also promised freedom from slavery. God was just. The "Judge of the world" was so moved with the horrors of slavery that he intervened personally on behalf of the children of Israel and delivered them out of the hands of their oppressors. So, too, God would deliver Africans in America. "He has heard the prayers that have ascended from the hearts of his people; and he has, as in the case of his ancient and chosen people the Jews, come down to deliver our suffering countrymen from the hands of their oppressors."[87] God knew their name.

Ministers and other black speakers consistently assured their listeners that though God was benevolent and in his benevolence forgave those who repented and changed their behavior, he was also a God of wrath who would not allow the wicked to go unpunished. These two dimensions, deliverance and retribution, were equally important in northern black Christianity. God would punish those who wantonly separated husbands and wives, parents and children. God was the "protector and avenger of slaves."[88] But how could a benevolent God allow black suffering? Few ministers were willing to tackle the question. The few who did eventually sided on the notion of eventual African Christianization. Perhaps God designed, Jones theorized, that knowledge of the gospel would be acquired by slaves so that "they might become qualified to be the messengers of it, to the land of their fathers." Or as Chloe Spear asserted, whites meant it "for evil, but God meant it for good."[89]

These clearly political sermons were unimaginable in early nineteenth-century white churches. Black preachers had to be able to express their firm conviction that slavery was not only a sin but also that God would wreak vengeance on its perpetrators. This was black evangelical Christianity. It was simultaneously spiritual and political. Richard Allen's intense commitment to Christianity and against what he called "spiritual despotism" remained solid.[90] Allen and his fellow pioneering clerics ensured that black evangelicalism's distinguishing feature was its explicit political agenda. The sacred and secular were inseparable.

Evangelicalism, with its stress on biblicism, conversionism, crucicentrism, and activism, is critical for understanding northern black reception and re-definition of Christianity. The other two elements in American Christianity, common sense moral reasoning and the republican ideals strongly evident in the Revolution, were essential for the development of an African American identity. As newly freed Christians coming of age during and immediately after the Revolutionary crisis, men and women set out to create their place in the new nation.

CHAPTER 2

Becoming American

CHRISTIAN REPUBLICANISM AND AFRICAN AMERICAN IDENTITY

As an American, I glory in informing you that Columbia boasts the first men who distinguished themselves eminently in the vindication of our rights, and the improvement of our state.

—Quoted in Dorothy Porter, ed., *Early Negro Writing, 1760–1837*

During the political crisis between Great Britain and her North American colonies, several black Christians living in the North embraced specific Revolutionary principles that coincided with their understanding and interpretation of the Bible. Consequently, these men and women created a dual identity that affirmed ties with their native "country" and testified, at the same time, to their growing identification with the emerging nation. Many free blacks in the late eighteenth and early nineteenth centuries designated themselves African and American, creating an identity based on their interest in developing and memorializing a collective ancestral past and establishing an identity for the present. The process of African Americanization occurred simultaneously with black Christianization during and immediately after the Revolutionary crisis, in which evangelical Protestantism had embraced certain republican political principles and common sense moral reasoning. Northern free blacks readily agreed with the republican ideals that included belief in human equality, a commitment to universal liberty, and opposition to rigid social hierarchy. They also embraced elements in the philosophy of common sense moral reasoning that stressed a universal innate moral sense. Now Christian, a significant population of northern blacks quickly identified as American.

This new national identity meant participating in the meaning and character of the new republic. Black Christians in the North stressed that freedom and equality were essential elements in the founding of the new nation and were the fundamental principles of the Bible. Black political evangelicalism would be the principle upon which they staked their claim to American nationality and citizenship.

The evolving multiplicity, ambiguity, and flexibility of Revolutionary thought and language opened the door for interpreting and incorporating key principles and concepts in ways that addressed the particular interests and needs of American evangelicals, black and white. Indeed, as Mark Noll demonstrates, Protestant Americans embraced republican ideals by folding them into their traditional theologies.[1] American Protestantism underwent major transformations in the eighteenth century. Until the middle of the century, American religious belief was essentially European; its theology was traditional, deferential to inherited authority, and suspicious of individual self-assertion. The center of formal religion throughout the colonies remained the prerogatives and actions of God. Beginning in the mid-eighteenth century, the religious fervor of the Great Awakening, combined with the growing intensity of the political crisis with Great Britain, contributed to the evolution of a distinctly American theology that integrated evangelicalism, elements of republicanism, and common sense moral reasoning. Events in the Revolutionary War cemented the alliance between republicanism and Christianity so that by the end of the 1780s it was routine for Christians to speak of republican and Christian values with one voice. Then, in the new century, common sense moral reasoning became integral to American Protestantism.

American revivalists often utilized republican reasoning in their promotion of reform. Presbyterian minister Jacob Green showed the extent to which Revolutionary ideology could be used to attack slavery. Green argued that slaveholders were "enemies to liberty, ergo are enemies to our present struggle for liberty, ergo are enemies to these United States. These slavish slave holders will watch for an opportunity to establish slavery and bondage in the United States." Concurrently, leading patriots employed traditional religious language to support republican policies. "From the time of the Stamp Act to the end of the War for Independence . . . patriot publicists skillfully and repeatedly linked Parliamentary actions to the devil." Even more profound, Thomas Paine, hardly a representative of traditional Christianity, successfully appropriated biblical narratives in *Common Sense* to justify and advocate revolution. Paine, who dismissed such fundamental Christian doctrines as the universality of sin, God's control over human affairs, and God's control in the timing of the millennium, recognized the necessity of finding common ground with American colonists. The Revolutionary War, Noll tells us, solidified and perpetuated a singularly American union of religious and political principles, as patriots and religious leaders characterized the struggle as an intensely religious cause. In late eighteenth- and early nineteenth-century America, republican thought and language were pervasive.

Moreover, by the early nineteenth century, theology in America had shifted even more from traditional reformed Protestantism (i.e., Calvinism), not only in its reception of republican ideals understood within a Christian belief system, but also in its acceptance of Scottish common sense moral reasoning, in which ideas about the nature of God, man, and society had changed. Common sense philosophy asserted man's universal capacity to arrive at "truth" by use of his own reason. Evangelicalism, republicanism, and common sense philosophy meant that Americans had refashioned fundamental Western reformed Christian doctrine in unique ways.[2]

Thus, when the small but significant number of people of African descent in the northern colonies and states converted to Christianity, the Christianity they learned, especially in the late eighteenth century, stressed key republican and common sense principles. The life-transforming conversions that many blacks and whites experienced at the height of the Revolutionary conflict only contributed to the confluence of evangelicalism and republicanism.[3]

Inevitably then, the crisis between colonists and Great Britain accelerated the evolutionary process of black Christians' identification with America. In New England, where slaves had right of petition and constituted, along with free blacks, 2.4 percent of the population, or about 16,000 out of a population of nearly 660,000, newly converted black New Englanders viewed the evolving crisis, like many whites, through the lens of evangelicalism. Enslaved blacks combined biblical principles and natural rights doctrine in their demands for emancipation, confirming the cementing of republicanism and evangelicalism in the Revolutionary era. Massachusetts slave petitioners in 1774 argued that "within the bowels" of a free Christian country" they had a "naturel right to be free."[4] Writing in the ironic mode, petitioners noted that they had been "unjustly dragged by the cruel hand of power from our dearest friends and sum of us stolen from the bosoms of our tender Parents . . . and Brought hither to be made slaves for Life in a Christian land."[5] Reflecting Locke's influence in the British North American colonies, Boston slave petitioners asserted their "naturel" right for freedom on the grounds of human equality and a doctrine of mutual consent. Slavery, they argued, violated natural law and Christianity. "That your Petitioners apprehind we have in common with all other men a naturel right to our freedoms without Being depriv'd of them by our fellow men as we are a freeborn Pepel and have never forfeited this Blessing by aney compact or agreement whatever."[6]

Petitioners argued that bondage was antithetical to Christianity; it prevented slave converts from obeying divine precepts. Both marital and parental responsibilities were dictated not by Christian principles but by financial interests of masters. Slavery ignored the "endearing ties of husband and wife" and children were denied parental love and guidance. Instead, they were "taken from us by force and sent maney miles from us wear we seldom or ever see them again there to be made slaves of for Life which sumtimes is vere short by Reson of Being dragged from their mothers Breest."[7] And, assuming their place within the larger Christian community, slave petitioners argued that bondage precluded true brotherhood. Their "deplorable" circumstances were such that they were "rendered incapable of shewing our obedience to Almighty God."[8] Particularly galling to slave petitioners, and probably most slaves, was that Christian patriots, many of whom were slaveholders, likened their increasingly precarious political status to that of enslavement in their appeals to the imperial government for relief from unacceptable duties and taxes. Colonists demanded liberty and freedom for themselves while holding others in abject bondage. It was hypocritical for "a People Profesing the mild Religion of Jesus A people Not Insensible of the Secrets of Rationable Being Nor without spirit to Resent the unjust endeavors of others to Reduce them to a state of Bondage and Subjection."[9]

Expanding on patriots' republican fears and admonitions concerning unlimited power, slave petitioners argued that slavery involved complete powerlessness and deprivation. While colonists complained that Parliament exceeded its bounds in taxing them, New England slaves asserted that real slavery transcended mere political and economic rights; it elided national and societal affiliations and invaded the most personal of human relationships. "We have no property! We have no wives! No children! We have no city! No country!"[10] Slave petitioners conspicuously stressed their Christian virtue in contrast to the degradation they experienced in slavery. They were determined "to keep all [God's] . . . Commandments," including obedience to "our Masters," as long as bondage persisted.[11]

Slaves noted the irony, too, that in submitting their many petitions they were imitating patriots in their petitions to Great Britain and meeting, regrettably, the same negative result. Yet, the very principles colonists used in support of their disagreement with the empire applied a thousand times more to them. They could not but express their "Astonishment that It has Never Bin Considered that Every Principle from which Amarica has Acted in the Cours of their unhappy Deficultes with Great Briton Pleads Stronger than A thousand arguments in favowrs of your petioners."[12] Invoking Lockean language of natural rights, they urged colonists to restore them "to the Enjoyments of that which is the Naturel Right of all men" so they would no longer be "chargeable with the inconsistancey of acting themselves the part which thay condem and oppose in others."[13] In May 1772, the *New London Gazette* published a poem of "a Negro" who argued on the basis of reason that the same principles for liberty that applied to colonists also applied to those in bondage. "Is reason yours, and partially your friend? Be not deceiv'd—for reason pleads for all."[14]

Evidence of a developing American identity was readily apparent in the slave petitions. New England slave petitioners wished colonists well in their "Glorious struggle for Liberty." They hoped a victory for patriots might mean actual freedom for themselves.[15] And as natural rights doctrine influenced New England slaves in their petitions for freedom, they began claiming rights of citizenship. These and probably many other New England slaves assumed equal right to the benefits of the legal system and argued for membership in civil society. Their rights were thwarted because of colonial "tyranny." Boston petitioners informed the court that, when free, they would participate in the responsibilities of citizenship. In language that challenged colonial laws defining degrees of freedom, slaves argued for the full application of the rule of law. They believed there was no law that permitted bondage in the Massachusetts colony. Slavery hindered them from reaping an "equal benefit from the Laws of the Land with other subjects." In expressing their intention to assume responsibilities of citizenship in America if granted freedom, the petitioners urged officials not to judge all blacks alike any more than they would judge all whites alike. Petitioners argued that the majority of blacks were sober, industrious, religious, and civic minded in spite of their abject condition and, if free, would "soon be able as well as willing to bear a Part in the Public charges."[16]

For these latter petitioners, American identity was still ambivalent, still evolving, however. With African identity secure and American identity in the early 1770s uncertain, they expressed interest in emigrating to Africa within three months after submitting the petition. "We are willing to submit to such regulations and laws, as may be made relative to us, until we leave the province, which we determine to do as soon as we can, from our joynt labours procure money to transport ourselves to some part of the Coast of *Africa*, where we propose a settlement." Yet by June of the same year, these petitioners reasserted the right to property ownership in America through their own "industry."[17] A year later, other slaves revealed that blacks' meaning of freedom coincided with the right to benefit from their own labor. They requested a land grant in Massachusetts that a man might "quietly sit down under his own fig tree [and enjoy] the fruits of his labour."[18]

Persistent in their interpretation of events through the prism of an evangelical Christianity and moving toward a dual identity during the Revolutionary War, northern blacks in a 1779 petition to the General Assembly of Connecticut condemned Americans not only for the "flagrant Injustice" of slavery, but also for keeping slaves in "gross Ignorance." Colonists had added to the wickedness of bondage done to "Africans" by preventing them from learning. These petitioners and others demanded their freedom based on their interpretation that Scripture asserted universal freedom and human equality, as "Creatures of that God, who made of one Blood, and Kindred, all the Nations of the Earth." Reflecting the growing acceptance of republicanism and common sense moral reasoning among evangelical Christians, these slave petitioners reasoned that they had the same intellectual capacities as their masters, so there was "nothing that leads us to a Belief, or Suspicion, that we are any more obliged to serve them, than they us, and the more we Consider of this matter, the more we are Convinced of our Right (by the Laws of Nature and by the whole Tenor of the Christian Religion, . . .) to be free."[19]

Free blacks applied the same Revolutionary principles as slaves and indicated that they identified even more with colonists in a common struggle. When the Massachusetts legislature in the 1770s appeared reluctant to enfranchise "Negroes, and molattoes" but not at all hesitant to tax those with property, New Englanders of African and Native American parentage Paul and John Cuffe petitioned the Massachusetts legislature in February 1780 for tax relief on the basis of no taxation without representation. The Cuffes unhesitatingly and successfully appropriated the language and ideals of rebel colonists. They were being taxed as citizens yet were denied privileges of citizenship, namely the right to vote. The Cuffes thought it ironic that the very reason colonists gave for resisting the British was used against the most vulnerable of the community. In that year, Massachusetts voters approved the removal of racial restrictions on suffrage in its newly established state constitution.[20]

The Cuffe brothers and many other blacks viewed the struggle against

Great Britain as a "Common Cause." They said that black men were fighting alongside whites for independence from "tyranny."[21] Even though most slave men fought in exchange for freedom on either the American or British side, some fought for what they perceived as a divinely inspired effort that would culminate in the creation of a new and different society. They fought for and supported, as Frederick Douglass would later argue, "the advent of a nation based upon human brotherhood and the self-evident truths of liberty and equality."[22]

Free blacks were more likely to fight for patriotic reasons. Though some were drafted, others were motivated not simply by the promise of a bounty or land grant but because they believed in the Revolutionary struggle. Twenty-one years old and recently freed from his indenture, New Englander Lemuel Haynes joined the Massachusetts militia and later the Continental Army in defense of the American colonies. Like many eighteenth-century free blacks, Haynes's parentage was both white and black. Abandoned by his white mother almost at birth and with no knowledge of his African father, he grew up in the rural home of a white Congregational deacon. Deacon David Rose included Haynes in family worship, Bible reading, and church attendance. Eventually, Haynes experienced conversion, was baptized, and joined the local Congregational church. During or perhaps shortly after his first military experience as a minuteman in Concord, Haynes memorialized the now famous struggle with a ballad. In "The Battle of Lexington," the young Revolutionary identified with the American cause and demonstrated his conviction that liberty was a natural God-given right.[23] "For Liberty, each Freeman Strives As it's a Gift of God And for it willing yield their Lives And Seal it with their Blood."[24]

Although Haynes was obviously influenced by the European American milieu in which he lived, James Forten, who grew up in a free black Pennsylvania household, identified just as fully with the American cause. At fourteen Forten joined the patriot forces in 1781 as a powder boy aboard the *Royal Louis*. When the British captured the ship during its second voyage, the young boy was fortuitously befriended by the British captain, who wanted to take him to England rather than let him suffer imprisonment with the other Revolutionaries. Forten chose prison and, according to one report, told the captain, "I have been taken prisoner for the liberties of my country, and never will prove a traitor to her interests."[25] He had joined up because, as he told his son-in-law much later, his "heart [was] fired with the enthusiasm . . . of the patriots and revolutionaries of the day."[26]

Northern blacks not involved in combat supported the Revolutionaries. In her poem to "His Excellency General Washington," the now famous Phillis Wheatley, enslaved since the age of seven in a Massachusetts household, urged the commander of the Continental Army to "Proceed, great chief, with virtue on thy side." New Jersey slave Peter Williams described his manumission and the liberation of his New Jersey town from the British as a "double joy to his heart."[27] According to his son, Peter Williams Jr., Williams's "attachment to the country of his birth was strengthened and confirmed by the circumstance, that the very day on which the British evacuated New York was the same on which he obtained his freedom by purchase, through the help of some republican friends of the Methodist Church; and to the last year of his life, he always spoke of that day as one which gave double joy to his heart, by freeing him from domestic bondage, and his native city from foreign enemies."[28]

Blacks who sided with the patriots perceived the Revolution as part of a divine plan. "Nothing short of a kind of miraculous interposition has brought us hitherto," Lemuel Haynes wrote.[29] Black Christians joined with other Christians in the British American colonies in drawing on the Bible for their understanding of the war and for interpreting republican political theory. For them, the principles of liberty and equality coincided perfectly with their understanding of Christian precepts they believed explicit in the Bible.

Thus, identification as Christian easily led to identification as American. With the growing emergence of Christian republicanism, Christian black northerners found common ground with the citizens of the new republic. Haynes readily embraced the patriot cause as his own and interpreted it within a religious mind-set. Although his ancestry, status, and choices distinguished him from most blacks of African descent in the northern colonies, Haynes developed one of the earliest and most representative northern free black evangelical arguments for the establishment of universal freedom and equality in the new nation. Haynes envisioned that America would be, from the start, a Christian republic of diverse peoples from Africa as well as Europe, all participating in the fruits of the current war.

In a 1776 treatise titled "Liberty Further Extended," the twenty-three-year-old former minuteman introduced his essay with the preamble to the Declaration of Independence. Then, like the New England slave petitioners for freedom, he argued that while colonists were engaged in a war against tyranny, it was imperative "to turn one Eye into our own Breast, for a little moment," to learn if tyranny existed within American society. If tyranny did exist, then this was the moment "while we are inspir'd with so noble a Spirit and Becoming Zeal . . . to tear her from us." Freedom, Haynes argued, was "an innate principle" established at creation. It was "a Jewel . . . handed Down to man from the cabinet of heaven, and is Coaeval with his Existance." It proceeded "from the Supreme Legislature of the univers" so only God could deny individual freedom. Indeed, every privilege of humankind originated from God and any laws that denied divine rights were "*void*." The enslavement of humans, Haynes reasoned, counteracted "the very Laws of nature."[30]

Concomitant with freedom was the divine origin of human equality. For evidence, Haynes cited the biblical reference that would be repeated by blacks throughout the nineteenth century: "It hath pleased god to *make of one Blood all nations of men, for to dwell upon the face of the Earth. Acts 17,26.*" Because humankind was "of one Species," the same laws applied to all. The Bible as interpreted through the lens of evangelicalism, with the values coming out of the Revolutionary crisis, provided Haynes and others the ammunition to attack slavery and inequality.

Haynes's main focus in "Liberty Further Extended" was on refuting eighteenth-century justifications for slavery. Even the "most cogent" arguments were, according to Haynes, "Essencially Deficient." Revealing the extent to which the language of race was still in its embryonic stage and examining and anticipating evolving theories of human variety that would become central to nineteenth-century racial ideology, the young Revolutionary soldier first attacked the excuse that skin color determined natural rights. He wanted to know where in Scripture existed the precept or practice that made a "Black man a Slave, any more than a white one."[31]

Haynes dismissed out of hand the idea that Europeans in West Africa were acting as peacemakers among warring African societies. Relying on the writings of eighteenth-century abolitionist Anthony Benezet, he noted that European slave traders would be contradicting their own interest. In fact, they were engaging in the "vile and atrocious" practice of creating wars among the nations to procure slaves.[32] Twenty-two years later, another black New Englander would argue similarly. In his speech on freedom, a member of the African Society in Boston said that the excuse that slave traders were protecting Africans from themselves or that Africans also had a system of slavery was merely a "cloak to cover" European wickedness. He added that the immorality of one group did not justify the immorality of another. "Is it a sufficient evidence that one neighbour hath a right to another, because he is so sagacious as to rob his neighbour of his wife and children, and sell them to another neighbour for half the value?"[33]

Likewise, Haynes found that the argument that slavery and the slave trade enabled the Christianization of pagans was without merit. The idea that slavery and the slave trade were a *"great Blessing instead of a Curs"* was particularly offensive to the New England Christian. Scripture and reason condemned such justifications. "Those Slaves in these Colonies are generally kept under the greatest ignorance, and Blindness, and they are scersly Ever told by their white masters whether there is a Supreme Being that governs the univers."[34] And, to those who argued that slavery was not contradictory to Christian principles because it was practiced among the early Christians, Haynes reasoned that the Apostle Paul discouraged the practice and recommended freedom "if attainable." The extent to which slavery existed and was prevalent, however, was still antithetical to "the unchangeble Laws of God, or of nature." It wasn't "strange" that humankind would "make that Become Lawfull which is in itself unlawfull," considering their moral depravity. Human property was "illicit, and was prohibited by the most obvious Dictates of Humanity." In fact, Haynes added, the status of slave was nonexistent. There were only those "who are pretended to be Slaves."[35]

Haynes's argument for the expansion or universal application of liberal principles showed the ways in which eighteenth-century northern black Christians reflected the changes in American Protestantism, with its incorporation of republican political principles and common sense moral reasoning, in their demands for a "true republic" that embraced Africans in the new nation as part of its citizenry. Appropriating Christian republicanism and utilizing common sense moral reasoning, blacks in the late eighteenth and early nineteenth centuries established the foundation of northern free black political thought that would last into the Civil War era.

Black northern Christians consistently expressed their firm belief in universal principles of freedom and equality by appropriating common sense moral reasoning in demanding their right to become full citizens of the body politic. A member of the African Society in Boston, in an 1808 speech on freedom, asserted the divine origin of human freedom and equality and added, "we . . . insist on the universality of freedom because we believe it to be the right of every rational creature." Northern blacks in the late eighteenth and early nineteenth centuries consistently argued for the expansion of the Declaration of Independence on the basis of biblical and liberal principles. One of the "Sons of Africans" called it "criminal" that those who love freedom for themselves prevent others from its enjoyment. The Sons of Africans and others repeated what had quickly become one of the mantras of early black political writing: "for *of one blood were all the nations of the earth formed.*" Prince Hall, probably manumitted in 1770 and founder of the African Masonic Lodge in the 1780s, repeated another biblical mantra, the Scripture verse that Chloe Spear found so comforting, for evidence of universal human equality when he reminded his fellow Masons in a 1797 speech that God "hath no respect of persons." Another biblical verse was repeated less often than the other two but was common nevertheless: "There is neither Jew nor Greek, there is neither bond nor free, there is neither male nor female: for ye are all one in Christ Jesus." In speeches, essays, sermons, petitions, and letters northern blacks persistently relied on the primary spiritual text of white America in their demands for black freedom, equality, and citizenship.[36]

The speaker to the African Society in Boston paralleled Haynes's other argument that if freedom is a right of one nation, it is the right of all nations. All men "are the Lord's." Color was no determiner of "the rights and privileges which Providence hath allotted." We "take the liberty to ask the objector against freedom . . . whether the complexion of one nation entitles them to the service and property of another: Or, in other words, whether the Africans ought be subject to the British or Americans, because they are of a dark complexion?" The arguments in support of African enslavement on the basis of skin color were "trivial . . . fallacious and groundless." While slavery was universally objectionable, "tyrants" exhibited "a spirit more fit to be a slave" than many of their "domestics." In his speech in New York City commemorating the abolition of the slave trade on January 1, 1808, Peter Williams Jr. expressed gratitude to white abolitionists for their role in restoring "our natural rights."[37]

Faced with clear evidence that republican doctrines would be limited to whites, northern blacks persisted in their vision of a "true republic" and claims of American identity and citizenship. In the 1796 bylaws of the African Society in Boston, the membership referred to their individual state citizenship and claimed national citizenship. They committed themselves to be "true and faithful citizens of the Commonwealth in which we live" and not to admit anyone who committed a crime against the "laws of their country." They were "Africans" but "fellow citizens" of the United States. Unaware that within a few years New York would essentially disfranchise black men, Joseph Sidney explained to a New York black audience in 1809 that America was "our country" and as such citizens had responsibilities and duties. Sidney wanted New York black men who met the property requirements to vote.[38]

When black Philadelphia preachers Absalom Jones and Richard Allen published and distributed their response to charges that black caretakers exploited white victims for profit during the 1793 yellow fever epidemic in the nation's capital, they implied evidence of civic virtue qualifying African Americans for citizenship. Contrary to popular opinion, the authors asserted that ordinary black men and women demonstrated the primary ingredient for republican governments: "virtue." Philadelphia blacks were "sensible that it was our duty to do all the good we could . . . [for] our suffering fellow mortals." As a matter of Christian charity and their duty as citizens, black interest was simply to serve, not to benefit from the dreaded disease as some whites had done. The former slaves pointed to Matthew Carey, the Philadelphia publisher who brought the charges, and noted that Carey was profiting from the sale of his pamphlet. They then showed that blacks, in contrast to whites, had used their meager means to help all patients regardless of their ability to pay.

Carey was not the only white who lacked virtue, according to their account; there were several whites who lacked a public spirit. On the other hand, poor blacks excelled in virtue.[39] "We can with certainty assure the public that we have seen more humanity, more real sensibility from the poor colored than from the poor whites. When many of the former, of their own accord, rendered services where extreme necessity called for it, the general part of the poor white people were so dismayed, that instead of attempting to be useful, they, in a manner, hid themselves."[40] In descriptive detail, Jones and Allen contrasted thoroughly humane black care with vicious and mean white behavior. "Many of the white people, who ought to be patterns for us to follow after, have acted in a manner that would make humanity shudder."[41]

As virtuous citizens, Africans in the United States, according to the ministers, consistently demonstrated their republican sense of civic duty. The true exploiters were those who claimed that people of African ancestry could not get yellow fever. The authors demonstrated statistically that blacks were affected and died with the fever like whites, and argued that officials squelched reports of illnesses to obtain black help. "Thus were our services extorted at the peril of our lives," the authors charged. "Yet you accuse us of extorting a little money from you." To underscore black Philadelphia beneficence and integrity, the clergymen attached a certificate of "approbation" from the mayor of the city whose testimony attested to the diligence, attention, and decency of deportment of Allen, Jones, and others.[42] Blacks, the ministers implied, were as qualified, perhaps even more so in some instances, as whites to become part of the polity.

Following the format of abolitionists' literature beginning in the mid-eighteenth century, Jones and Allen ended their "A Narrative of the Proceedings of the Colored People During the Awful Calamity in Philadelphia in the Year 1793; and a Refutation of Some Censures Thrown upon Them in Some Publications" with an appeal to slaveholders. In language and tone similar to Benezet and Haynes, the authors appealed to slaveholders' sense of patriotism and a "self-love" that would benefit themselves and the larger society. Slavery, they argued, threatened the entire country and the guilt of slavery would fall on future generations.[43] "If you love your children, if you love your country, if you love the God of love, clear your hands from slaves; burthen not your children or your country with them."[44]

Many northern blacks couched their antislavery campaign within Christian republican principles as Americans. They argued that the new republic's willingness to accept slavery threatened its very existence. Combining Christian republicanism and Lockean terms of liberal society in which individual rights coalesced with the public good, northern free blacks argued that slavery was antithetical to the development of civil society; it was ultimately not in the interest of individuals, including slaveholders, and therefore the larger society. While embracing individualism and distinctions between private and public interests, they, like Locke, believed certain private interests in the "long range" were harmful to society. Slaveholding was just such a vice; ultimately, it harmed the entire nation.

Repeating the argument of the New England slave petitioners, early republic free blacks consistently reminded white America of the unfinished business of the new republic in allowing for the continuance of slavery. Utilizing (as did most Americans) the vocabulary of the Revolution, with words such as "tyranny" concerning those with power, free blacks argued that as human beings, equal with all others and holding natural rights, slaves experienced persistent tyranny in their person and family. Moreover, slaves were unable to contribute to their families or "church and state"; instead, slavery "spread ignorance . . . poverty and distress in the world." Rather than establish a peaceful society, the existence of slavery created persistent fear throughout the country. In an 1827 speech, William Hamilton explained that unlike whites in the North, where the "virtuous" sleep without fear, southern whites experienced "the wicked dream of being pursued by furies." A "poor, single, solitary man of colour, cannot enter their country, but through their dread of soul, they seize him and imprison him. They are like him that has murdered his neighbour, who starts at every one that looks him in the face."[45]

More explicit than Jones and Allen, Haynes stressed the absolute necessity of a virtuous citizenry. After becoming a Congregational minister in Rutland, Vermont, Haynes delivered several sermons in honor of various American political events. In two sermons, one celebrating American independence and the other celebrating George Washington's birthday, he stressed the importance of a virtuous citizenry for the republic. In his *The Influence of Civil Government on Religion* (1798), *The Nature and Importance of TRUE REPUBLICANISM* (1801), and *DISSIMULATION ILLUSTRATED* (1814), Haynes noted that the question for citizens was what is good for the whole society; "selfish" and self-centered men were not friends to God or their country. God established civil government "as a source of virtue." Government's role was to "suppress vice and immorality—to defend men's lives, religion and properties."[46] A republican government's main role was to establish and protect the people's natural rights. "This is that noble independence and republicanism taught in my text."[47]

Thus, the U.S. government failed in its primary role. Rather than destroy slavery during the Revolution and establish a "true republic," the nation's founders allowed the persistence of the one institution that corrupted the entire nation. The government failed at its most basic level: denying individuals the "natural right" of liberty and equality. The source of every societal problem was selfishness, "avarice," and "greed," Haynes and other blacks argued, and slavery exemplified voracious greed. Slavery, most black Christians believed, was more than a pernicious, exploitative, and oppressive labor system; it was a preeminent sin and prevented the development of "true republicanism" in the young nation. In a speech memorializing the 1827 abolition of slavery in New York, William Hamilton, the first president of the New York African Marine Society, described slaveholders as the incarnation of greed for money and power. Slaveholding was passion gone mad and therefore dangerous. "Authority and gold are their gods, their household gods, their sanctuary gods, and the highest gods of their sanctum sanctorum."[48]

A 1799 petition of the "People of Colour, Free men, within the City and Suburbs of Philadelphia to the President, Senate, and House of Representatives," requested the abolition of the slave trade, slavery, and an end to the kidnapping of free blacks in the northern states. The petitioners called upon the "guardians of our rights, patrons of equal and national liberties," to recognize that slavery affected the "welfare" of the country.[49]

Haynes argued that the antithesis to a republican government was a monarchy in which unnatural distinctions between men were established in law. Rather than grant the dignity of all men, monarchs and despots kept their constituents in ignorance and poverty so that they "know but little more than to bow . . . and crouch . . . for a piece of bread." The Vermont Congregational clergyman pointed to "the poor Africans, among us" as an example of how despotism existed in America. The only reason Africans were "being subjected to slavery, by the cruel hands of oppressors," was because selfish, avaricious men denied them their natural rights.[50] Thus, virtue, a primary element within republicanism and critical for the functioning of the new republic, was missing from the start. Black evangelicals in the late eighteenth and early nineteenth century clung to the belief of divine intervention as they worked to change public opinion toward all blacks by calling upon shared Christian republican values.

Black writers and speakers consistently emphasized the necessity of virtue for a "true republic," often using founding fathers to illustrate virtue or the ways in which it was lacking. As they had done with Christianity, northern blacks separated the behavior of most of the white proponents of Revolutionary ideals from the principles themselves. George Washington and Thomas Jefferson came under particular scrutiny. Writers and speakers praised George Washington for his patriotism exhibited in military and national leadership. Exemplifying virtuous citizenry, Washington represented the patient and unassuming president who symbolized the enlightened slaveholder by manumitting his slaves. The first president was, according to Haynes, "an enemy to slaveholding, and gave his dying testimony against it, by emancipating, and providing for those under his care." New Yorker Joseph Sidney, speaking at the commemoration of the abolition of the slave trade in January 1809, applauded Washington and other patriotic Federalists for personally applying the principles of the Revolution.[51] Washington revealed respect for "our African brethren" by manumitting his slaves.[52]

But not even Washington held the most prominent place among white Americans in early black political thought. This status was reserved for early abolitionists. Abolitionists were divine instruments engaged in disinterested service to humanity, the essence of virtue. Several northern blacks writing about the most respected abolitionists agreed with Peter Williams Jr. that John Woolman and Anthony Benezet headed the list of the "humane and respectable men." Expressing pride in his American nationality, Williams recounted how these men engaged in the most important work of abolition with "disinterestedness, engagedness, and prudence."[53]

Thomas Jefferson, on the other hand, was condemned or ignored while his words in the Declaration of Independence held a place next to the Bible. Peter Williams referred to the "sons of '76 [who] . . . pronounced these United States free and independent" as being inspired by God. They uttered the noble sentiments: "we hold these truths to be self-evident, that all men are created equal; that they are endowed by their Creator with certain unalienable rights; among which are life, liberty and the pursuit of happiness." Blacks repeatedly and sarcastically referred to Jefferson the slaveholder who spoke of liberty and democracy. Jefferson was foremost among those Virginians who cried the loudest for liberty and equality while enslaving thousands: "No people in the world make louder pretensions to "liberty, equality, and the rights of man, than the people of the South! And yet, strange as it may appear," Joseph Sidney explained, "there is no spot in the United States where oppression reigns with such unlimited sway!" The leader of the "enemies of our rights" was Thomas Jefferson, "the great idol of democracy" and slaveholder of "several hundreds [of] . . . our African brethren."[54]

In 1813, Lemuel Haynes placed much of his disapprobation for James Madison in a speech titled "DISSIMULATION ILLUSTRATED," delivered before the Washington Benevolent Society on the anniversary of George Washington's birthday. While Haynes did speak about Washington, the antithesis of dissimulation at the end of his talk, the speech mainly concerned his belief that hypocrisy rather than Christian republicanism had become the unabashed national principle during the War of 1812. President Madison was the primary representative of "dissimulation." A strong Federalist like most New Englanders, Haynes believed that party dissension and political self-interest had displaced the ideals of virtue. Public officials, rather than serving as exemplars of placing public good over private interests, were now willing to "sacrifice a state, yea, a world, to avarice and ambition." If it was the nation's duty to wage revenge on Britain for impressments, then, by this same logic, it was the duty of slaves to "rise and massacre their masters." The war exemplified hypocrisy. "It is a species of dissimulation, when we justify that in ourselves, which we condemn in others."[55]

Identifying as African and American, newly freed northern black Christian men and women intensely engaged in concerted effort to establish their place in the new republic. Conversion to evangelical Christianity meant that they shared fundamental values and interests with the dominant white majority. In fact, they had become more American than African culturally and politically. American identity, however, meant defining the new republic through the lens of black evangelicalism and resisting enslavement and other inequalities. Black Christians intended to work within their communities to fulfill the republican ideal of civic virtue. In several ways, individual interests converged with the desire to model African American citizenship by establishing institutions contributing to civil society.

Along with the formation of separate churches, a core group of men and women demonstrated their belief that they were part of American society by creating fundamental economic and social institutions in the major northern cities. The foundation for this incredible burst of activity in the late eighteenth and early nineteenth centuries was driven by black Christianity in which the blend of the political and sacred meant God would resolve the problem of national hypocrisy, white Americans would not only eliminate the slave trade but also abolish slavery, and blacks would gain equality. Northern blacks' firm conviction that their place was in the new republic and that their identity was African *and* American reflected their evangelical faith. By the end of the 1820s, schools, churches, two separate black religious denominations, mutual relief societies, charitable organizations, and literary societies had been established. The men and women leading these various organizations believed that they would exemplify as evangelical Christians the virtuous citizenship required of republicanism.

Mutual relief societies were established early on to address the most basic needs of the growing newly freed population. In Newport, Rhode Island, former slave and music teacher Newport Gardner became concerned that essential economic and social needs of blacks were not being met by the city's established institutions. To bring order and unity to Newport's emerging free black population, he and several other Newport men established the African Union Society in 1780 to help members in times of financial stress and provide a means of record keeping for Newport's black population. Evidently, records of births, marriages, and deaths of northern blacks were not considered a state or municipal responsibility. Men and women in other cities rapidly followed the Newport example. Groups such as the Philadelphia Free African Society,

Boston African Marine Fund, Philadelphia Daughters of Africa, and others responded to the imperatives of a growing free black urban population.[56]

In a culture of Christian mutuality, practicality, and charity, economic security was the major focus of these earliest organizations. For instance, the Daughters of Africa, a group of two hundred workers, was concerned solely, it seems, with cooperative relief. In case of sickness or the death of one of its membership, the society cared for the member or any orphaned children.[57] In the 1796 "Laws of the African Society" of Boston, the organization stated clearly that it existed "for the mutual benefit of each other." The constitution of the Colored Female Religious and Moral Society of Salem, organized in 1818, stated in Article VII that the "Society is formed for the benefit of the sick and destitute of those members belonging to the Society."[58]

As in the case of the Philadelphia Free African Society, almost immediately these "social bodies" involved themselves in more than financial protection. Many of the organizations attempted to resolve nearly all the problems confronting northern blacks. The aspects of life most direct, personal, and significant were considered first. Besides addressing the needs of sick members and their orphaned or widowed family members and establishing means of record keeping, many organizations purchased or rented burial grounds to prevent the indignity of having their members buried in segregated spaces reserved for blacks, indigents, and criminals. In 1790, the Philadelphia Free African Society petitioned the mayor for the right to rent burial land for their members. A few months later this same group also established procedures for performing marriages at their monthly meetings.[59]

Children, perceived as the hope for the future, were of primary concern to the fledgling societies. Because of disruption by war, parental death, enslavement, and poverty, large numbers of black children were under the control of city and county officials. Black mutual relief societies sought to care for the orphans of its membership. The younger generation would help transform the prevailing conditions of poverty and ignorance into those of industry, autonomy, and respect. Prince Hall, founder of the first black American fraternal order, urged his fellow Masons in 1792 to make the education of "our rising generation" a first priority by foregoing unnecessary expenditures for recreation and using the funds to finance black youth education. A member of another organization argued that "the future elevation . . . of the people of colour" depended upon the "intellectual, moral and religious improvements" of black children. The Pennsylvania Augustine Society for the Education of

People of Colour organized in 1818 because they were "sensibly impressed with the high importance of education for the improvement of our species."[60]

Education of children would help ensure the future of African Americans in the republic. But discrimination in schools was as prevalent as in the other critical social and economic American institutions. Consequently, black men and women collectively and individually established schools for black children. Six years after Prince Hall explained the importance of education to his fraternal brotherhood, he opened a school in his home. Black taxpayers were particularly concerned about paying taxes for schools that refused admission to black children. Along with other black Bostonians, Hall, a Methodist minister and Revolutionary War veteran, had grown tired of waiting for the state legislature either to provide schools for black children or to permit attendance at established schools. As early as 1787, he and others petitioned the legislature to admit black children to the public schools. As taxpayers, they had "the right to enjoy the privileges of free men." Feeling the "want of a common education," they were concerned about the prospects for their children if they remained in ignorance "in a land of gospel light." Refusal to admit was "for [no] other reason [than] . . . they are black."[61]

Although black education immediately after slavery remained largely a consequence of white American religious and philanthropic efforts, African Americans opened schools for children of both sexes in New England, New York, and Pennsylvania in the late eighteenth and early nineteenth centuries. In the early 1790s, Pennsylvania blacks built a schoolhouse before building any other institution. Others simply opened schools for all children. Katherine Ferguson, a former New York slave, established an orphanage and school for New York City children, black and white. In 1808, the Newport African Benevolent Society founded a school that continued in operation until 1842, when the city officials finally agreed to use tax monies for a separate black school. Sarah Mapps, a free person from birth and educated by private tutors, opened a private school in Philadelphia for black children in 1820. Mapps was unusual, though. Most black women were domestics, not teachers.

African American women's support for black education was mainly financial for children in the few black-controlled schools and especially for schools operated and run by white organizations and churches. Women held bazaars, fairs, and banquets for funding black education. In Newport, women established the African Female Benevolent Society "for the good of our posterity." They also formed organizations to provide for the most basic needs of indigent black students. In New York City, the African Dorcas Association supplied clothing for children attending the African Free School, which had been established in 1787 by the New York Manumission Society, a white abolitionist organization.[62]

Increasingly, students and parents expressed dissatisfaction with the quality of white teachers' instruction and their inability to participate in the governance of the white-dominated educational systems designed for blacks. Members of the African Benevolent Society in Newport were determined to control the quality of education for their children. In 1808 the Newport African Union Society worked with the African Benevolent Society to provide a school "for any person of colour in this town." The constitution of the African Benevolent Society made sure that blacks would maintain power over the school. With membership limited to "any person of colour, whether male or female," and full power given to the directors of the society, which consisted of "four white and seven coloured persons," the ABS ensured that black members held the bulk of power over the direction of the school. The Rhode Island Missionary Society, a Quaker organization, worked closely with the African Benevolent Society in establishing the school. The fact that some prominent white men played an important role in the directorship of the school, particularly in the area of finances, suggests their cooperation and, perhaps, the necessity of white participation to protect African American financial interests in Newport.

The Pennsylvania Augustine Society for the Education of People of Colour, organized by prominent black Philadelphians, including James Forten, Russell Parrott, John Gloucester, and others, wanted an alternative to the "defective system of instruction" available for black children. Revealing the limited education considered appropriate by Philadelphia white officials for black children, the society stated that they would establish a curriculum that included the "useful and scientific branches of education" along with the arts. The school was to be almost completely under black control.[63] Besides wanting their children to have an educational curriculum equal with that of other Americans, northern blacks wanted their children to learn shared values of freedom, equality, and justice that they believed constituted both Christian and republican principles. Education of children reflected northern black determination to participate in American life and society as equals.

Black parental objection to white teachers centered on the quality of teachers available for black education. They believed white teachers were often incompetent, prejudiced, and quick to administer excessive punishment to black students. In fact, most whites considered teaching in black schools demeaning, so teachers, in general, were hard to find. They were usually paid less than their counterparts teaching white students, and were often less competent and were transitory, working only a few months before quitting. As a result, black parents often withdrew their children from schools after a trial period. Parents in Providence, for example, charged that the white teacher was racist; he had threatened his students with severe punishment if they dared greet him in public. Black parental and community dissatisfaction continued in Providence until a black teacher opened a school in the 1830s. In New York City, black parental discontent came to a head in the late 1820s. Parents demanded the removal of the white teacher who caned a student because the student referred to a black man as a "gentleman." They also expressed concern that the school had become a training ground for colonization plans to remove free blacks to Liberia. In 1832, black parents took control of the African Free School and replaced the teacher with a black teacher. The school's attendance, already high, increased sharply.[64]

Black evangelical political interests, so strongly expressed in the demands for separate churches, became evident in the demands for community control over black education. Racism and incompetence among white teachers, along with an insufficient curriculum, were antithetical to the plans of the newly freed northern black population's political interests. African Americans living in the North viewed education as one of the primary means toward full participation in American social, political, and especially economic institutions. This was why black control of the African Free School in New York was so critical. Children needed to learn their equal place in American society and, as Americans, benefit from a liberal arts curriculum that prepared them for a variety of positions. As important, children needed to know their self- and collective worth. Forced to accept denigration of their children and themselves in slavery, former slaves joined with those who had never experienced slavery in establishing schools under black control. In the third decade of the nineteenth century, the number of schools fitting their vision increased; by then more African Americans were schoolteachers and administrators. Children needed to learn to critically assess the nation's limitations about slavery and to understand how to confront discriminatory legislation. This was the period of promise. Much needed doing and, as far as possible, northern black preachers, teachers, and businessmen organized and prepared to meet post-slavery exigencies of a growing northern black community. According to William

Douglass, one of the earliest black historians, African Americans in the north envisioned a future of promise and intended to establish the foundations of community life in their own time. "Worthy men . . . animated with some of the spirit of those days, resolved to introduce a new order of things among themselves."[65] Christian leaders had successfully created a collective identity and were now engaged in common cause for gaining the benefits of inevitable citizenship.

Besides mutual relief organizations, schools, churches, and burial grounds, northern black organizational activity included prototypes of banks and even an attempt to create a fire company. In 1818, several young black Philadelphia men formed a fire company because black homes were inadequately protected by the city. Although resounding white opposition quickly ended the plan, the organization illustrated black resolution and determination to meet the necessities of the emerging free community. Needs were evident everywhere and diverse organizations attempted to address them. Some of the cooperative insurance societies made provisions for donating surplus funds to charities or investing them in real estate or black businesses.[66]

Driven by their belief in divine providence, leaders were determined to alter their conditions and especially that of future generations. Consequently, they exhibited measured optimism about their future in the new nation. Relying on their Christian faith for an interpretation of the recent past and the present and placing less stress on state and national laws and policies that would have discouraged and dissuaded them, black preachers and others cited particular political events as signs that the new nation was undergoing major transformation. The Revolutionary War, abolition of the slave trade, and the abolition of slavery in the North were all signs of the beginning of the end of European American oppression of Africans and their descendants. Slavery would end and so would racial discrimination. In 1809, Joseph Sidney referred to the abolition of the slave trade as "a stride . . . towards the total abolition of slavery in America!" George Lawrence asserted four years later that the United States, "founded on the principles of liberty and equality, and declaring them to be the free gift of God, . . . must enforce it; I am confident she wills it, and strong forbodings of it is discernible." A speaker the year before encouraged those still in bondage that a time was coming "when universal freedom should take place . . . when they shall be all their own men." In the same year, another speaker hoped God would "hasten that glorious time" when Christianity "shall cover the *earth*."[67]

Some of this optimism reflected the belief of some northern blacks, like many other Americans, that their country would introduce steps leading toward the millennium. The republican government was the fulfillment of divine guidance culminating in a thousand-year reign of peace on earth. Haynes reflected the view of many Christians when he expressed hope that America would model Christianity for the whole world. "May we not almost predict that this will be the blissful region that will introduce the golden age, or peaceful kingdom, that shall break in pieces all the haughty empires of the world and . . . America become the glory of the whole earth."[68]

A significant number of black men who became wealthy or were financially secure at the turn of the century, the elite of the northern black population and disproportionately represented in the formation and control of northern black institutions, found reason for optimism by generalizing from their own personal experience. Newport Gardner, a former slave who purchased his freedom and that of several family members after winning a lottery, became a schoolteacher, minister, and property holder, making him a prominent leader of the Newport free black community.[69] Paul Cuffe, another New Englander and one of the petitioners involved in the dispute over taxes and the franchise in Massachusetts, also earned a great degree of prosperity through his own hard efforts and fortuitous circumstances. The son of Cuffe Slocum, an Ashanti who eventually gained his freedom, and Ruth Moses, a Wampanoag, Paul grew up on a 116-acre farm in Dartmouth. When his father died in 1772, he became a seaman at fourteen and used his seafaring skills during the war to trade between the mainland and the small islands, often eluding the British blockade. Practicing industry and frugality, Paul turned the trading business into a profitable venture. In the early nineteenth century, Cuffe and his wife, Alice Pequit, a Pequot, owned several fishing and whaling vessels as well as a house, school, and farmlands.[70]

The lives of James Forten and Prince Hall reveal similar patterns of individual striving, relatively favorable circumstances, and financial success. Forten, probably as financially successful as Cuffe and also involved in the maritime industry, was prominent in the Philadelphia black community. Born to free parents in 1766, Forten, whose great-grandfather arrived as a slave in the 1680s, received a fragmented education in the African School established by Quakers in the early 1770s. He learned how to repair sails from his father, fought in the Revolutionary War, later apprenticed himself to a sail maker, and eventually became owner of the sail-making company at age thirty-two.

As a manufacturer, Forten and Sons employed over thirty black and white workers. Within a few decades, Forten was wealthy. Although knowledge of Prince Hall's parents and place of birth is uncertain, he became prominent within the Boston free black community and is known as the founder of black Freemasonry in the United States. Working for a time as a steward on vessels and fighting in the Revolutionary War, he eventually became involved in trade (probably as a secondhand clothes dealer) and was one of the city's few black property holders.[71]

Other men, like Richard Allen and Absalom Jones, were also industrious, frugal, and among the city of Philadelphia's few black property holders, especially in the early years of the republic.[72] With constant references to the Pauline Scriptures, Allen constantly admonished free blacks to work hard and stay sober. Entrepreneurial in spirit, often "with wide-ranging business interests,"[73] Protestant principles of hard work, frugality, sobriety, and piety dictated the direction of these men and many others like them who helped establish the structures of the free black communities in the northern states. Their personal lives suggested to them that it was possible for former slaves and free blacks who started with little or nothing to gain financial security and prominence among northern blacks and some whites.

Although most of the men mentioned above avoided simplistic generalizations from their own personal experience, several did think that model free black behavior would influence the timing and process of change. They believed northern free black behavior could contribute to the abolition of slavery and black citizenship. Convinced that they exemplified the virtuous citizens needed for the republic, men like Hall and Allen believed the majority of free blacks should copy their lead. And too, they recognized (to their dismay) that whites made no distinctions between blacks. Anticipating what historian Kevin Gaines has identified as the problem with late nineteenth-century "uplift ideology," a few late eighteenth- and early nineteenth-century northern black leaders hinted that free blacks should prove worthy of freedom and equality.[74]

In speeches, autobiographies, and sermons, some elite men admonished the laboring poor northern black majority to exhibit characteristics that would ensure success. A critical function of black organizations involved modeling and inculcating values of stewardship, charity, industry, sobriety, and frugality, eschewing conspicuous consumption and display. Repeating the admonitions of white abolitionists, these organizations argued that free black behavior played a primary role in eliminating racial discrimination and ending slavery.

Not surprisingly, ministers were foremost in this regard. In their 1794 publication, Philadelphia ministers Richard Allen and Absalom Jones explained that "much depends upon us for the help of our colour more than men are aware: if we are lazy and idle, the enemies of freedom plead it as a cause of why we ought not to be free."[75] Thirteen years later Joseph Sidney told black New Yorkers that it was their "duty" to act with sobriety, honesty, and industry; this would demonstrate that they knew the value of freedom. The "Ethiopian cannot change his skin yet his heart may nevertheless become an habitation for all virtues which ever adorn the human character."[76] While these writers admitted free black vulnerability to dominant white political, economic, and social interests, they insisted that black behavior mattered in the abolition of both slavery and racial discrimination.

At the same time, ministers, teachers, and businessmen consistently admonished whites not only that greed was the cause of slavery and that blacks who engaged in criminality or vice did so because of the lack of alternative choices, they also stressed that African Americans were like all people, reflecting a broad spectrum of human personality and behavior. All blacks should not be judged by the actions of a few.[77] Asserting African American individuality and diversity would become a constant refrain throughout the new century and the next. In stressing the diversity of the black population, the emerging black middle class tried to distance themselves from the poor free black majority to demonstrate the degree to which people of African descent could become virtuous citizens of the republic if given the chance. Virtue and Christianity were synonymous for these men and women. Yet, as historian Leslie Harris has noted, New York City blacks involved in "remaking the race" were actually creating social divisions within the black community.[78] Class differences would become even more apparent in the antebellum era.

The organization of the American Colonization Society (ACS) in 1816 tested black evangelical confidence in inevitable abolition and full inclusion into American society. The ACS challenged fundamental black assumptions and activities. While several African American leaders stressed positive changes over the negative, including the Fugitive Slave Law that threatened all free blacks, the Naturalization and Militia laws' being restricted to whites, the passage of antiblack immigration laws in the newer states like Ohio and attempts at passing them even in the older states, they could not ignore this new organization.[79] In December 1816, prominent northern and southern whites, for a variety of reasons, met in Washington, D.C., to form an organization that would sponsor the removal of all free blacks to Africa. As an idea developed in the late eighteenth century mainly for religious reasons, the colonization scheme in the nineteenth century represented more diverse interests. Motivated by a combination of economic, humanitarian, and religious interests, the ACS membership conflicted sharply with black notions of national identity and place in the new republic. Rather than work toward the abolition of slavery and the betterment of the free black community, members of the colonization society argued that ameliorative plans were futile.

Combining blatant racist language with expressions of humanitarian concern, depending on the audience, colonizationists claimed that free blacks were an inferior people who could not change their degraded status in America because of a naturally strong racial prejudice. While some members expressed hope that slaveholders might emancipate their slaves more willingly if they were removed from the South, others, particularly slaveholding members, supported the organization because emancipation was not at issue. They believed the very existence of free blacks threatened the stability of slavery. Some colonizationists not only agreed to this qualification but also argued that slave values would increase when free blacks were removed.[80] A healthy and viable free black community, in spite of the many constraints, contradicted a developing proslavery ideology that represented people of African ancestry as incapable of independent thought and action.

Northern blacks were particularly alarmed, not only because some of the most prominent politicians in the nation were members of the new organization, but also because of the ACS's tactics for gaining financial support and increased membership. Spokesmen for the ACS traveled throughout the country appealing to the racist fears of white America. They depicted free blacks as a rapidly increasing population of subhuman, degraded brutes that weakened the strength of the republic. Slaveholders, according to some colonizationists, deserved "sympathy rather than our indignation."[81] When recruiting free black support for the plan, ACS spokesmen avoided racist appeals and concern for the slaveholders in their speeches. Instead, they stressed the necessity of black evangelism to Africa—only "coloured missionaries" could save Africa.[82]

Meeting at Bethel Church within a month after the ACS was organized, three thousand black Philadelphians, with Russell Parrott and James Forten in charge, unanimously expressed their belief that "any measure or system of measures, having a tendency to banish us . . . would not only be cruel, but in direct violation of those principles, which have been the boast of this republic." Emigration to Africa was not a return to a native homeland. America was their country as much as any other immigrant's, voluntary or involuntary. "Our ancestors (not of choice) were the first successful cultivators of the wilds of America, we their descendants feel ourselves entitled to participate in the blessings of her luxuriant soil." Participants at the meeting abhorred the "unmerited stigma" colonizationists cast on free blacks. The so-called "dangerous and useless part of the community," as colonizationists represented all free blacks, had been willing to endanger their lives for their country in the recent war with Great Britain even though they did not enjoy all the rights of a free people.[83] Besides, abolition was "progressing." "Every year witnesses the release of numbers of the victims of oppression, and affords new and safe assurances that the freedom of all will be in the end accomplished."[84]

In addition to reasserting their American nationality and their optimistic vision for the future of an inclusive America, the Philadelphians resolved that they would "never" willingly separate from slaves. "They are our brethren by the ties of consanguinity, of suffering and of wrong; and we feel that there is more virtue in suffering privations with them, than financial advantages for a season."[85] Philadelphia blacks argued a year later at another large anticolonization meeting that the true intention of colonization was to further secure slavery. Should colonization succeed, slavery "will be thus rendered perpetual."[86] Colonization would repeat the evils of the slave trade in breaking up families. "Parents will be torn from their children—husbands from their wives—brothers from brothers—and all the heart rending agonies which were endured by our forefathers when they were dragged into bondage from Africa will be again renewed, and with increased anguish."[87] Moreover, Philadelphians at the meeting rejected the idea that colonization was appropriate for newly emancipated slaves. Without education and Christianity, slaves were unprepared for emigration to an African colony.[88]

As evangelical Christians, many anticolonizationists found recruiters' warnings that whites would never change their negative attitudes toward blacks and that, therefore, blacks' status would not improve to be precise contradictions to the Christian belief in the transformative power of God. Through divine intervention, white America would change not only policies but also attitudes and live up to its national principles as stated in the Declaration. Colonizationists' assumptions undermined the premise on which black Christians based their faith and ignored individual and collective efforts in gaining freedom. The ACS ignored the many educational, religious, and charitable organizations free blacks established at great sacrifice. Thus, unwittingly and in complete contradiction to their own goals, colonizationists pushed many northern blacks even more toward American identity and their determination to become full participants in American society.

The majority of northern blacks retained their vision of an inclusive America in spite of some black interest in emigration to Africa, either through their own initiative in the 1780s or later through the ACS. When approached by some New England emigrationists about emigrating to Africa because Africans in America were "strangers and outcasts in a strange land" and slaves were treated in the "most inhuman and cruel manner" and living in "heathenish darkness and barbarity," Philadelphian Christians responded: "With regard to the emigration to Africa you mention, we have at present but little to communicate on that head, apprehending every pious man is a good citizen of the whole world." The members added that rather than request God's help for emigration to Africa, northern blacks should pray that "the Lord thereby be pleased to break every yoke, and let the oppressed go free."[89]

Emigration, however, was not rejected out of hand. Forten, Allen, and others supported some emigrationists' schemes that provided opportunities for poor blacks and/or entrepreneurial possibilities for the wealthy. Cuffe's program of settlement and trade interested several wealthy northern blacks and poor blacks who believed they had no future in the United States. Later, the Haitian government's invitation to free blacks to settle in Haiti gained the tepid support of leaders. Emigrants began sailing to Haiti in late summer of 1824, and by 1826 about six thousand from New England, New York, Philadelphia, and Baltimore arrived in Port-au-Prince.[90] Emigration to Haiti proved a disappointment to at least two thousand Americans, who returned within the decade. Emigrants demonstrated just how culturally American they were. Besides having to learn a different language, Catholic Haiti was a problem for some. Also, the emigrants, many of whom were urban, were expected to live in the rural areas.

The colonization society did attract black support in spite of its racist propaganda. Several hundred emigrated to West Africa, some for religious reasons—to evangelize Africans and provide for the spiritual welfare of the American emigrants. But most northern blacks emigrated because they wanted economic and political advantages not available in the United States. "Our freedom is partial," wrote one Illinois emigrant, "and we have no hope that it ever will be otherwise here."[91]

The colonizationists' scheme and especially their propaganda would strongly affect elite northern black attitudes toward future emigration in general and African American national identity in particular. In the 1820s, when the ACS established their colony, Liberia, African American identity shifted emphasis to underscore an American nationality. By the 1820s, black Christians engaged in establishing and developing viable institutions in cities were increasingly confronted with the reality that their efforts were insufficient for the task. America was not changing for the better. Rather than reject their vision for an equally inclusive free America, black evangelicals supported their conviction of inevitable change through a gospel of activism.

CHAPTER 3

They Want Us Slaves Forever

EVANGELICAL REFORM AND THE EXPANSION OF SLAVERY

I must observe to my brethren that at the close of the first Revolution in this country
. . . there were but thirteen States in the Union, now there are twenty-four, most of
which are slaveholding states, and the whites are dragging us around in chains and
. . . handcuffs, to their new States and Territories to work . . . their farms . . . to be an
inheritance to them and their children forever.

—David Walker, *WALKER'S APPEAL*

To the horror of those involved in creating free black communities, rather
than gradually declining, as was occurring in the North, slavery in the South
was expanding dramatically after the first decade of the new century, and
arguments defending slave labor as a positive good for the nation and for the
slaves evolved and intensified. Likewise, the American Colonization Society
persisted in its racist appeal to "return" free blacks to Liberia, the West African
colony established in the 1820s. Instead of moderating or redirecting efforts,
however, men and women who took on roles of leadership accelerated their
drive toward a free and equal society in which African Americans participated
fully. Many northern black men and women became full-fledged national
reformers, persisting in their vision of what Haynes called a "true republic."
In this period, as before, evangelicalism informed reformers' objectives and
means of protest.

Confronting American society was difficult for individuals of African descent in any period, but for those early nineteenth-century men and women
convinced of immanent change and preparing themselves and those in like
circumstances for their role as citizens of the republic, antebellum society

proved almost beyond comprehension. The process of reckoning with the limited meaning of northern black freedom that varied from state to state required time for evaluation and reflection during an era when prejudice against blacks, a consistent problem in the eighteenth and early nineteenth centuries, intensified in the years before the Civil War.

As historian Leon Litwack shows, African Americans in the North were relegated to the most menial jobs, denied access to public education, and not allowed to migrate to the newly established states of the Northwest and West without great difficulty. While political democracy expanded to grant all white men the suffrage in the antebellum years, most African American men were disfranchised. By 1840, about 93 percent of northern free black men were denied the vote. Only in Massachusetts, New Hampshire, Vermont, and Maine could black men vote on an equal basis with white men. Black men gained the franchise in Rhode Island in 1842, but in New York, where white men gained universal suffrage, black men had to meet certain property and residence requirements. In New Jersey, Pennsylvania, and Connecticut, black men were completely disfranchised. Legal discrimination against northern free blacks complemented political disfranchisement of black men. In Illinois, Ohio, Indiana, Iowa, and California, African Americans could not give court testimony when a white person was a party in a case. Oregon forbade African Americans to own property, make contracts, or bring lawsuits.

Racial discrimination in jobs and housing reflected even more white antipathy toward African Americans. While the nation was growing incrementally and expanding opportunities for whites, America's black men, women, and children faced consistent economic discrimination. Many men and women who had worked at skilled jobs as slaves found they could not practice their skills in freedom. By 1855, about 87 percent of those who had jobs in New York City, for example, worked in menial or unskilled labor. A similar pattern existed throughout the North. Only a relative few were able to practice their trades. And increasingly African Americans were forced to live in a few segregated areas of the cities, under the most adverse living conditions. And, as mentioned earlier, black children were not admitted to most public schools. After much black agitation and a significant African American population developed, states began providing for separate black schools.[1]

Many blacks blamed the American Colonization Society for spreading antiblack propaganda in the guise of paternalistic benevolence. The colonization society became more popular in the late 1820s, establishing local and state chapters. In 1829, Congress debated the feasibility of financing the removal of all free blacks to Africa.[2] By 1830 there were about 125,000 free blacks living in the North.[3] That number nearly doubled in the next thirty years. Additionally, black migration to eastern cities persisted; by then northern slavery had almost completely disappeared. Fugitive slaves, mainly from the Upper South, contributed to the growing northern black population. Black community organizers complained that state officials still had not devised "means" for the freed people.[4] Migrants needed jobs, housing, and community, but generally found only the latter. The community leaders' program of institution building during the early years of northern emancipation was insufficient to meet the needs of the fast-growing free black population in the antebellum era. Likewise, leaders' concentration on developing churches, schools, literary societies, mutual benefit organizations, and so on did not directly attack intensified racial prejudice and violence.

Consequently, community leaders reassessed their efforts and basic assumptions about their future in American society. By the 1820s they concluded that concentration mainly on black community development was no longer tenable. Their vision of imminent inclusion in the great republic was being thwarted by the twin evils of expanding slavery and growing racism. Groups of men and women in different cities and at different times started developing what became, by the first years of the third decade, a reform movement encompassing three main objectives: free black community development, abolition of slavery, and equal rights. Retaining their vision of a truly free and equal Christian society, northern blacks intensified and expanded their efforts through an evangelical lens—God wanted them to do more.

The transition from concentration within community to a more aggressive reform outside the black communities occurred in mini-stages. Believing that slavery negatively impacted all blacks, slave and free, members of mutual relief societies throughout the North began making abolition a major focus of their multifaceted organizations. While earlier organizations had addressed the abolition of slavery generally, organizations established in the 1820s and 1830s made it a top priority. The Massachusetts General Colored Association, established in 1826, for instance, signaled an attitudinal change from the expectation that providence would resolve the problem of slavery to determining that black collective effort must play a larger role. A member of the association argued that "the inhuman system of *slavery*, is the *source* from which most of our miseries proceed."[5]

The incorporation of abolition into mutual relief and benevolent societies combined with the creation in 1827 of the first black newspaper, the *Freedom's Journal,* which served as a regional forum and information center for developing strategies, providing job and housing ads, and offering news of interest to African Americans. As importantly, the newspaper's publishers and editors also established the *Journal* to influence public opinion. They would counter insidious and pervasive negative stories about people of African ancestry. Presbyterian New York minister Samuel E. Cornish and John B. Russwurm, a recent graduate of Bowdoin College, editors of the first black press, indicated their evangelical foundation in the newspaper's flag, "Righteousness Exalteth a Nation," forewarning of a more assertive Christian republican position in the struggle against racial prejudice and discrimination. Blacks would speak for themselves. First they addressed the problem of misrepresentation even by their white "friends" who condemned racism in theory but practiced it daily. It was critical for friends and those "who make it their business to enlarge upon the least trifle" so as to discredit "any person of colour" to learn the "simple representation of facts." "We wish to plead our own cause. Too long have others spoken for us. Too long has the publick been deceived by misrepresentations in things which concern us dearly." And because "the civil rights of a people" were "the greatest value," the editors would place the issue before the public and encourage those men who could vote to use their elective franchise independent of the influence of any party. For Russwurm and Cornish, partisan politics would have no place in their newspaper. Rather than party interests, the Constitution of the United States would be "our polar star."

Besides re-presenting African Americans, Cornish and Russwurm explained that the purpose of the paper was to provide a national forum or "public channel" among northern blacks. "It is our earnest wish to make our Journal a medium of intercourse between our brethren in the different states." The editors noted that issues concerning blacks would be "candidly discussed and properly weighed." Moreover, the editors would stress particular virtues they deemed essential for participation in the human family. Blacks had a duty as a "spoke in the human wheel" to perform their part in contributing to civil society. Christianity, education, and frugality, they explained, would contribute to the moral, religious, civil, and literary improvement of African Americans.

Additionally, the editors underscored black dual identity and suggested an emerging pan-Africanism. Africa and Haiti would loom large in the education and informational focus of the paper. Articles of interest to blacks would include international topics that provided "useful knowledge of every kind, and everything that relates to Africa." Because knowledge of Africa was becoming "more known," the racist stereotypes of ignorant natives would be dispelled. "Hayti," too, as a new republic was progressing "in all the arts of civilization," and South America, "where despotism has given place to free governments, and where many of our brethren now fill important civil and military stations," would also help counter ideas of intellectual black inferiority.[6]

The first issue of the journal included the first of a series of articles about Paul Cuffe, who displayed the personal, civic, and professional qualities that the editors felt black Americans should emulate. Cuffe demonstrated industry, frugality, sobriety, and Christian charity. Russwurm and Cornish hoped their readers would do likewise. The first issue of *Freedom's Journal* also contained notices of deaths, accidents, ship arrivals and departures, and an announcement of the opening of a new school in New York City for "colored children." Articles other than inspirational biographies included reports of missionary activity in Sierra Leone and graphic accounts of the brutality of American and British slavery. Quickly, though, *Freedom's Journal*, and the black newspapers that immediately followed, focused on the abolition of slavery.[7]

Yet it was a strident voice in Boston, not the newly established press, that heralded the transition to a more vocal, impatient, and aggressive generation of evangelical African American reformers determined to abolish American slavery immediately. David Walker, the owner of a small new and used clothing store in Boston, a member of the Prince Hall Masonry Lodge #459, the Massachusetts General Colored Association, and the African Methodist Episcopal church, and a circulation agent for and contributor to *Freedom's Journal*, concluded that white Americans intended to keep blacks enslaved "forever." Born in North Carolina as the child of a slave father and free mother, Walker was "legally free" but, like other free black children, quickly learned that freedom and blackness were contradictory terms and, if not understood properly, especially in the southern part of the United States, could mean enslavement or death. In spite of multiple proscriptions, Walker's parents had inculcated values of personal self-worth in their young son, and at some point he learned to read and write. Reading broadly and traveling widely throughout the South and North before landing in New England, Walker arrived with a wealth of experience.[8]

Viewing the enslavement of Africans and their descendants within a republican evangelical mind-set, Walker repeated the late eighteenth- and early nineteenth-century view that slavery undermined the achievement of a true republic. He was convinced that the existence of racial slavery meant not only the perpetuation of proscribed conditions for all blacks but the declension of the young nation. Voracious reading, especially of the Bible and world history, supplemented by firsthand observations, contributed to Walker's development of a more international perspective shared by many black reformers of his generation. Like northern blacks active at the turn of the century, he viewed sub-Saharan Africans and those of the diaspora as a unified people vulnerable to European oppression throughout the globe. Consequently, within this pan-African stance, Walker asserted an agenda of international black liberation. Yet, because he felt that blacks in the United States were the "most degraded, wretched, and abject set of beings that ever lived since the world began," concentrated effort must begin where it was most needed. Similar to earlier evangelicals and several who became prominent later, Walker embraced mil-lennialists' notions of a world salvation, the process of which was interrupted by white American greed for money and power. Blacks were physically en-slaved, but whites were in spiritual bondage.

In a speech before the Massachusetts General Colored Association in 1828, Walker had already established the theme of his later work. Blacks, free and enslaved, were responsible for their own liberation, and the means to achieve this goal were enlightenment and collective action. By the fall of 1829, Walker had written, published, and distributed the *APPEAL . . . TO THE COLOURED CITIZENS OF THE WORLD, BUT IN PARTICULAR, AND VERY EXPRESSLY, TO THOSE OF THE UNITED STATES OF AMERICA*. In important ways, Walker's *APPEAL* was a jeremiad warning white America of coming judgment if slavery persisted: "I tell you Americans! that unless you speedily alter your course, *you* and your *Country are gone!!!!!*" But mainly it was an epistle to blacks world-wide to gain personal and collective awareness of actual black status and unite to end white oppression. Walker utilized the evangelical trope of conviction, repentance, and transformation as a means for change (a method that would become known as "moral suasion"). Black and white comprehension of their distinct and related condition was the prelude for reform. If not, the hell of perpetual slavery or imminent damnation awaited.

Walker epitomized black evangelicalism with his firm commitment to the United States and in stressing that slavery threatened the virtue of the Ameri-can people and therefore the nation. All Americans, black and white, were guilty of the continuation of slavery, and thus the divine plan for the United States as a model for the world moving toward the millennium was thwarted. Believing they were powerless to end slavery and racial discrimination, some blacks behaved as if their individual freedom was all that mattered. Walker insisted that too many free blacks accepted their circumscribed existence. Content with "low employments" and minimal education, these individuals indulged in extravagant clothing and luxuries for themselves rather than contributing to change. Consequently, black youths had little inspiration toward achievement beyond menial labor and were apathetic about slavery. The fact was, Walker argued, all blacks were slaves. "If any of you wish to know how FREE you are, let one of you start and go through the southern and western States of this country."[9] Writing in an intensely jeremiadic tone throughout the *APPEAL*, Walker added slaves to the list of those with culpability. Some slaves were more concerned about protecting themselves than even members of their own family. Slave informants and those who lied against other slaves to improve their own position and were "servile" only perpetuated the "wretched" system. Slave servility was especially treacherous in Walker's mind; it undermined familial and communal responsibility. Fathers beat their sons, "mothers their daughters, and children their parents, all to pacify the passions of unrelenting tyrants." But this kind of treachery among slaves was also practiced among some free blacks who helped slave catchers find fugitives for money. Greed was not a characteristic exclusive to whites.

Self-interest, servility, and deception were not, however, the defining characteristics of most blacks. Walker believed that the majority of blacks were courageous enough to sacrifice their lives for the cause of freedom. Extending Thomas Jefferson's lament about the republic's involvement in slavery, Walker wrote, "But when I reflect that God is just, and that millions of my wretched brethren would meet death with glory . . . I am with streaming eyes, compelled to shrink back into nothingness before my Maker and exclaim again, thy will be done, O lord God Almighty."[10] Like most antebellum evangelicals, Walker placed the onus on individual black Christians who were lacking in intense effort. What was needed, he believed, was an enlightened male leadership that would educate and unite all blacks in the United States: "Men of colour, who are also of sense, for you particularly is my APPEAL designed. . . . I call upon you therefore to cast your eyes upon the wretchedness of your brethren, and to do your utmost to enlighten them. . . . Let the Lord see you doing what you can to rescue them and yourselves from degradation."[11]

Walker argued that "enlightened" men were responsible for making blacks cognizant of widespread black degradation and for providing the black masses with a clear understanding of the cause of slavery: greed. "The fact is, the labour of slaves comes so cheap to the avaricious usurpers, and is (as they think) of such great utility to the country where it exists, that those who are actuated by sordid avarice only, overlook the evils, which will as sure as the Lord lives, follow after the good."[12] Whether enslaved or in quasi-slavery, southern blacks were consistently thwarted in their attempts to improve their conditions because avaricious whites profited from economic and political interdictions against blacks. The same thing happened in the North. Walker cited cases of northern blacks who worked, saved, and acquired property only to have it taken from them by unscrupulous whites. Whites took black property at will "even if it is a *mud hole.*" Inherited black property was even more vulnerable. The property "most generally falls into the hands of some white person. The wife and children of the deceased may weep and lament . . . but the estate will be kept snug enough by its white possessor."[13] Apparently referring to a recent case, Walker challenged black and white Bostonians to refute his charges.

Walker combined his faith in knowledge with a firm conviction in the ultimate divine liberation of all black people. While belief in divine intervention was not new among reformers, the difference was in Walker's strong reliance on human effort. Revivals throughout the North, led by Charles G. Finney and other Protestant ministers, increasingly stressed human responsibility in personal salvation and then applied this sense of responsibility to "sins" in society. Evangelical reform in the 1820s to 1840s emphasized human activity instead of passivity, ability over inability.[14] Infused with this same spirit, Walker applied antebellum evangelical emphasis to black freedom. Rather than blaming God for not living up to black expectations, Walker and the reformers who followed decided that the problem was limited exertion among both blacks and whites. The times called for accelerated effort. More than ever before, black evangelicals decided blacks, slave and free, educated and uneducated, had a major role to play in changing their adverse conditions and therefore the nation. Like other reformers, Walker stressed black education as the key to freedom.

Abolition was a simple process in Walker's mind. Once enlightened, slaves would cease labor, thus ending the abhorrent system. Walker readily admitted that a slave strike could result in nothing short of a bloodbath, but felt that those not willing to die for liberty deserved slavery. For Walker, slavery was worse than death. As a Christian, Walker was ambivalent about whether slaves should initiate rebellion. He circumvented controversial theological questions by reasoning that slave resistance would be self-defense.

Yet, the *APPEAL* was not so much a call for insurrection, as contemporary whites thought; Walker saw himself as a John the Baptist preparing the way for inevitable and complete black freedom. He believed the struggle for abolition would most likely be violent, beginning in the United States and spreading to the Caribbean, South America, and Africa. Solidarity through enlightenment provided by men of sense, slave or free, was the beginning of the end of international white oppression. The end of all oppression, though, lay ultimately with the Christianization of the world. Walker believed blacks would play a primary role in the coming millennium because most white Christians were nearly beyond redemption. Thus, blacks would be the chosen instruments to Christianize the world. "It is my solemn belief, that if ever the world becomes Christianized (which must certainly take place before long) it will be through the means, under God of the *Blacks*, who are now held in wretchedness, and degradation." Before his untimely death (probably of a heart attack, though contemporaries thought he was poisoned because of the price on his head by southern governors), Walker had successfully printed and distributed two more editions of his cry for reform, enlightenment, and black solidarity to southern and northern blacks.[15]

Walker's significance lies not only in his role as the symbol of a transition toward a more aggressive evangelical abolition movement in which human endeavor replaced reliance on divine intervention, but also as a forerunner of particular ideas and language that became central in antebellum abolitionist propaganda. Walker argued that the church was primarily responsible for the continuation and expansion of slavery. One section of the *APPEAL*, "Our Wretchedness in Consequence of the Preachers of the Religion of Jesus Christ," was a vociferous attack on white clergy, whom Walker blamed as much as slaveholders for the continuation of black oppression in the United States. Clergymen condoned slave patrols that prevented Christian slave meetings, excused slaveholders who whipped slaves for praying, and taught slaves, when they spoke to them at all, to obey slaveholders. For Walker, even worse than clergymen's condoning slavery was the fact that they themselves were often slaveholders. There were American clergymen, "pretended preachers," who not only held black men, women, and children as their "natural inheritance," but who treated their slaves as badly as "any Infidel or Deist in the world."

Others, seeing how preachers of the gospel treated slaves, felt no compunction about doing the same. Established institutions, particularly religious, were critical for ending slavery. Walker believed that if clergymen would do "their utmost to erase it from the country; not only in one or two cities," but raised "one continual cry," the country would be saved.[16]

And like late eighteenth-century and early nineteenth-century black reformers, Walker revered the Declaration of Independence as reflecting biblical principles of human liberty and equality. Unlike early and later leaders, though, Walker stressed the revolutionary implications within the Declaration and the Bible. "See your Declaration Americans!!! Do you understand your own language?" Citing the passage which asserts American citizens' right or "*duty*" to alter or abolish government if the government becomes destructive, Walker asked if British oppression was at all comparable to black bondage. "Now, Americans! I ask you candidly, was your sufferings under Great Britain, one hundredth part as cruel and tyrannical as you have rendered ours under you?" As the forerunner of aggressive black activism and abolition in general, Walker revealed that black reformers would continue to draw upon fundamental American values—first and foremost, evangelicalism—in their demand for the expansion of the principles of liberty and equality.

Additionally, Walker reflected and anticipated a type of late nineteenth-century black millennialism, or what religious historian Timothy Fulop calls, "progressive millennialism," a belief that reflects traditional millennial thought that is "optimistic about the power of Christianity to transform and perfect American society, but . . . is not naive and takes a more religiously prophetic stance toward the United States" emphasizing "the role of the church, evangelism, missions, and reform in giving birth to the millennium on earth." According to Fulop, progressive millennialism can include pan-Africanism and strong social criticism of the United States. In particular ways, though, Walker and antebellum reformers like him reflected how the "nationalistic evangelical millennialism" tradition, evident at the end of the eighteenth century, had, according to historian Ruth Bloch, "become deeply embedded in the thought and the character of the American people."[17] Walker was not only certain of the coming millennium and the prominent role of America, but also that black Americans would play a special role in perfecting the world.

The *APPEAL* is important, too, for revealing how northern blacks maintained their dual identity while colonizationists consistently stressed only one. Walker's identity was African and American and he viewed himself and others of African ancestry as one people. Perhaps, even more than earlier reformers, and certainly more than many who would follow, his pan-Africanism was more evident and vigorous. In the *APPEAL,* Walker's reference to Americans was to white Americans, but at the same time the United States was the country of blacks as well as whites. Black northern reformers would soon stress American nationality more, however, as members of the American Colonization Society promoted the view of blacks as being alien to American citizenship.

Walker's opposition to colonization, if anything, was more vitriolic. In fact, he was wary of black emigration of any sort. He used the same arguments as early anticolonizationists but added a stinging condemnation of black American emigration. Claims of American nationality remained dominant. The difference was that Walker argued that blacks, not whites, had a greater claim to citizenship. And, black emigrants were almost traitors to the struggle for abolition and equality. "America is more our country, than it is the whites—we have enriched it with our *blood and tears:*—and will they drive us from our property and homes, which we have earned with our *blood* . . . and keep back millions of our dear brethren, sunk in the most barbarous wretchedness?" Walker's attitude shows that colonizationists pushed northern blacks toward an even stronger American identity that compromised earlier notions of alternatives for settlement. Walker asserted that the movement was better off without the emigrants who were ignorant enough to let the "whites *fool* them off to Africa."[18]

Other black reformers reflected Walker's gospel of activism. African Americans needed to do more. In 1832, reformer Peter Osborne explained to a black church in New Haven that "with the Declaration of Independence in one hand, and the Holy Bible in the other, I think we might courageously give battle to the most powerful enemy to this cause."[19] Osborne encouraged the congregation to maintain their hope that blacks would gain freedom and equality in the United States. There were favorable signs throughout the nation, he said. Presumably pointing to the rise of immediatism among white abolitionists, Osborne argued that it was "high time for us to be up and doing."

Contrary to Walker's imagination, the Christian "men of sense" he called upon for black enlightenment were most immediately represented by a New England woman, Maria Stewart, perhaps his most devoted follower. As a young Boston widow, Stewart's pietistic political writings and speeches signaled the diversity and complexity of black reform in the antebellum era. Contrary to Walker, Stewart demanded that black men expand principles of freedom and equality across gender lines. She saw herself as one of Walker's disciples called upon to prepare the way for black freedom. Like Walker, Stewart's activism was based thoroughly in evangelical Protestant thought and language. Her conviction of being "called" meant a commitment "for the cause of God and my brethren." Like her hero, she was prepared for martyrdom. "Many will suffer for pleading the causes of oppressed Africa, and I shall glory in being one of her martyrs; . . . [God] is able to take me to himself, as he did the most noble, fearless, and undaunted David Walker." [20]

If Walker's *APPEAL* heralded an aggressive abolitionism that was threatening to whites, Stewart's various abolitionist and equal rights speeches in Boston indicated that even a hint of female assertiveness in the public sphere was threatening to some black men. In an era when women did not speak publicly before male audiences, Stewart was reluctant to take on the mantle of Walker. Cautious at first, the young reformer spoke solely to black women's groups, but by the early 1830s she began speaking to "promiscuous" or mixed (men and women) audiences.

With all the fervor of Walker, Stewart repeated and amplified his condemnations of black self-interest and disunity and argued strongly for black solidarity. She believed that whites' claim that black Americans were often their own worst enemy was accurate. Blacks lacked solidarity to achieve common interests. Rather than support one another's attempts for self-improvement, northern blacks tore one another down, dealing "treacherously" through an "envious and malicious disposition." Stewart wanted African Americans to develop virtues of kindness and gentleness, and to "promote love and friendship." This was how solidarity was established. Political agitation had to be built upon essential Christian principles. "No gentle methods are used to promote love and friendship among us, but much is done to destroy it." [21]

Both Stewart and Walker reveal the degree to which the ideal of a unified ethnic community under the collective name "African" was fraught with problems if not contradictions in the antebellum era. Early community leaders helped unite diverse people of African descent around the historical idealization of a common "African country," mainly by reminding northern blacks of persistent common oppression through slavery and quasi-free black status. As the nineteenth century wore on, Africa for various reasons receded into the background for most northern blacks, making common oppression the primary reason for black unity and thus subjecting a shared African identity to greater circumspection. Yet unity remained elusive. The problem, as New

York City physician and intellectual James McCune Smith would note later, was that northern blacks were oppressed differently. Each northern state had laws that defined black rights and status in distinction from whites, but the laws and racial customs were not uniform throughout the North. In most New England states, for example, black men had the right of franchise. In these and other states, cities, or towns, it was often easier for certain black men and women with particular social connections to gain an education and/or operate businesses, thus making it possible to own and maintain property. As several African Americans gained some modicum of financial security, differences in socioeconomic status increasingly interfered with the development of a united front. The emerging black middle class formed similarly to the white middle class in that social values, based largely in evangelicalism, served as its foundation. The ideals of a virtuous citizenry were values embedded in evangelical Christianity: piety, frugality, sobriety, and industry formed core characteristics of the emerging middle class, black or white.[22]

Late eighteenth-century black community leaders hoped to inculcate these virtues in the northern black masses as they embraced and practiced them for themselves. In the early to mid-nineteenth century, concentration on these virtues as means for improving individual and collective black socioeconomic status would distinguish African Americans even more than income and education. But education and income increasingly contributed significantly to the emerging class divide that would only become more pronounced after the Civil War. Thus, even though she lamented the barriers placed before them, Maria Stewart was disgusted with northern blacks who, in her mind, did not try hard enough to improve their lot in life. At the least, they could practice the four virtues, especially piety.

Revealing also that she embraced significant elements of the gender conventions of the dominant society, Stewart gendered her advocacy as Walker had done, holding out particular censure for black men. In short, she felt they were cowards. Rather than act as the protectors and providers for women, too many black men, according to Stewart, lacked the characteristics necessary for agitation; they weren't acting like men. The most extreme reaction to black initiative would be death, but inaction made death inevitable. Black men might as well die for something than for nothing; they did not measure up to the standard of masculinity.[23] Stewart not only reflected the prevailing gender ideology and challenged the existence of black masculinity but also expanded its meaning. David Walker, Stewart believed, epitomized black manhood; he acted "wholly in the defense of African rights and liberty."[24] Commitment to the cause of abolition and black equality was a prerequisite for black manhood.

Additionally, Stewart extended Walker's idea of activism toward pragmatic efforts in the North. She looked specifically at economic methods for improving black socioeconomic status. Black poverty might diminish through the establishment of cooperative dry goods and grocery stores funded by money wasted on "nonsense." Because blacks contributed immeasurably to the growing American economy, black men should claim black rights and create practical programs through cooperative effort.[25]

Walker assumed black men would play the primary role in reforms; Stewart, as other antebellum women would do, stressed the important contributions of women. In extending her message to black women, she expected women to act in both the private and public spheres of antebellum society. She argued that women had a particular and prominent role in the abolition of slavery, in securing equal rights, and in community development. Like the republican mother of the Revolutionary era, women should exemplify noble and exalted faculties at home. "O, ye daughters of Africa, awake! Awake! Arise! No longer sleep nor slumber, but distinguish yourselves. Show forth to the world that ye are endowed with noble and exalted faculties."[26]

As wives and mothers, black women were responsible for encouraging gentleness and mutual concern in the family and community. Mothers were especially charged with motivating black children toward industry and learning. Both parents, though, in Stewart's mind, were ultimately obligated for training children in proper values. Black youth were failing the community. Young women were displaying crassness and vulgarity instead of a "delicacy of manners," while young men were concerned with petty wrongs, content with ignorance, and interested only in self-gratification..

Both young men and women, Stewart believed, would benefit from an education that included the arts, humanities, and sciences. Stewart stressed even more, however, the necessity of women's education and black women's access to jobs other than menial labor. Domestic work offered little in return for the continual "hard labor" that "irritates our tempers and sours our dispositions." That so many black girls like her were forced to abandon their higher aspirations and accept menial roles pained Stewart and motivated her toward expanding black women and girls' educational and employment opportunities. She visited the shops of white businesswomen and asked them to hire black girls who had "the most satisfactory references." White businesswomen responded that they had no personal objections (if it were up to them), but that they feared community reprisal. Thinking of the white middle-class majority, Stewart challenged the notion of white women's powerlessness and implicitly challenged white women to become more intellectually engaged and socially active. She and other black women viewed white women's limited status as privileged compared to their own. "O, ye fairer sisters, whose hands are never soiled, whose nerves and muscles are never strained. . . . Had we had the opportunity that you have had . . . what would have hindered our intellects from being as bright, and our manners from being as dignified as yours?"[27]

While Walker's strong language may have riled some black men in Boston, similar words and sentiments from a young woman in her early twenties were intolerable. Unprepared for an outspoken female reformer who claimed a leading role in the abolitionist movement, several black men in Boston rejected Stewart's activism in spite of her testimony of divine calling. In so doing, they motivated Stewart to develop the first public American feminist statement in the United States. Several men apparently believed that though women were important to the movement, they should not play leadership roles. Stewart dismissed such reasoning as illogical and unsupportable. After persistent conflict, however, she decided to move to New York, where she gained more education and later began teaching. Before acquiescing to black Boston's gender proscriptions, Stewart, using the Bible as her guide, spoke publicly in defense of women's rights. Her "Farewell Address" on September 21, 1833, anticipated and reflected a growing feeling among black and white women in America that republican principles of freedom must apply to women as well as slaves.

Stewart referenced biblical history for evidence of female leadership and rejected the contemporary biblical argument that women should remain in private life. There were numerous historical examples of women in positions of influence, and the Apostle Paul's admonition restricting women to private speaking had been superseded by Christ himself. "What if I am a woman; is not the God of ancient times the God of these modern days? Did he not raise up Deborah, to be a mother, and a judge of Israel? . . . And Mary Magdalene first declare the resurrection of Christ from the dead?" In the fifteenth century, Stewart added, the spirit of the age meant that women played roles of prominence in cultural, intellectual, and spiritual realms. "What if such women as are here described should rise among our noble race?"[28]

The same time that Maria Stewart was creating a stir in the early 1830s in Boston's African American community, male delegates from various organizations and states began meeting in "national" conventions annually to discuss ways "to improve the situation and condition of the people of colour." Although they were responding more directly to Ohio's Black Laws that resulted in the violent expulsion of free blacks, the first national meeting, in September 1830, solidified the shift away from a primary focus on internal community needs and toward external issues, mainly equal rights and the abolition of slavery. By then, members in several organizations had established that advocacy for equal rights and the abolition of slavery would join community improvement to form the three main means for achieving their vision of a truly free and equal nation in which people of color fully participated. The American Society of Free Persons of Colour, representing delegates from Pennsylvania, New York, Rhode Island, Connecticut, Delaware, Virginia, and Maryland, announced that black efforts involved the aggressive pursuit of these three ends. The times called for more assertive action, and abolition, equal rights, and free black community development were interconnected and vital elements for the accomplishment of their goals. Perhaps responding to the denunciation of Walker's tract, reformers at this national convention emphasized that their struggle for emancipation excluded violence. They would "pursue all legal means for the speedy elevation of ourselves and brethren to the scale and standing of men."[29]

Significantly, convention delegates, most of whom were Pennsylvanians, believed they were capable of reaching their tripartite objectives. As Walker and Stewart demonstrated, black optimism in the antebellum period was not like the optimism of the early activists. While several early leaders continued in the movement a few more years, a younger, more aggressive generation steadily replaced them. This second generation increasingly placed greater confidence in individual abilities as agitators for social and, importantly, political change.

Partly because they were products of the idealistic Revolutionary age of early leaders and mainly because they lived within a growing and vibrant black community in which many black men and women exhibited some measure of control over their lives, many young people in their early twenties and thirties were convinced they had the necessary talents to effect change in America. Child slave fugitive and activist minister Henry Highland Garnet, for example, grew up in New York City in the 1820s and 1830s, where free blacks had established several cooperative relief and literary societies, founded churches, and actively supported the New York African Free School. Garnet's mentor,

Theodore Wright, was the minister of the Shiloh Presbyterian African Church and was actively involved in abolitionist, anticolonizationist, educational, and political causes.[30]

Many second-generation leaders were, in fact, children of pioneer community organizers. All five of the children of Philadelphia sail manufacturer James Forten and his wife, Charlotte, were involved in the abolition movement. Margaretta, Sarah, and Harriet, like their mother, were members of the Philadelphia Female Anti-Slavery Society, and brothers Robert and James Jr., with their father, were active members of the Philadelphia Anti-Slavery Society. New York carpenter William Hamilton, an early organizer of black cooperative relief societies and supporter of black education, had two sons, Robert and Thomas, both of whom followed their father in advocating abolition and black education. They would gain prominence as editors and publishers of the *Weekly Anglo-African* in the late 1850s and 1860s. Boston tailor William G. Nell was cofounder of the Massachusetts General Colored Association in the mid-1820s, and his son, William Cooper Nell, became an abolitionist, a strong advocate of integrated public schools, and active, like his father, in fighting for better conditions in the black community.[31]

Self-confidence, however, did not obviate belief in divine assistance. While not viewing themselves as divine instruments like Walker and Stewart, many of this second generation were as religious as the first. They were usually members of evangelical churches that embraced the ideals of individual responsibility for social change. Although most reformers were either Baptist or Methodist, some were Episcopalian, Presbyterian, or attended meetings of the Society of Friends. Teacher and abolitionist Sarah Mapps Douglass and her mother, Grace Bustill Douglass, attended Philadelphia Quaker meetings, and the Forten family had religious ties to St. Thomas African Episcopal Church.[32]

The activism of Stewart, Walker, the Fortens, and the Douglasses illustrate the greater complexity and diversity among the second generation. Many more women, several slave fugitives from the South, and several free black men and women from the Upper South participated in various aspects of the cause. In spite of black male protestations and Maria Stewart's semiretirement from public life, a few women played dominant roles, and southern free blacks and fugitive slaves brought greater urgency and saliency to the movement through firsthand accounts.

Moreover, this generation was better educated than its predecessor. Through formal education and/or private tutoring, self-study, and the literary societies, most had more than the rudimentary education of their forebears. Some attended the few high schools that admitted African American youth, several were college educated, and a few had higher degrees from prestigious institutions. Theodore Wright earned a degree at Princeton Theological Seminary; James McCune Smith, unable to obtain medical training in the United States, earned his medical degree from the University of Glasgow. A few others earned degrees from Oberlin, Amherst, and Bowdoin.[33]

If the education of second-generation activists distanced them from the first generation and the larger uneducated northern black majority, financial status further separated them and their families from most northern blacks in the antebellum era. Former slave and successful Philadelphia baker Cyrus Bustill made sure that all his children learned self-supporting skills that ensured financial stability. While most activists were working or middle class, a few, especially in Pennsylvania, were wealthy. Businessman and editor of the *National Reformer* William Whipper owned a prosperous lumber business in Columbia, Pennsylvania.[34] This emerging middle and upper middle class dominated black reform disproportionate to their numbers and developed a close-knit social network in which individuals generally maintained their status through intermarriage. They often opened their homes to one another's children so that they could take advantage of educational opportunities and provided hospitality to convention delegates so that they could attend meetings or conventions without suffering the indignities of racial discrimination at local hotels and restaurants. And like those of a later age, they formed social organizations and activities that shielded themselves and their children from blatant discrimination or the glaring gaze of racists, who viewed them as spectacles for their personal curiosity, disgust, or amusement.[35]

Yet in the early years of antebellum activism, the 1820s to the late 1830s, continuity rather than change defined the northern free black agenda. Black political evangelicalism remained the foundation of black reforming strategies. Perhaps because the aging Richard Allen was so prominent at the national convention and had a significant degree of power in the various black communities as bishop of the African Methodist Episcopal church, the initial strategy for improving black socioeconomic status was similar to the goals and practices of earlier organizations that sought to improve the character of blacks individually and collectively. For addressing concerns and interests of the growing black communities, the convention delegates established a fact-finding committee with state and local branches to collect data on black educational, occupational, and financial status and report back to the governing board. Other committees addressed the needs of the poor by forming local societies that were responsible for conveying admonition and advice from the larger body to individual communities. In other words, the twin goals of organizing the interests and concerns of growing free black communities and teaching Protestant middle-class values to the impoverished northern black majority in preparation for participating fully in American society were coordinated across the North in the early 1830s.[36] Convention delegates viewed reform through the prism of black evangelicalism, in which the sacred and secular, the moral and political, converged to establish virtuous black citizens who claimed the natural rights under the Declaration of Independence and the Bible.

At critical points in the antebellum era, the black press complemented and reflected the black evangelical agenda of black community leaders. In the earliest years of black journalism, between 1827 and 1842, these newspapers concentrated in large measure upon inculcating an evangelical morality. All the short-lived but important black newspapers of the era, including the *Freedom's Journal* (1827), the *Rights of All* (1829), the *Weekly Advocate*, which soon after became the *Colored American* (1837), the *National Reformer* (1838), and those that failed almost before the first printing, were quite different from the popular presses developed around the same time. By the 1840s the penny press reflected a switch in newspaper writing from mainly editorializing to gathering news, often sensational, that appealed to the white masses; the black press, on the other hand, was more concerned with teaching morality. Beginning this trend, the editors of the *Freedom's Journal* indicated the newspaper was devoted "to the dissemination of useful knowledge among our brethren, and to their moral and religious improvement." The *Journal* planned to "dwell," not "dictate," on "general principles and rules of economy" and encourage black parents to promote education as "an object of the highest importance to the welfare of society."[37]

The black newspaper editors' concern about black morality reflected their evangelical experience and understanding. Presbyterian minister Samuel Cornish was especially important because he dominated the black press in the early years. He was coeditor in the first year of the *Freedom's Journal*, sole editor of the *Rights of All*, and, in its earliest years, also editor of the *Colored American*. The banners of the various papers Cornish edited symbolized his evangelistic zeal among blacks and the larger American society and revealed the dominance of evangelicalism in antebellum black reformers' thought.

While coeditor of *Freedom's Journal*, the newspaper's creed was "Righteousness Exalteth A Nation." When he left in September 1828, John Russwurm, an educator not a preacher, had changed the newspaper's banner by April to "Devoted to the Improvement of the Colored Population." In 1829, Cornish reestablished his editorial position with a new paper, *The Rights of All*. This time he extended the *Freedom's Journal* banner. To the old banner of "Righteousness Exalteth A Nation" he added "Sin Is a Reproach to Any People." When he replaced his short-lived *Weekly Advocate* with the *Colored American* in 1837, Cornish returned to the shortened version in the newspaper's banner, "Righteousness Exalteth A Nation."[38]

Moreover, Cornish, representing the broadening of the reformer's agenda in the antebellum years, illustrated his republican Christian view of African Americans' equal place in the United States in editorials utilizing the metaphor of the wheel. American society was the "human wheel," with interrelated and interdependent spokes. The efforts of both blacks and whites, as two distinct spokes in the wheel, were necessary to make a strong, viable nation free of slavery and inequalities. Cornish argued that the "great republik" was a body politic requiring the functioning of all body parts for a healthy nation. "Viewing this great republik as composed of so many different grades and capacities, the editor considers that . . . it is all important . . . that every constituent must become perfect, as far as human perfectibility goes, before the body politic can become perfect."[39]

Evangelicalism dominated antebellum northern African American thought because it continued to address the political and spiritual interests of black Christian reformers and, too, because ministers continued as major forces of the black movement between the 1780s and the late 1830s.[40] Besides spiritual reasons, men and women interested in a degree of independence and in playing a principal role in the community and the larger society chose the ministry, or for certain women, itinerant preaching, made possible in part because evangelical churches were not as strict about formal education as the more traditional denominations. As noted earlier, Baptists and Methodists stressed the conversion experience and divine "calling" more than clerical training.[41]

Convention delegates decided that one of the means of communicating the three-pronged goals of immediate abolition, community development, and equal rights would be through a weekly journal, to aid in "the cause of our oppressed brethren."[42] Unable to achieve this immediate end because newspapers failed before they barely began, they relied on letters, petitions, and speeches as the primary tools for demanding the abolition of slavery and equal rights.[43] They believed that the nation's two foundational documents supported their cause. In the 1831 convention, for example, the Committee on the Condition of the Free People of Colour of the United States recommended that "the Declaration of Independence and Constitution of the United States, be read in our Conventions; believing that the truths contained in the former are incontrovertible and that the latter guarantees in letter and spirit to every freeman born in this country, all the rights and immunities of citizenship."[44]

Black reformers viewed the abolition of slavery and equal rights as interrelated goals and insisted that white abolitionists share their sentiment. Possibly stimulated by David Walker's seemingly insurrectionary tract, a new generation of white abolitionists aggressively advocated immediate abolition in the 1830s. William Lloyd Garrison and his supporters significantly affected and were affected by black activism. Garrison's sincerity and, more importantly, his support for immediate abolition and equal rights gave black reformers renewed hope that conditions might change fairly quickly. Several white abolitionists were now advocating the program blacks believed would create full and complete black freedom.

When Garrison solicited financial support for his newspaper, the *Liberator*, several black abolitionists wholeheartedly supported his efforts with money and subscriptions, and some became local circulation agents. Wealthy Philadelphians James Forten, his son-in-law Robert Purvis, and prosperous Pittsburgh barber John Vashon helped keep the abolitionist paper afloat in the first years of circulation. Actually, in the early years of the newspaper northern free blacks were the majority of the *Liberator*'s subscribers. When Garrison asked James Forten for support in December 1830 before the paper's first issue appeared on New Year's Day, Forten expressed hope that the paper would change public opinion affecting blacks. "I learn with the greatest regret, that so much prejudice exists in the Eastern States, but may the 'Standard you are about to erect in the eyes of the Nation' be the means of dispersing those clouds of errors, and of bringing many advocates to our cause."[45]

According to Presbyterian minister Theodore Wright, northern blacks gained a "new impulse" when whites joined the movement. "At that dark moment we heard a voice—it was the voice of Garrison, speaking in trumpet tones! It was like the voice of an angel of mercy! Hope, hope, then cheered our path! The signs of the times began to indicate brighter days."[46] White antislavery support in the 1830s reinvigorated black reform, especially when

Garrison, under black reformers' influence, switched to anticolonization. Garrison and several other like-minded white Americans expressed full support for equal rights. Garrison's public declarations that slavery and prejudice were a national disgrace endeared him to most northern blacks. His assertions that it was "the sacred duty of the nation to abolish the system of slavery now, and to recognize the people of color as brethren and countrymen who have been unjustly treated," reflected black evangelical ideals and suggested the real possibility of white transformation in the not too distant future.[47]

As a consequence, antislavery became, for the first time, a racially integrated movement. Opponents of slavery before 1830 worked in racially segregated organizations, but after 1830 some black abolition societies became auxiliaries of mostly white-run societies. In 1833, for example, the Massachusetts General Colored Association became a "subsidiary" of the New England Anti-Slavery Society.[48] In the new organizations, black and white abolitionists worked together and agreed that methods of persuasion through the use of speeches, petitions, and pamphlets were the means to end slavery. Similar to other reformist organizations working within an evangelical revival model, local, state, and national antislavery societies coordinated speakers' circuits, published newspapers and other literature, organized mail campaigns, and generated and sent petitions that poured into Congress.

By the 1850s, several black men and a few black women were prominent speakers on the antislavery circuit. Massachusetts barber Charles Lenox Remond became one of the first full-time abolitionist lecturers.[49] But freeborn blacks like Remond, the son of a wealthy Salem businessman, would be superseded when former slaves, especially recent fugitives, took the lectern. Several, such as Henry Bibb, William Wells Brown, Samuel Ringgold Ward, and particularly Frederick Douglass, traveled throughout the North and Great Britain, with and without white colleagues, generating support for the American abolition movement. Fugitives from slavery recounted horrifying scenes of American slavery, demonstrating slave discontent, documenting slaveholder brutality, and, more importantly, arguing for the slaves' right to freedom.[50]

Slave narratives were not just appeals for the abolition of slavery but were in some ways evangelistic tracts pointing the way toward individual and national redemption. Some escaped slaves who authored or told their stories exposed the growing discrepancy in the nineteenth century between the assumption within republicanism of the necessity of a virtuous citizenry and stress on private interests. Republicanism assumed a moral sense, a civic responsibility that would preclude unrestrained individualism at the expense of the common good. But by the antebellum era, private interest, according to fugitive slaves, had almost won the battle.[51] African Americans and other abolitionists, more implicitly than explicitly by this time, clung to the Christian republican ideal of virtue. American citizens would soon conclude that slavery ultimately harmed the republic. They appealed to the Christian majority to check the "vice," the "greed," the "extravagance" of "self-indulgent" slaveholders and end slavery. The language, the scenes of slaveholders' sexual exploitation of slave women, the travails of slave mothers forced to part with daughters and sons, the fiction of slave marriage in which husbands and wives were easily separated by sale, and the family life of the enslaved in general illustrated in graphic detail the consequences of unlimited power.

Slavery, according to the slave narratives and other black abolitionists' writings, threatened the most precious of national principles, liberty. Herein was the core of natural rights in the heart and soul of America writ large. The all-powerful slavery would destroy the new republic and enslave everyone in its midst. Similar to eighteenth-century leaders Absalom Jones and Richard Allen, writers like Frederick Douglass illustrated the belief that if slavery did not end, the entire country would be engulfed in its powerful tentacles. Douglass depicted his slave mistress Sophia Auld in his 1845 *Narrative* as the embodiment of the innocent republic, full of generosity and kindness. She was a "pious, warm, and tender-hearted woman. There was no sorrow or suffering for which she had not a tear. She had bread for the hungry, clothes for the naked, and comfort for every mourner that came within her reach." Yet, in the arms of slavery, Auld, with all her "heavenly qualities," became vicious, if not evil, with a heart of "stone." Slavery, Douglass asserted, "proved as injurious to her as it did to me."[52] For the public good and the general welfare of the nation, slave narrative writers and other abolitionists asserted, slavery must be abolished. The abolition movement would save the nation, according to black abolitionist John Mercer Langston. It was established not to free the slave but for "the preservation of the American Government, the preservation of American liberty itself."[53]

Slaveholding was not just wrong but a sin—and for black evangelicals, the greatest sin. Black and white abolitionists demanded that the nation stop sinning immediately. New York grocer, printer, and writer David Ruggles believed slavery absolutely immoral. Abolitionists must use "evangelical weapons" to attack the system. Other means were ineffective among licentious slaveholders. In fact, Ruggles argued, slavery would end if northern white women used their power and influence on the nation and particularly on southern white women, whose behavior was quite different when in the North as opposed to the South. In their own homes and interacting with slaves, southern women were vulgar and cruel, exacting the "severest labor." They inflicted tortuous punishment "with an indescribable savageness of ferocity." In allowing slavery, Ruggles wrote in his pamphlet *The Abrogation of the Seventh Commandment by the American Churches,* Americans, especially American churches, sanctioned adultery. There was no parallel in the historical records, a people professing Christianity and permitting the most unchristian acts. For blacks, slavehold-ers' repentance involved manumission regardless of the consequences. While some white abolitionists' notion of immediacy was at times vague, black aboli-tionists usually meant instantaneous action. National repentance necessitated acknowledgment of the sin and immediate emancipation.[54]

But abolitionists generally lacked a clear program for the actual process of immediate emancipation, however defined. Some black abolitionists believed freed slaves would be ready for immediate citizenship. A committee "Report on the Condition of the People of Color in the State of Ohio" at the 1835 Ohio Anti-Slavery Convention referred to African American residents of Cincinnati, many of whom were fugitive slaves or slaves who had purchased their freedom and were living financially independent lives, as examples of what would hap-pen if slavery was immediately abolished. Black Cincinnati residents were more than capable of participating fully in society.

> The question is often asked, Can slaves, if liberated, take care of themselves? We cannot answer this question better than by pointing to the colored population of Cincinnati. It is amusing to see the curious look which an emancipated slave assumes, when he is asked this ques-tion. He seems at a loss to know whether he shall consider it a joke or an honest inquiry. "We did," they say, "take care of ourselves and our masters too, while we were in fetters. We dug our way out of slavery— and now that we are free, all we ask is a fair chance." We know of no class of men who are better qualified to take care of themselves.[55]

Abolitionists also pointed to well-known fugitives like Frederick Douglass, Henry Highland Garnet, William Wells Brown, and others as "living examples of the practicability" of immediacy. Some black abolitionists, however, hinted that slaveholders should divide their land among former slaves. Presbyterian ministers Theodore Wright and Samuel Cornish thought masters should manumit and then hire former slaves for wages. This would be the means for freedmen and women to gain a foothold and gradually advance in the social order.[56] Wright and Cornish argued that rather than incur an immediate transformation of the southern socioeconomic structure or cause the decline of the southern black population, the southern economy would continue as before, at least in the short run, only with waged black workers. Those who thought blacks would simply "waste away" ignored the role of slavery. The "social structure of the South is already formed; and . . . one of the elements of it is the colored population to whom certain offices have been assigned; and that they can perform these offices as well in a state of freedom as in a state of servitude."[57]

A writer to the *Colored American* noted in 1838 that most of those who discussed the subject of immediate abolition avoided the political and economic status of freedmen and instead resorted to the issue of compensation to the slaveholder. He added, in "this matter, we acknowledge no master but God." Abolitionists generally believed compensation to slaveholders was improper because it implied support for the right to own fellow humans; it rewarded sin.

Antebellum black abolitionists' critique of slavery was similar to that of late eighteenth-century slave petitioners and other late eighteenth-century black abolitionists who condemned slavery. All humans were ultimately accountable to God and society. Slavery precluded individual responsibility and choice. It not only robbed spouses and parents of fundamental familial responsibilities, but it also denied individual Christians the duty to obey God rather than man. Demanding obedience that only God could command, the slaveholder inserted himself in the place of God, thus eroding the pillar of Christian faith.[58] Black and white abolitionists believed the North was as guilty as the South for the institution of slavery. All American economic, political, and social institutions supported the system in one way or another. The United States' political economy, in particular, came under condemnation. New England cotton manufacturers and the mercantile industry, involved in the processing, selling, and shipping of slave-produced goods, were as responsible as those who bought and sold slaves. And so were politicians who interpreted or established laws that protected slavery. Slavery affected national and international communities. In fact, Pennsylvania businessman William Whipper argued that slavery "paralyzed the virtue of the whole world."[59]

Similar to Walker, other black abolitionists stressed black Americans' contributions to American economic growth. In counterattacking colonizationists' charges and demanding full citizenship, several activists claimed their rights on the basis of the "blood, sweat, and tears" of their enslaved ancestors.[60] New York Presbyterian minister Henry Highland Garnet argued that black soldiers' contributions to the Revolution and the War of 1812 gave blacks the rights of citizenship. But even if no blacks had fought in these wars, blacks' contributions to American agricultural prosperity entitled them to freedom. More than any other group, African Americans contributed to "the agricultural prosperity of the country. . . . Who is it that will deny that they here stand preeminently entitled to blessings of life and liberty?"[61]

Black reformers generally viewed the thriving American economy as a sign of divine blessing. And rather than criticize capitalism or suggest ways in which the economy greatly benefited from exploited labor, abolitionists condemned amoral or excessive capitalism. The flaw in the nation was the existence of forced labor and all the horrors that came with it, not the system itself. Abolitionists believed that the white southern majority, the nonslaveholders, was negatively affected because slavery created unfair labor competition. Poor southern whites, according to black lawyer John Mercer Langston, had no means or opportunity for "acquiring wealth" as long as slavery existed. Denied public education and jobs, they existed in a state of "ignorance" and "indolence."[62]

Instead of attacking the economic system, black evangelical reformers addressed the failures of social institutions, namely the church. Even Walker, though he and most others regarded the profit motive as critical for understanding the persistence and perpetuation of slavery, believed the problem was individual and collective greed. Avarice, in this evangelical age, was a matter of morality and as such required condemnation, conviction, repentance, and regeneration of individual and collective souls. The churches, responsible for influencing and upholding morality, had accommodated or supported slavery, thus undermining a virtuous citizenry so essential for the perpetuity of the republic. In the appendix to his 1845 *Narrative*, Frederick Douglass distinguished between religion and "*slaveholding religion*," between the "Christianity of this land and the Christianity of Christ." As such, he argued, "We see the thief preaching against theft, and the adulterer against adultery. We have men sold to build churches, women sold to support the gospel, and babes sold to purchase Bibles for *the poor heathen! All for the glory of God and the good of souls.*" Abolitionist Sarah Remond said that the American church was infinitely more corrupt than any other American institution.[63]

Moreover, most black reformers shared the Enlightenment ideal of inevitable human progress. Like other Americans, they believed the world's civilizations were constantly improving, knowledge was increasing, and democracy was replacing tyranny. The United States would have been in the forefront of world progress if not for the entrenchment and spread of slavery and prejudice. James Forten asserted in 1830 that in the world the "spirit of freedom is marching with rapid strides, and causing tyrants to tremble, may America awake from the apathy in which she has long slumbered."[64]

Following Walker's admonitions, black evangelicals believed that African American Christians had a particular role in the path toward human progress. That role, according to New York Episcopalian minister Alexander Crummell, was to teach white Christians "the great element of humanity." Then the United States would regain her leading role in the march toward progress. In 1843, James McCune Smith told the Philomathean Society of New York City, a young African American men's literary society, that the black American destiny was to save the republic through antislavery exertions. The abolition of slavery would "tend to perpetuate the Republic." Smith was certain that blacks would bring about "true Republicanism." "We will save the form of government, and convert it into a substance." In the June 10, 1837, *Colored American* editorial, Cornish explained that black Americans were special instruments of Christ to save America and therefore further the gospel. "We have a whole nation to redeem," he asserted, "and some thousands of clergymen of all denominations to save from the fatalities of *time-serving*, of pride, and of avarice, engendered by this spirit of caste." The cause was broader than abolition and equal rights; it was a movement "for the establishment of peace on earth and good will to men. . . .Then shall be the reign of perfect peace."[65]

While most white abolitionists could not imagine black Christians guiding America toward the millennium, many more whites joined the movement in the 1830s and 1840s. Yet slavery continued unabated and racism was not only evident outside abolitionists' circles but within the movement itself. Many white abolitionists often demonstrated ambivalence or outright antagonism toward interacting with blacks on levels of equality. They accepted the idea— sometimes reluctantly—of blacks in the organizations and welcomed them as speakers if they adhered to white counsel, but generally rejected them as colleagues. Too often white abolitionists indicated that they embraced notions of black inferiority.[66]

Still, several black abolitionists consistently acknowledged white allies.

Some white abolitionists' speeches and actions indicated they believed, like blacks, that the quest for equal rights was an integral part of the abolition movement and that they were actively involved with blacks in combating discrimination in education and public accommodation and in political disfranchisement. David Ruggles's negative experience on Massachusetts rail cars convinced him and others that several white abolitionists were consistently engaged in resisting racial discrimination. When Ruggles, a former grocery store owner who became secretary of the New York City Vigilance Committee, an organization created to help fugitives in the informal transportation and communications network termed the "Underground Railroad," was dragged from a "white car" on the segregated New Bedford railway line in 1841, white abolitionists, including Garrison, publicly condemned the rail company. Then, as one of several acts of civil disobedience, an integrated group of abolitionists met on the car from which Ruggles had been ejected.[67]

Even so, many black abolitionists were certain that most whites were not fully committed to equal rights, despite the rhetoric and activity of a few. Theodore Wright repeated the refrain of black reformers when he addressed a national abolition gathering in 1837. Wright reminded whites that equal rights and abolition were part of the same cause. Too many new members were supporting antislavery because of the spread of slavery into Texas, currently a self-declared republic, but were not willing to "take their stand on the principle of recognizing man as man. . . . A rush is made into the abolition ranks. . . . Anti-Texas . . . converts are multiplying. Many throw themselves in, without understanding the breadth and depth of the principles of emancipation. I fear not the annexation of Texas. I fear not all the machinations, calumny and opposition of slaveholders, when contrasted with the annexation of men whose hearts have not been deeply imbued with these high and holy principles."[68]

Black reformers argued that whites were hypocritical in opposing slavery in the South while ignoring its equivalent in the North.[69] Part of the problem, as many black abolitionists saw it, was that whites were allowing side issues to undermine the movement. From the beginning, there had been philosophical differences among abolitionists. These differences became decisive by the late 1830s when many abolitionists considered moral suasion, or the appeal to Christian morality, inadequate as a means to end slavery and looked to political means. At the same time, Garrison became more radical in his approach to solving multiple social issues. His avowed nonresistance and vociferous attacks on religious institutions created dissension within abolitionism, especially among many in the middle states who believed political means could effectively end slavery. To complicate matters, several white abolitionist women insisted on gender equality within the movement. Garrison and several other men supported feminists' efforts. Women like Angelina and Sarah Grimké, Elizabeth Cady Stanton, and Abigail Kelley were determined to participate equally with male colleagues, not as separate and subordinate entities in the female antislavery societies and national conventions but within the more powerful male local and national societies.

Conflict over these issues culminated in a split within abolitionism and led to the formation of a second antislavery society. The American and Foreign Anti-Slavery Society, established in 1840, retained separate organizations for the sexes and supported political activity, including third parties, to end slavery.[70] While a significant number of black abolitionists supported women's rights generally, most stopped short of becoming involved in the divisive issue of sexual equality. This was not the time, several argued, for free women to place their interests over those of millions of slaves. It was difficult enough fighting against the tide of racial prejudice. The movement could not have yet another controversial issue.[71] When Frederick Douglass summed up the history of American antislavery in 1855, he argued that the women's rights issue was separate from abolition, and feminists—men and women—should not have allowed it to interfere with the progress of the movement. Douglass, an advocate for women's rights and speaker at the first women's rights convention at Seneca Falls in 1848, believed women should have placed slaves' interests above their own restricted freedom:

> Thus was a grand Philanthropic movement rent asunder by a side issue, having nothing, whatever, to do with the great object which the American Anti-Slavery Society was organized to carry forward. Before I would have stood in the way of such an attitude, and taken the responsibility of dividing the ranks of Freedom's army, I would have suffered my right arm to be taken off. How beautiful would it have been for . . . [a] woman, how nobly would her name have come down to us in history, had she said: "All things are lawful for me, but all things are not expedient![72]

Cornish thought that abolitionists in New England were engaged in a controversy over issues secondary to the "noble cause of humanity and righteousness." Charles B. Ray, editor of the *Colored American* when the abolitionists' split finally occurred, complained that so much energy was spent in conflict that little was accomplished to end slavery. Ray did not believe two societies were necessary even though he became a strong supporter of political measures instituted by the American and Foreign Anti-Slavery Society. He thought moral suasion was one of several means to end slavery. The "sectarian jealousies" all tended to cause abolitionists to forget the main purpose of the movement—"the slave and the outraged free colored community." Ray wanted abolitionists to "agree to disagree." Many black abolitionists, he added, were discouraged and losing hope. "Augustus," writing to the *Colored American* editor from Pittsburgh, asked what would happen "if our friends divide among themselves and exhaust their energies combating each other?"[73]

Yet, white abolitionists' racism, divisiveness, and near neglect of equal rights were not the only cause of concern among black reformers. Conflict among blacks themselves over means to achieve emancipation and equality created intense debate. Perhaps even more troublesome, especially for those committed to consensus, was that reformers expended great energy over terms of distinct American identity. This latter issue would help distance them even more from the African identity of their late eighteenth-century forefathers while the persistence of slavery and growing racism would reveal the political side of black evangelicalism.

CHAPTER 4

We Do Not All of Us Think Alike

EVANGELICALISM AND CONFLICTING STRATEGIES FOR CITIZENSHIP

Resolved, That it is our earnest desire that Africa may speedily become civilized, and receive religious instruction. . . . That we will resist all attempts made for our removal to the torrid shores of Africa, and will sooner suffer every drop of blood to be taken from our veins than submit to such unrighteous treatment.

—Quoted in "Sentiments of the People of Color"

By the late 1820s and especially the 1830s and 1840s, many northern blacks had distanced themselves from Africa. While there is no doubt that the "back to Africa" focus of the American Colonization Society (ACS) accelerated black commitment to American national identity, conversion to republican Christianity with its expansive principles coming out of the Revolution had already ensured that American identity would supersede African identity. Consequently, the second generation leadership's emphasis on American nationality undermined the late eighteenth- and early nineteenth-century leaders' evangelical goal of a unified ethnic community with a common "African" identity based in more than shared oppression in and out of slavery. In the minds of early community leaders, African identity coexisted with the leadership's hope for shared Christian republican values that combined the political with the sacred to establish and prove a virtuous citizenry. Second generation leaders' stress on their Americanness, instead of their unity under a common African identity, coincided with an emerging middle class in which greater stress on Protestant morality and education distanced some even more from the northern poor black majority. Although black evangelicalism remained fundamental to reformers' thought and action, evangelicalism was often more implicit than explicit in reformers' intense debates about identity and separate institutions. Indeed American identity became integral to the discussion over means to achieve equal status in American society. Combined with the controversy over whether people of African ancestry should establish separate organizations, reformers debated, seemingly incessantly, about whether they should use distinct terms of identity. For a few, Africa was no longer relevant.

Of course, time and space played a significant role in northern blacks' sense of West and West Central Africa. By the second decade of the new century, most people of African descent in the northern part of the United States had no direct memory of Africa. In these years and earlier, African-born men and women were increasingly a tiny minority, replaced by a majority born in the new republic. Already more European culturally than their southern counterparts and with large numbers migrating to urban areas, more and more northern blacks lived and worked in even more diverse communities with a white majority than had been the case in the seventeenth and eighteenth centuries, when significant "clusters" of the slave population existed in New England and the middle colonies.[1]

With West and West Central Africa distant generationally and geographically and the American Colonization Society's proclamations that free blacks had no place in the United States, American identity intensified for many northern blacks, especially ministers, teachers, editors, and other community leaders. Fewer and fewer referenced Africa as their "country" or romanticized an African past.[2] The collective African identity based in a shared past that was to unify them was quickly being replaced with greater emphasis on black contributions to America. In one of the first responses to the organization of the ACS, Philadelphia blacks stated at their 1817 anticolonization meeting: "Whereas our ancestors (not of choice) were the first successful cultivators of the wilds of America, we their descendants feel ourselves entitled to participate in the blessings of her luxuriant soil, which their blood and sweat manured."[3] Bishop Richard Allen, prominent at this early Philadelphia anticolonization meeting, repeated the 1817 response at an 1827 meeting and added another dimension that would generally replace the idyllic African country references of earlier writers and speakers. In his letter to the editors of the *Freedom's Journal*, Allen affirmed black Americans' right to the land where they had shed "blood, sweat, and tears" and added that, as a largely uneducated people, most black Americans were unfit to convert "heathen" Africa.[4] In his

1828 Thanksgiving sermon to blacks in Providence, Rhode Island, clergyman Hosea Easton consistently referred to the United States as "our country" and complained that white ministers insulted blacks in America "by saluting them as Africans or Ethiopians. While in fact they are Americans, and perhaps distantly related to some of the white members, by reason of the brutal conduct of their fathers."[5]

Boston protestors explained in detail "why we object to the plan of dragging us to Africa—a country to us unknown, except by geography." Challenging the earlier assertion of a dual identity, they wanted to know how "American born citizens are African." In their objection to colonization, Brooklyn protestors combined their rejection of Africa as their country with claims of citizenship. They knew "of no other country in which we can justly claim or demand our rights as citizens, whether civil or political, but in these United States of America, our native soil." Objecting to the status of "foreigner," they stated that Africa was "a country unknown to us in every respect."[6]

> We are not strangers; neither do we come under alien law. Our constitution does not call upon us to become naturalized; we are already American citizens; our fathers were among the first that peopled this country; their sweat and their tears have been the means, in a measure, of raising our country to its present standing. Many of them fought, bled, and died for the gaining of her liberties, and shall we forsake their tombs, and flee to an unknown land?[7]

In Hartford, activists stated that they were the "legitimate sons of these United States, from whence we will never consent to be transported." Contrary to colonizationists' claims, protestors argued that they were not naturally physically adaptable to the African climate. Many protestors believed Liberia was a land "detrimental" to their health. They referred to reports of black American colonists in Liberia who sickened or died "on their arrival, to the pestilence usual to that place."[8]

In their vigorous protestations, black anticolonizationists revealed how deeply they were immersed in significant fundamentals of American culture, particularly religious values. Reflecting the nineteenth-century belief that Christianity and civilization were synonymous, protestors never questioned the colonizationists' goal of evangelism. They simply argued that "the poor ignorant slave" was unequipped to "instruct in the principles of Christianity and the arts of civilized life."[9] Richard Allen claimed blacks in the United States were American in "habits, manners, and customs." They would "never consent to take our lives in our hands, and be the bearers of the redress . . . to that much afflicted country."

For those who found racial prejudice in the United States intolerable, protestors generally recommended Upper Canada, "a place far better adapted to our constitutions, our habits, and our morals; . . . where you will be surrounded by Christians, and have an opportunity to become civilized and christianized."[10] Besides the additional possibility of a colony in the western territories of the United States, Haiti was another choice for blacks unwilling to tolerate racial prejudice. Africa was not completely ruled out, though, as Boston protestors noted that free people could "go where they please."[11] Having converted to Christianity or as second- or third-generation Christians, these protestors showed that the ACS merely quickened the pace at which American identity and critical aspects of American culture were becoming central.

Not surprisingly, an "African" designation was used less and less in the names of most new organizations in the 1830s. While "people of color" was a distinct term of identity in the eighteenth century, "colored" or "people of color" became more prominent in these years. And although "African" was not removed from the names of older organizations, newly established newspapers, literary societies, mutual relief societies, and even some churches used "Colored" as a distinguishing form of American identity. The *Colored American*," "Colored Reading Society," "Colored Female Union Society," "American Society of Free Persons of Colour," "Colored Female Charitable Society," and "Colored Presbyterian Church" are just a few examples of the many organizations and newspapers established in these years. Several organizations used no distinguishing designation at all. The "Brotherly Union Society," established in 1833 by the "coloured men of the county of Philadelphia," the "Female Literary Society," and the "Humane Mechanics Society" referenced no distinct term of identity or "collective name" that distinguished black organizations from the numerous social and fraternal organizations in the larger society. Petitioners, especially those protesting the ACS goal of free black removal, did, like other protestors, retain some form of distinctive name, generally identifying as "people of colour."[12]

Northern reformers reached some sort of informal consensus in reducing the use of African identity for the names of new organizations and newspapers, but vigorous controversy ensued when individual reformers publicly rejected any form of ethnic particularity. Most thought black experience and especially activism required distinctive terms of collective identity for strategic reasons and political/social interests. They believed that they were Americans yet distinct from other Americans because of their past and present oppression and should unite around an identity to demand inclusion and the abolition of slavery. The majority also thought blacks should maintain separate black organizations for addressing profound inequities. Black churches were particularly essential for expressing black evangelical values founded in Scripture that provided the foundation for freedom and equality. Others argued that as Americans they were like people of European ancestry and needed only one term of identity, American. The issue came to a head in the mid-1830s when Pennsylvania businessman/reformer William Whipper said that black Americans should consider themselves simply American and never form separate organizations for any reason. The human problem of sin was universal, according to Whipper, and as such must be dealt with through national moral transformation. Whipper's focus on moral reformation reflected the values of many evangelical Americans in the 1820s and 1830s.

During the years that black men and women were rethinking solutions to the problems of slavery and discrimination, evangelicalism surged and moral reformation became a national cause. As Mark Noll explains, the "central religious reality for the period from the Revolution to the Civil War was the unprecedented expansion of evangelical Protestant Christianity. No other period of American history ever witnessed such a dramatic rise in religious adherence and corresponding religious influence on the broader national culture." If evangelicalism surged, Methodism soared. Beginning as a minor sect only a generation before the Revolution, Methodism grew to become the most "pervasive form of Christianity in the United States." At the same time evangelicals (Baptists, Methodists, Presbyterians, most Congregationalists, and many Episcopalians) shared core beliefs. They all believed the "Bible taught a message of rescue and deliverance, and that this message provided moral guidance, personal empowerment, and direction for self and society."[13]

Methodism, the doctrine that influenced many if not most northern blacks, enticed believers with a vision of individual and social perfection. For Methodists, individuals were obligated to strive toward perfect love and holiness; they viewed good works as signs and conditions of their gradual progress toward this end.[14] Retaining belief in the eventual millennium, evangelicals with perfectionistic tendencies in the 1830s to the Civil War stressed moral reformation not only for individual converts but the entire nation and even the world. Religious awakenings spread all over the country, convincing evangelical clergymen that "the Spirit of the Lord was mightily at work, ushering in the millennium through the hallowing of America."[15] Clerics combined millennial expectation and radical moralism to imagine a perfect society, one in which God's justice, peace, and love triumphed.

Congregationalist Charles G. Finney, the popular evangelist of the early nineteenth century, helped make perfectionism pervasive among northerners in Jacksonian America. When Finney asserted that Christian perfection—absolute obedience to the law of God—was attainable in this life, he was engaging in the public debate concerning the biblical idea of righteousness and of sanctification, "a central preoccupation of religious thought in the United States" in these years. Finney insisted, as religious historian Timothy Smith has shown, that "Christians must obey the moral law of God in all of its rigor. Anything less contradicted the plain sense of Scripture and undermined the foundation of God's moral government."[16] Finney's acceptance of the Wesleyan stress on "perfect love" in the early 1830s strongly influenced moral reformers, including radical abolitionists. William Lloyd Garrison and those labeled "Garrisonian," many of whom were directly connected to Finney as evangelists or students, indicated the biblical and perfectionistic foundations of their crusade. Even before he accepted a professorship at the abolitionist intellectual hotbed Oberlin College, Finney, combining common sense reasoning with evangelical fervor, asked if God would require repentance and holiness if humans were incapable of obeying. While at Oberlin, he declared the Holy Spirit exerted a "divine moral suasion" by presenting "truths" to the mind. By then Garrisonians had been engaged in "moral suasion" for some time in their demand for an "immediate" end to slavery.[17]

Connected to moral perfectability for some Americans was the crusade against alcohol consumption that attracted the largest and most diverse group of supporters of any antebellum reform. Reformers of all kinds: abolitionists, proslavery advocates, feminists, and free-thinkers viewed drinking as a serious problem in American society. Seeking simplistic answers to complex issues, temperance advocates argued that the high per capita consumption of alcohol was the cause of increasing poverty and vice. According to these reformers, intemperance would eventually cause the erosion of political freedom and thus subvert human progress.[18]

As it did with other Americans, moral perfectability strongly influenced many black evangelical reformers, who decided that black drunkenness re-inforced white prejudice. Because of white America's penchant for sweeping stereotypes, one black drunkard, reformers believed, affected the future of all African Americans.[19] The 1831 national convention delegates placed tem-perance alongside education and "economy" as essential for "the elevation of mankind." But more than other black reformers, William Whipper and some of his Philadelphia colleagues perceived moral reform as the primary means for elevating free black status in the mid- to late 1830s. Whipper made temperance the overriding issue at black conventions. He wanted blacks to establish local, state, and national temperance societies, a goal to which other blacks were not averse, and generated support among prominent white abolitionists who con-sistently advised blacks to practice the "virtues of temperance and economy."[20]

Whipper connected moral reform, especially temperance, to the abolition of slavery and racism far beyond what most white moral reformers could imag-ine and simultaneously challenged eighteenth-century black community lead-ers' interest in furthering a black evangelical agenda that necessitated separate institutions. While accepting the idea that temperance was as important as hard work and frugality, several convention delegates became dissatisfied with what seemed like a redirection of the convention's goals. The situation was exacerbated when it became evident that Whipper's moral reform involved not only temperance but also antagonism to separate black institutions, includ-ing conventions. Within a short time, antiseparatism became a main tenet of the moral reformers. Ignoring distinctions between black evangelicalism and white evangelicalism, Whipper argued that Christianity was inclusive, not exclusive; there was no justification for an institution restricting member-ship on the basis of "complexional variation." "Caste distinctions" supported slavery and racism. Northern free blacks could lead the way in ridding the nation of the curse of "distinctional caste." Arguing that blacks were as guilty as whites in establishing segregated institutions, Whipper asked how blacks could justifiably condemn a practice in which they engaged. "Can we hope to be successful in reforming others before we procure a reformation among ourselves?"[21] Whipper failed, however, to explain whether he believed blacks should simply join white organizations, including churches, or whether blacks should create organizations that were not designated with some distinctive terminology.

Whipper's broad interracial evangelical program for national reforma-tion was inspired by Garrison and other radical white abolitionists who supported racial integration as much as abolition. Garrison's motto for the *Liberator*—"OUR COUNTRY IS THE WORLD—OUR COUNTRYMEN ARE MANKIND"—encompassed the humanitarian ideal that awakened Whipper. It "was the key that opened the moral world to my view." When he read the *Liberator*'s motto Whipper envisioned a society founded in a "common brotherhood" without national, cultural, and color distinctions.[22] Whipper invited white Garrisonians to join his newly established "national" moral reform society. Their unwillingness—a point of derision among some black reformers—only underscored Whipper's belief that he and his black Philadelphia supporters would lead the way in freeing the nation from the "heathenish spirit of caste." According to Whipper, his new society was the only organization committed to true reform. "We design to occupy a sphere of moral reformation of this age and country, that has but partially claimed the attention of those that have preceded us."[23]

Whipper's vision of a perfect society reflected specific themes in antebellum evangelical Christianity. His new society's "Declaration of Sentiment" rejoiced that blacks were in a country "where the liberty of speech and press" were protected by law. They were "thrown into a revolution where the contest is not for landed territory, but for freedom; the weapons not carnal, but spiritual; where the bow is the power of God, and the arrow the instrument of divine justice."[24]

Indeed, Whipper's moral vision shared the basic premise of both northern white and black evangelical reformers. Most agreed that virtue was essential for the success of the republic. The evangelical "preoccupation with divine law" represented, according to Timothy Smith, "a religious revitalization of that essentially moralistic argument among the founding fathers over how to keep the unrestrained passions of the common people from destroying the order and security necessary to a republican commonwealth."[25] Whipper was caught up in the optimism of the age, driven by evangelical millennial beliefs. He was convinced that the best means to end all oppression, slavery and racism included, was through the transformation of the individual heart and working outward to the community, nation, and then the world. This work would not be done in separate black organizations but through the actions of all moral reformers. Unlike Whipper, most black evangelicals maintained the goal of early black evangelicalism: working within the black institutions to address the spiritual, political, social, and psychological needs and interests of northern blacks. If whites joined blacks, black evangelicalism would be compromised for all the reasons stated in the late eighteenth century. African American leaders needed separate space to reinterpret the Scriptures and define the republican vision that placed blacks solidly in the human family deserving of freedom, equality, and American citizenship. This, they felt, was God's divine plan.

Response to Whipper was tempered at the 1834 and 1835 conventions, but according to the recording secretary "animated" discussion took place. It was then that Whipper succeeded in pushing through his motion for the national convention to abandon any term that identified northern blacks as a distinct population within the larger society. By 1836 the "American Moral Reform Society" was born as the new organization open to all Americans committed to national moral reformation, including temperance, abolition, and equal rights.

But the year before, black attendance at national conventions had already dwindled significantly. Although other reasons prevailed, including white mobs endangering the lives of delegates and the destruction of black churches, it seems clear that several if not most delegates were unhappy with Whipper's new society. In 1837, the majority of those who had been involved in the national conventions and several who participated in the new reform society expressed strong reservations about the American Moral Reform Society. Whipper's goals, they asserted, were antithetical to black interests.[26] They rejected Whipper's organization mainly because of its antagonism to separate black organizations and the use of a distinct black identity, rather than its goal of moral perfectability. In fact, reformers' consistent stress on education meant moral and intellectual development. Christian principles in the minds of reformers since the late eighteenth century involved constant moral betterment. Intellectual achievements were insufficient without the "cultivation of the mind and morals combined."[27]

Opposition centered largely in New York. Samuel Cornish, fellow minister and shoemaker Charles Bennett Ray, and barber and businessman Philip Bell vigorously defended separate black institutions. To them, Whipper's ideals were unrealistic, vague, and impractical. These men reestablished a black newspaper in 1837, the *Colored American*, from which they launched their attacks on anyone opposed to separate black action, institutions, and distinct terms of identity. At the same time, they called for a return to national black conventions that followed the guidelines of the 1831 and 1832 meetings. As someone who had served as vice president of the American Moral Reform Society in 1835 and had attended the meetings in 1836 and 1837, Cornish was skeptical of the purposes of the society from the start. Whipper's plans were "visionary" and the society disorganized. The organization, he added, "originated in defective, inefficient views of the condition and wants of our people."[28]

In letters to the editor, reformers from various regions of the country joined Cornish in supporting separatism. Lewis Woodson, a Pittsburgh minister and businessman writing under the pseudonym "Augustine," believed Whipper and his supporters were committing "errors of considerable magnitude." Black status in America was distinct. "We have been held as slaves, while those around us have been free." History and Scripture both demonstrated that only those who experienced oppression could resolve the problems confronting them. Solutions, according to Woodson, necessitated black unity through meetings controlled by blacks and restricted to black participation.[29] Like other antebellum reformers though, Woodson ignored the more complex "African" ethnic identity that earlier leaders so assiduously tried to construct. Shared oppression necessitated common goals. Gone was discussion of a shared idyllic past as a means to unite blacks and condemn whites. Yet, Woodson implied that blacks still needed to control their organizations to abolish slavery and gain equal rights and, as importantly, influence African American individual and collective sense of worth, all part of the black evangelical agenda founded in Scripture.

Baltimore minister, teacher, and former vice president of the American Moral Reform Society William Watkins believed Whipper, Purvis, the Fortens, and other moral reformers failed to comprehend the enormity of the black American condition. The times required concentrated efforts, not broad, sweeping programs that purported to include all of American society. The situation was similar, Watkins argued, to two men falling overboard, one black the other white. Five white men all rush to the aid of the drowning white man and ignore completely the drowning black man. As the only black man on board the steamboat, he reaches out both hands, not to the white man, "who has already abundant help," but concentrating all his "energies in one vigorous effort to extricate" the black man, who needed help, too.[30]

In spite of opposition, Whipper persisted. As sole editor of the *National Reformer*, the American Moral Reform Society's paper, Whipper and the editors of the *Colored American* engaged in continuous debate in the late 1830s and early 1840s over the benefits and problems of separatism and distinct terms of American identity.[31] The debates indicate that Whipper and his Philadelphia colleagues were in the minority and that the debate itself moved both groups toward a more certain American identity. Most activists believed, as Watkins argued, separate activities and organizations were the most effective means for blacks to discuss solutions to American slavery and American caste.

Moreover, they consistently asserted that blacks must be in the forefront of the movement. *Colored American* editor Charles B. Ray summed up the feelings of separatists when he insisted that separate black initiative was imperative. American society created the caste system, and until it was abolished, blacks should meet to devise means distinctive to their interests as Americans: "While we believe that, being of the American nation we ought to identify ourselves with the American people and with American interests, yet there are and will be special interests for us to attend to, so long as American caste exists, and we have not equal rights in common with the American people."[32]

This antebellum controversy indicated that the black evangelical vision of a future American society and culture that shared fundamental values of freedom and equality for all people persisted. Yet, individuals of African ancestry still needed separate space to develop the Christian morality that included individual and collective esteem unavailable in white-dominated institutions. Just out of the Oneida Institute, a manual labor school, future Presbyterian minister Henry Highland Garnet attempted to dismiss, once and for all, the antiseparatist/separatist controversy. Writing under the pseudonym "Sidney," Garnet strongly condemned Whipper for undermining black unity.[33] He wrote that history proved that "internal dissensions" caused the defeat of any movement. The real issue involved means, and there was sufficient historical evidence to show that the "exclusive effort" of the oppressed resulted in success. For proof, Garnet pointed to the American Revolution, the Irish freedom struggle, and British West Indian emancipation, the latter being "chiefly through the influence of colored men—the oppressed" contending "for their rights."

Then Garnet attacked the other sticking point: distinct terms for black American identity. The idea of a dual identity was not the problem, he argued. Instead, distinctive terminology was a useful political means for building and maintaining solidarity among the oppressed. The question of "color" had diverted attention from and trivialized the movement, he charged. The multitudinous and complex problems blacks faced were being ignored while activists engaged in a topic "devoid of reason" and "disreputable" to them as a people.[34] "The people are perishing by oppression, and our leaders, one opposing the other, upon a *word*; they are metaphysicising upon *things*, when they should be using the resistless energy of principle, to vindicate their wronged and deeply injured brethren . . . instead of giving living productive action-proposing idle theories!"[35]

Garnet suggested that distinct terms of identity, especially references to skin color, embarrassed Whipper. There was nothing about distinct terminology to be ashamed of. The words were not the cause of prejudice, and removal of the language would not eliminate prejudice. Speaking for most reformers, Garnet maintained that black Americans would continue to use terminology that satisfied their common interest. Moreover, the fact of human diversity necessitated white acceptance of difference, not accommodation to racial prejudice.[36] Americans were of different colors and ethnicities. "We say our people should not give way the least to the stout-heartedness of our oppressors in this matter. If they have prejudices, they must get over them. As for our color, as God has given it to us, thus we are pleased with it. . . . Surely the term colored is not disgusting to Mr. W. and his friends. They cannot be ashamed of their identity with the negro race!"[37]

Garnet was unsuccessful in eliminating either the issue of separatism or the constant quarrels over distinct terms of identity. He and other reformers continued to lament that the latter issue was trivial and unnecessarily divisive. "How unprofitable it is for us to spend our golden moments in long and solemn debate upon questions whether we shall be called "Africans," "Colored Americans," or "Africo Americans," or "Blacks.""[38]

White abolitionists generally ignored debates about distinct identity among black reformers, but several objected strongly to separate black meetings. When Garrisonians opposed blacks meeting in separate organizations in the *National Anti-Slavery Standard* "except where the clearest necessity demands it," separatists countered with charges of racial paternalism. *Colored American* editors argued that underlying white opposition was the implicit belief that black leadership was incapable of determining a state of exigency without white counsel. Ray and others charged Garrisonians with being "dictatorial" and "authoritative" in spirit. The writer of the article in the *Standard*, Ray wrote, "feels himself doubtless the colored man's superior and adviser."[39]

The controversy surrounding separate versus integrated institutions was far more complicated than the language implied. It was central to northern black identity and goals, involving evangelical reformers' vision of their place in American society. At the same time, these debates suggested that by the late 1830s black reformers believed racism would be more difficult to end than slavery. The problem was how to challenge racial segregation and not appear to practice it at the same time. Of course, their concern was of less import when whites denied people of color access to jobs, schools, theaters, and so on or restricted them to inferior seating and engaged in other blatant racist practices. But when blacks specifically restricted meetings, they were hard put to defend their actions.

Not too long after his escape from slavery, Frederick Douglass joined in the debate over the question of separate black organizations, and at first reflected the Garrisonian antagonism to African American reformers meeting separately. He and Garnet, also a fugitive from slavery, represented opposing sides of the separatist controversy in the 1840s. Douglass eventually argued that separate conventions, churches, social organizations, and schools should only be instituted as a matter of extreme exigency. Blacks contributed to prejudice when they restricted activities to blacks. At the same time he and others discouraged blacks from attending white churches with segregated seating and discriminatory practices in the sacraments; Douglass argued that separate religious organizations and schools were great "evils." The "negro churches and negro schools in the community are all the pernicious fruit of the wicked, unnatural, and blasphemous prejudice against our God-given complexion; and as such stand directly in the way of our progress and equality."[40]

Black Americans should attend white institutions whenever possible, and black churches and schools should be organized only when nothing else was available. Like Whipper, Douglass believed separate black organization and activity only contributed to attitudes of white superiority and to black feelings of inferiority. Proslavery forces wanted to keep blacks isolated; blacks should not oblige. Douglass argued that while in the past there had been a need for black institutions, that was no longer the case. Those who hated slavery should put away anything that symbolized it. As Garrisonians in the early to mid-1840s, Douglass and Whipper still believed the root cause of racial prejudice was slavery. Hence racism and slavery were not yet separate issues for either man. Whipper's organization, the American Moral Reform Society, voted that any schools the society might establish should provide access to all Americans. Charles Lenox Remond, a Garrisonian for much of the antebellum era, told a black audience at the 1855 celebration of Boston's school desegregation that black schools and churches were "proslavery" and a barrier to abolition.[41]

Yet Douglass, Remond, Whipper, and other Garrisonians were forced to accept the reality of persistent institutional racism. At first Remond and Douglass participated in separate meetings primarily to find ways to eliminate them. Others opposed to separate institutions except when necessary avoided black organizations almost completely. Charlotte Forten's father, Robert, was so opposed to segregated schools that he sent Charlotte, at sixteen, to live with Charles and Amy Remond in Salem, Massachusetts, where she could attend a recently desegregated secondary school. Before that time, Charlotte had private tutors even though there were black schools in Philadelphia. Douglass followed a similar course with his children. William C. Nell, perhaps the most avid antiseparatist Garrisonian and a leader in the Boston school desegregation case, attended a segregated school as a child but vowed to fight segregation for future black children.[42]

Most reformers, including Garnet, agreed that separate schools accommodated white segregationist policies but believed segregated schools were better than no schools. Besides, few black families had the financial means and social network of the Forten or Douglass families. As a consequence, most black northerners established schools and other organizations without apology or hesitation. In 1849, Ohio convention delegates strongly opposed segregated black schools but argued they had no choice except to establish and support them.[43] Illinois state convention delegates in 1853 were forced to support segregated schools for the same reason. They resolved "That while we adopt this plan for the education of our children, we desire to have it distinctly understood, that we do so from necessity . . . and shall continue to protest, against those unjust, unconstitutional and undemocratic laws by which we and our children are proscribed."[44]

Still, for some northern blacks, separate black schools remained essential. Black schools, like churches, were necessary to further the black evangelical agenda. Concerned about the quality of the curricula and teachers, parents and others insisted upon separate schools under black control with black teachers. In a letter to the *Colored American*, "A Friend" suggested that the issue of black-owned and black-controlled schools be added to the agenda of the proposed 1840 national convention. Black schools were necessary, the writer argued, because black teachers served as role models for African American children and a black education board would create and maintain a curriculum that prepared black children for any field of endeavor.[45] Children would learn, early on, that their place was in the republic and develop the virtues essential for participation in the body politic.

In Philadelphia, when Quaker goldsmith Richard Humphreys bequeathed $10,000 in 1832 for training black boys in various skilled occupations and agriculture, the city's black artisans demonstrated the free black community's wish that black children gain an education that fulfilled the black evangelical vision. At first, the Quaker trustees of the estate established a "farm school" several miles outside Philadelphia with the initial plan for agricultural training and elementary education for black orphans. This early plan failed. It began with only a few students, who started running away when the trustees switched their policy and restricted student activities to farm labor. Forced to close in 1846, the trustees did not reorganize until 1848, at which time they asked black tradesmen to apprentice black youths. The artisans agreed and quickly proposed an evening school in which "literary subjects" were taught with "well trained persons" as teachers. Apparently frustrated that their initial plan failed, the trustees gave the artisans full authority in selecting teachers and overseeing the entire effort. The tradesmen formed a "Board of Education Auxiliary to the Guardianship of the Estate of Richard Humphries. . . ." The evening school, a type of high school, opened in the fall of 1849 with a black teacher and an enrollment of thirty students.

Not satisfied with just an evening school, the artisans successfully pushed for a day school. In 1852, the Institute for Colored Youth (ICY) opened in Philadelphia with African American principal Charles A. Reason—formerly professor of Greek, Latin, mathematics, and natural philosophy at racially integrated New York Central College. Reason created a curriculum that reflected the interests of black parents and reformers. It had a strong academic emphasis and signaled a complete break with the agricultural component specified in Humphreys's will. By the end of the decade the Institute offered a substantive primary and secondary education for girls and boys, with black teachers of both sexes offering courses in bookkeeping, natural philosophy, Latin, Greek, higher algebra, trigonometry, natural sciences, and rhetoric. Grace Mapps headed the Female Department and her daughter Sarah headed the elementary school. When Reason left the school, he was replaced by Ebenezer Bassett, a black graduate of Connecticut State Normal School and a former student at Yale College. Bassett added more mathematics courses, and Robert Campbell, a Jamaican who had only recently moved to Philadelphia, taught the science courses. Philadelphian blacks vigorously supported the Institute for Colored Youth; Reason had opened the school to the entire community through a library and lecture series, both established in the first year of the school's opening.[46]

So while most reformers and other African Americans resented exclusion of their children from schools established for whites, many not only believed in the exigency of separate action but also indicated that they wanted separate black schools under black control taught by black teachers. Demand for black control of the curriculum and insistence that the schools have black teachers reflected the majority's interest in having black students fully prepared for equal participation in American society, intellectually, socially, and emotionally. These convictions remained after the Civil War. At the 1865 state convention in Pennsylvania, a delegate proposed the convention pass a resolution supporting separate black schools because "as we know by experimental knowledge, . . . colored children make greater advancement under the charge of colored teachers than they do under white teachers." As in the pre–Civil War era, this proposal sparked lengthy debate. Concerned that the resolution would appear discriminatory, some delegates requested an amendment specifying that no discrimination on the basis of color would be made in the employment of teachers. Response to the amendment was loud and clear: most blacks wanted black teachers. One delegate made the telling statement that those who opposed the original resolution "would be ashamed to meet their constituents" when returning home if the amendment passed. Philadelphian educator Octavius V. Catto, a teacher and former ICY student, provided the compromise amendment. The resolution was "just and proper" in spirit, Catto said, but the "phraseology" required changing to prevent the wrong assumption that the convention supported the hiring of only black teachers solely on the basis of their color. The fact was that black teachers were preferable because they understood the needs of black students and were more concerned with their welfare. To avoid all misunderstanding, Catto offered an amendment addressing delegates' concerns. It passed unanimously.[47] "In the appointment of teachers for these schools, colored persons, their literary qualifications being sufficient, should receive the preference; not by reason of their complexion but because they are better qualified by conventional circumstances outside of the school-house."[48]

Unlike with schools, controversy surrounding separate churches and social organizations was nearly ignored. Residing in a highly racially polarized society, the majority of African Americans preferred socializing among themselves in critical areas of their lives. While American identity became more entrenched, the late eighteenth-century evangelicals' belief that black experience in oppression created a distinctive religious worldview precluding social comity between whites and blacks persisted.

Yet, few early and mid-nineteenth-century black religious leaders who left records appreciated West and West Central African contributions to Christian liturgy. White church racism was the usual reason given publicly for separate black religious institutions. Antebellum black evangelicals, like their late eighteenth-century counterparts, wanted to avoid further oppression by developing institutions and social relationships that contributed to their sense of dignity and worth by interpreting Scripture through an egalitarian lens that rejected a racial interpretation. While black evangelicalism was distinct in the critical ways discussed above, clergymen did not view its distinctiveness as a separate cultural environment that incorporated West and West Central African religious practices.

Though more implicit than explicit, inculcating and demonstrating virtue remained a primary goal of several influential and increasingly better educated black clergymen. The language of virtue within and outside the church, however, began stressing concerns that reflected values of an emerging middle-class respectability, particularly restraint, decorum, and order. Several ministers viewed with alarm certain West and West Central African liturgical practices evident in many black churches. A practice that may have contributed to the solidarity they deemed so essential for political action was, according to many reformers, overly emotional and detrimental to the well-being of black congregations.

In the early 1850s, Daniel Payne, A.M.E. preacher, educator, and former student of Lutheran Theological Seminary in Pennsylvania, was sent to a Baltimore church after serving in New York. Soon after his arrival, Payne began condemning the "bad customs of worship" in the church. The singing and prayer bands "existed in the most extravagant form." Black congregants resisted Payne's attempts to change their traditions and they had him replaced.[49] The possibility that the Baltimore Ebenezer African Methodist Church blended African and European religious practices is fairly certain. As a missionary to freedmen and women in the 1870s, Payne met the same "extravagances" he had confronted in antebellum Baltimore and, predictably, was appalled. After observing a "ring shout" in which the worshippers formed a ring as they stamped their feet and clapped their hands "in a most heathenish way," Payne stopped the service. "I told [them] . . . that it was a heathenish way to worship and disgraceful to themselves, the race, and the Christian name." In that instance, the worshippers stopped the ceremony, but would not sit down, as Payne requested. Instead they walked "sullenly away."[50]

Unaware of the complexity of a developing syncretic religion among mainly poor and working-class blacks, Payne and other educated evangelical clergymen decried deviation from European American Protestant liturgical norms. Their stress on restraint, order, and quiet reverence in the house of God helped undermine even further the possibility of an ethnic identity with distinct cultural elements that may have contributed to a stronger politically viable and unified northern black populace.

Daniel Payne was also among those demanding an educated clergy. In this reform effort he and others revealed even more the degree to which an evolving middle-class respectability distanced educated black ministers from the northern black majority. They indicated that in many ways they were more culturally European American than their constituents. The ministers' notions of separate institutions and distinct identity remained primarily ideologically and politically specific, with no appreciation of West and West Central African cultural contributions. Ministers and other reformers connected the blending of African religious practices to the high rate of uneducated clergymen and what they considered emotional excess. The editorial pages of the *Colored American* were filled with complaints and admonitions about the need for an educated clergy. William Watkins, Lewis Woodson, and Daniel Payne led this campaign. This dilemma of poorly educated preachers would haunt educated black clerics and activists/reformers into the twentieth century.[51]

The problem for these clerical reformers was that though a few more black men were admitted to colleges in the late antebellum era, most colleges restricted admission to whites. Also, attending college took money and preparation that most blacks lacked. So these reformers fought on two fronts. They demanded an educated clergy and the overturn of racial discrimination in college and seminary admission policies.[52] Related to the concern for an educated clergy was the desire that community leaders exemplify a restrained decorum in the pulpit and in the community. Evangelical preachers and teachers were role models for the community, especially the youth. Payne's concern about positive role models centered on emotionalism in the liturgy of many African Methodist Episcopal churches. Uneducated ministers, he argued, relied on emotionalism because they lacked the intellectual development to understand and interpret Scripture. Congregations, in turn, Payne believed, considered those who made the "greatest noise and the most extravagant gesticulations" the most pious. Payne and other African Methodist Episcopal leaders responded by attempting to impose quiet restraint in worship services. In

1841, the Indiana A.M.E. Conference passed a resolution against ministers' prolonging the evening services and "the singing of fugue tunes and hymns."

Insensitive to the different cultural interests of many of their constituents, many educated black ministers, like other reformers, wanted all blacks to emulate their moral, educational, and economic aspirations. More culturally European American than their congregations, clerical reformers expected congregations to embrace their notions of superior liturgies and ways of behaving. They increasingly stressed orderliness, punctuality, cleanliness, and sobriety. They became more concerned about order than black unity and esteem, the bedrock of black evangelicalism that would enable the fulfillment of the political agenda. As educated men concerned about the spiritual growth of their membership, they wanted distance from liturgical practices they considered inferior or pagan.

Unlike white reformers, black reformers were driven by the consistent worry that most whites were unwilling to distinguish between African Americans of varying education, socioeconomic achievements, or cultural differences. They were all judged as uneducated, poor, and morally inferior. Thus black reformers' admonitions about decorum and restraint to poor and working-class blacks were fraught with intense frustration and contradiction. They unwittingly reinforced white notions of black inferiority in their denunciations of syncretic Afro-Euro religious and nonreligious practices by asserting the superiority of European culture and the inferiority of elements of sub-Saharan African cultures in an era that treated cultures and peoples as one.

Payne's concerted advocacy for an educated clergy was evident at almost every A.M.E. convention. He and his more educated supporters successfully passed resolution after resolution explaining the importance of education among the clergy and in the community. Payne and his supporters, though, were not simply establishing ecclesiastical policy that reflected their concern about white perceptions. They truly wanted black ministers to develop intellectually. But when they tried establishing a policy of ministerial self-study, other ministers at conventions balked and relented only when the college-educated men threatened to leave the church. The policy was unenforceable, though, and Payne and others continually complained that the black community was afflicted with too many ministers who regarded intellectual pursuits lightly. Douglass's opposition to black churches included concern that uneducated ministers perpetuated ignorance. These men lacked the "mental qualifications" to instruct their own congregations. Furthermore, uneducated ministers, he argued, encouraged an anti-intellectual bias among blacks; they were making a virtue out of ignorance.[53] To these reformers, uneducated preachers were counteracting evangelical goals of inculcating the virtues necessary for civic involvement. Other conference resolutions admonished clergymen to make sure their congregations arrived on time to all meetings and that they dressed simply, "neatly and cleanly."

Even though some ministers ignored cultural differences that would have given greater support for separate black churches, a few had to acknowledge that most black congregants preferred their own churches. Some, when confronted with the possibility, explicitly rejected the idea of any white membership. After opening a school for black children in Philadelphia, a white schoolteacher started worshipping at Bethel A.M.E. church and later joined one of the classes. Many Bethel members, particularly the women, strongly resented her presence. They questioned whether whites could become members. The church pastor, affirming the right of people of all colors to join the religious body, soon learned that church women acting collectively wielded unquestionable power. As major financial supporters, women parishioners simply withheld money until the pastor acquiesced.

When Amos G. Beman, pastor of a Hartford, Connecticut, black Congregational church, married an Englishwoman after his first wife's death, he learned that his congregation would not tolerate a black pastor with a white wife. The women forced Beman's resignation almost immediately. These women showed that reformers' strategies for inclusion into American society and identity as Americans were complex and multifaceted. Separate organizations established as a means for resolving some problems contributed to contradictions in principle and practice that were, at least on the surface, akin to some forms of prejudice.[54]

Antagonism toward white presence in culturally specific and intimate areas of northern black lives revealed how important black space had become. The formation of free black communities, so desired by the leadership, offered northern blacks a refuge from subjugation, a means of avoiding the white gaze of black inferiority. The establishment of black institutions for creating unity and providing the leadership space to inculcate the understanding and values of black evangelicalism with its conflation of the sacred and the secular, however fraught with contradictions and utopianism, promised temporary transcendence from consistent exposure to the ideology of black unworthiness. Churches and other social organizations gave African Americans the ability to attend to other concerns of human endeavor, personal and private.[55]

Apparently, separate and clearly social organizations, often connected with black churches, required the same distance from whites. There was little controversy about the existence of strictly black societies. Not admitted to white social organizations, blacks had been developing their own private social organizations since the eighteenth century and before. It seems, too, that many northern black abolitionists preferred their own abolitionist societies. Charles Remond condemned Massachusetts blacks for segregated antislavery societies.[56] These separate societies persisted because they were integral parts of other black social organizations. Besides, most black northerners must have viewed with no small degree of skepticism some reformers' interest in interracial abolitionist societies when they repeatedly condemned white abolitionists for treating them as inferiors.

In keeping with black evangelicalism's goal of full black participation in the body politic, most reformers who supported separate black institutions and distinct terms of identity in the 1840s identified fully as Americans. They were American in spite of their proscribed status. Like David Walker, Garnet and others consistently affirmed allegiance to the United States, a country that would eventually live up to Christian republican principles. In his 1848 speech to the Troy Female Benevolent Society, Garnet expressed profound patriotism. "Some people of color say that they have no home, no country. I am not among that number. . . . America is my home, my country, and I have no other. I love whatever of good there may be in her institutions. . . . I mourn because the accursed shade of slavery rests upon it. I love my country's flag, and I hope that soon it will be cleansed of its stains, and be hailed by all nations as the emblem of freedom and independence."[57]

Most evangelical reformers in the two decades before the Civil War, like those before them, consistently embraced some hyphenated form of American identity, some type of terminology that differentiated them from white Americans. This dual identity was at once political and social. Identity merely as American inadequately portrayed their unique experience and status. Yet American identity challenged the European American conviction and constant refrain that the nation was a "white man's country." Blacks demanded American nationality for all the reasons they had stated repeatedly since the eighteenth century. It was the land their forefathers bled and died for as soldiers and workers. Those who persisted in their identification as African and American challenged not only the idea that blacks did not belong in the new republic, but also that blacks, like whites, did have a homeland, a space from which they all originated. Terms other than African, such as "Colored," provided means of developing and maintaining long hoped for unity in addressing critical grievances. They *were* distinct Americans. Additionally, activists intended to name themselves, not have it imposed by those who oppressed them.[58]

White America exacerbated the problem of black identity by turning almost any term in reference to blacks into a pejorative. In 1837, Cornish explained that "colored" was preferable because he and his colleagues of the *Colored American* wished to appeal to a specific group of Americans and because the terms Negro, African, and black had become terms of "reproach" in American society.[59]

While conflicts over terms of identity and separate black institutions persisted, most abolitionists agreed by the 1850s that political means would help achieve their goal of abolition and full inclusion into American society. The political dimension of black evangelicalism in which biblical precepts supported political goals of freedom and equality dominated in the two decades before the Civil War. Finding moral suasion inadequate, New York reformers were in the forefront as they explicitly linked political and economic rights. The *Colored American* editorialized in 1837 that if the franchise were extended to blacks, it would do more to improve poor black conditions than anything else.[60] Evangelicals Garnet, Ray, Theodore S. Wright, Alexander Crummell, and others at the New York state convention in 1840 argued that black employment lay in the power of the ballot. "To the non-possession of the elective franchise may be traced most of the degradation to which we, as a people, have been for years subjected." State conventions became the forum for finding an effective means for gaining the franchise.

Conflating evangelicalism and republicanism, the Albany delegates' first resolutions in 1840 denounced the 1821 New York constitutional clause that provided for universal white male suffrage but required black men to own property worth at least $250.[61] Delegates resolved that "all laws established for human government, and all systems, of whatever kind founded in the spirit of complexional cast, are in violation of the fundamental principles of Divine law, evil in their tendencies, and should therefore be effectually destroyed."[62] They added that the "monied restriction" of the state's franchise law was an "invidious and proscriptive" act since the very means by which a people obtain and protect their financial resources were "held up before us as requirements for the use of the privilege."[63] Black evangelical reformers protested against disfranchisement throughout the antebellum period and after.

Reformers persistently based their right to the franchise on a firm belief in free black citizenship based in Christian republicanism. Like white Americans born in the United States, northern black men argued their rights of citizenship by virtue of birth. They were entitled to all privileges and immunities provided in federal and state statutes based on the preambles to the Declaration of Independence and the Constitution.[64] A few disagreed that the Constitution provided free black citizenship. Frederick Douglass and other black Garrisonians regarded the Constitution as a proslavery document in the 1840s. After Douglass broke with Garrison, he joined the majority of black reformers and appealed for black rights on the grounds that the Constitution protected them as it did other Americans.[65]

Sometimes appealing to nativist tendencies, like many other Americans in that era, northern blacks argued they were more American than the recent immigrants flooding the eastern shores. They were particularly irked that immigrants could vote and hold political office within a matter of years of their arrival in the country while blacks could not. In demands for the franchise, they repeatedly invoked black men's sacrifices on the battlefield in various wars, especially the Revolution, for proof of loyalty and patriotism. Men of color, William C. Nell argued, were more able than the "ten thousand per annum who swarm our genial shores." Coming from the "tyrannical despotisms of Europe" and having lived under "the besotted and deadening sway of European kings," immigrants could not appreciate "the value, and exercise the privilege of voting" as could black Americans. Nell wanted to know what immigrant could give evidence of deep devotion to the nation. With education, skills, and some means, middle-class blacks especially resented any "vagabond from Europe" being given rights denied to them.[66]

In 1855 black Californians met specifically to find ways to gain the right of court testimony. Their resolution summarized not only an affirmation of their status as American citizens and anger over taxation without political rights, but also a nativist bias. "You receive our money to educate your children, and then refuse to admit our children into the common schools. You have enacted a law, excluding our testimony in the Courts of justice of this State, in cases of proceedings wherein white persons are parties. . . . At the same time you freely admit the evidence of men in your midst, who are ignorant of the first principles of your Government—who know not the alphabet."[67]

"Taxation without representation," reformers consistently charged, was the unconstitutional effect of black disfranchisement. Ohio convention delegates in 1849 "believed with the Fathers of '76, that taxation and representation ought to go together." Antebellum politicians had strayed so far from the Christian republican principles of the Revolutionary age that they were endangering the republic. Just as black evangelicals increasingly claimed a purer Christianity, they began asserting a purer patriotism. African Americans would preserve the liberal principles upon which the nation was founded. Young white Americans, New York physician/reformer and intellectual James McCune Smith noted, were unaware of the meaning of the Declaration of Independence and the Constitution. The American educational system preferred rote learning to teaching reflective thought because if read reflectively, both documents would reveal how far the nation had strayed from its sacred principles. Increasingly, as did the Revolutionary generation before them, reformers regarded their movement as a vigil averting the tide of complete Christian republican declension.[68] Almost every state convention, in these years, organized a campaign for the franchise. In the early 1840s, Garnet created an efficient, albeit unsuccessful, voting rights campaign that included audiences with Albany politicians.[69]

For black male reformers, political-economic rights involved a question of their individual manhood. In an era when "manliness" was defined as rugged individualism, independence, and the ability to provide for and protect women and children, male activists' demand for the franchise, the right to serve on juries, and the right to bear court testimony involved sociopsychological dynamics as well. It was as important to black males that they achieve political rights to protect and provide for self and family as it was to them that they distinguish themselves from the dependent status of women and children. All elements blended together in various protests. They would never, black men argued, accept the political status of "half men." Without the vote a man was not a man.[70]

Revealing that their gender conventions were similar to that of the dominant society, black men showed that they thought within the existing patriarchy. They simply rejected a racially specific patriarchy. Men were leaders, protectors, and providers. It was their Christian responsibility and duty as men. Contrary to the reality in which most black women worked hard to provide for their families alongside men, women ideally belonged in a separate domestic sphere with no political or economic rights. Samuel Cornish editorialized in his *Weekly Advocate*, the 1837 precursor to the *Colored American*, that women had a powerful influence for good or evil in society. Gone were the days when a woman "had no rights, when her talents were not appreciated." Now, every woman had all those "rights and privileges to which her talents, and her worth entitle her."

Black women, in conventional American gender language, were especially essential in the "enterprise" for improving the status, morals, and education of the African American population. Their duties in the home as Christian mothers were critical, according to Cornish. "Let our beloved female friends rouse up . . . exert all their power . . . to show the world that there is virtue among us." Robert Banks, who designated himself "a colored man" in his published address to the "Buffalo Colored Female Dorcas Society," told the society's members that, as wives, they were the "ornament" of their husband's life, "the kind protectress of his peace and comfort, and her heart is the home of his affection and love." Perceiving a traditional role for black women, these activist men were determined to demonstrate they were men by defining black women's status as being the same as that of middle-class white women, subordinate and domestic, not as coproviders who should have political rights.[71]

Reflecting the growing feminist movement of the 1840s, some black women exacerbated the question of black masculinity when they challenged male dominance in conventions and churches. Black women, constituting the northern urban black majority, were often heads of households or wives who usually had more steady employment as domestics than husbands because of the competitive, unstable world of day laborers, the only work available to most black men. When Mrs. Sanford[72] was granted the right to speak to the 1848 Ohio national convention, she told the all-male delegates that women needed the elective franchise as much as men. Married women needed the right of "property in the marriage covenant, whether earned or bequeathed." The vote and legal right to independent property ownership when married was not necessary, she advised, to "domineer" or "dictate," but because there were "duties around us, and we weep at our inability." Sanford urged delegates to broaden the struggle to "unqualified citizenship." She invoked the language of the Declaration of Independence and Christianity in her demand for "inalienable rights." After Sanford spoke, delegates, led by feminist and president of the convention Frederick Douglass, voted to invite "females hereafter to take part in our deliberations."[73]

But only a handful of women participated, and they still were not welcome as delegates in subsequent state and national conventions. In the Ohio 1849 state convention, Jane Merritt explained that women were not interested in being mere spectators at the conventions. Those who were invited to attend wanted a voice in the proceedings. Inviting women merely as spectators was "wrong and shameful." They would henceforth boycott the conventions, Merritt said, unless women participated. Again debate followed and all male delegates adopted a resolution "inviting the ladies to share in the doing of the Convention." On paper at least women were acceptable delegates. But some New York males at the 1855 state convention were unwilling even to go that far. When Barbara Steward, a New York teacher and an antislavery lecturer, tried to be admitted as a delegate, she was promptly removed on the grounds that the convention was "not a Woman's Rights convention."[74]

Most male delegates to the various conventions, it seems, did not want reminders of their precarious male status in American white patriarchal society. Holding to the gender conventions of the dominant society but placed in a tenuous position that made it impossible for men to adhere to standards they interpreted as their manly Christian duty, many black male reformers were determined to experience control in areas that provided, at least for particular moments, some psychological sense of their manhood.

In the last two decades before the Civil War, resolution after resolution passed in the several state and national conventions showed the mostly male reformers' frustration and dismay about their proscribed status in the nation they called their own. Attempting to grasp how white America could claim a republican Christian heritage while brutally enslaving millions and engaging in harsh discriminatory practices against free blacks exceeded the comprehension of most blacks. For them, the issues were simple and straightforward.[75]

Some activists began viewing support of political parties, not just the franchise, as an effective means for the abolition of slavery. Garnet led in this endeavor. He was involved from the beginning with the abolitionist Liberty party and later supported the Republican party, surmising that the Republicans' position against the spread of slavery would result in its abolition. He first tried to get black national and state convention delegates to endorse political parties that supported abolition. This proved a difficult task in the early 1840s because of Frederick Douglass and other Garrisonians, who rejected participation in the political process. At the 1840 New York convention, for example, Garnet urged endorsement of the newly established Liberty party. Debate about the issue revealed that some delegates believed supporting a minor third party was futile and that endorsement of the Liberty party would diminish chances for the success of a Whig candidate who supported at least some of their interests.

But most delegates believed endorsement of political parties, even the Liberty party, was premature. First of all, endorsement undermined black political independence in New York. Democrats were always quick to charge that blacks were tools of Whigs. Second, they still believed gaining the franchise for all black men, not just those few who owned property worth $250, was more important than political endorsement. It was the cart before the horse. Black New Yorkers needed support of the entire electorate, Democrats and Whigs, so tact and skill to most delegates was uppermost. Garnet's proposed resolutions condemning the two main political parties only jeopardized the primary goal of gaining the franchise.[76]

Even so, Garnet persisted and was successful three years later at the national convention in Buffalo. By this time Frederick Douglass was gaining critical influence in the abolitionist movement and, like many other Garrisonians, was opposed to "political action." After a lengthy debate the convention adopted a resolution calling upon "every lover of liberty to vote the Liberty ticket so long as they are consistent to their *principles*." In the following year, Garnet was less successful at the New York state convention; New York City reformers Ray and Wright remained adamantly opposed to blacks endorsing any political party.[77]

Reformist evangelical clergyman Garnet did eventually succeed. In keeping with black evangelicalism, he convinced most abolitionists that political means was an essential strategy for abolishing slavery and gaining equal rights. Garnet had been suspicious of relying solely on moral suasion for some time. Political power was a more effective means, and the Liberty party in the early and mid-1840s was the only party Garnet thought blacks could conscientiously support. The abolitionists' party principles included a commitment to equal rights as much as abolition. Later, by the 1850s, when Garrison was less influential among black abolitionists, Douglass and other abolitionists came to regard political parties as legitimate and viable alternative strategies for influencing public opinion. Then, some reformers, like Douglass, supported the Free Soil and later Republican parties.[78] While admitting that these parties were concerned with white interests, these reformers believed the party platforms were steps in the direction of freedom and full equality for black Americans.

Insistence on political party support and endorsement was only one of two strategies Garnet brought to the 1843 national convention. His other proposal, a violent overthrow of slavery, generated even more excitement and debate.

Besides indicating interest in exploring various means for achieving equality and abolition, Garnet's proposal also revealed the degree to which evangelicalism as the sole means for American reformation was losing ground among American reformers. By the mid- to late 1840s, American evangelicalism had already peaked as the primary means for achieving the perfect society. Moral suasion would become an antiquated idea of a past generation, while the political dimension of black evangelicalism took on a more practical role for equal rights and the abolition of slavery.[79]

But in the antebellum era, the problem that came to dominate black thought as much as slavery was a growing and pervasive racial ideology that threatened even more the black vision of an egalitarian American republic. Some black theorists of race, especially evangelicals, unwittingly incorporated elements of racial theory that supported black subordination. Thus, for some reformers, commitment to American nationality meant becoming increasingly enmeshed in American culture and values that perhaps made a more astute critique of racism nearly impossible.

CHAPTER 5

They Despise Us for Our Color

THE PROBLEM OF RACE AND BLACK
EVANGELICAL REFORM

> In order to pursue my subject I must, for the sake of distinction, use some of the
> improper terms of our times. I shall, therefore speak of *races*, when in fact there is but
> one race, as there was but one Adam.
>
> —Henry Highland Garnet, *The Past and Present Condition*
> *and the Destiny of the Colored Race*

Sarah Mapps Douglass was an accomplished, self-confident woman. As
a member of the Female Literary Association and the Philadelphia Female
Anti-Slavery Society, a contributor to the *Liberator*, and most of all a teacher,
she opened an academy for black girls, the only such high school in Philadelphia and for a time in the country. When she became a teacher of English
and science at the successful Institute for Colored Youth in Philadelphia in
the 1850s, Douglass added anatomy and physiology to the course offerings
and, after taking courses at the Female Medical College of Pennsylvania and
Penn Medical University, gave lectures on the female body to black women
in her home. Asked to lecture about the same topic in New York, she stirred
up a bit of controversy. Lecturing on female anatomy was considered by some
"inconsistent with the delicacy of woman's character." Nevertheless, Douglass
received "hearty thanks" from her audience, who believed all women should
learn the structures of their body and "those natural laws pertaining to their
bodily and mental well-being."

But education and position were no protection from racial discrimination
and the haunting, frustrating feelings they created in individual black lives.

White America constantly reminded Douglass that race mattered in the North, and that it mattered more and more in the years before the Civil War. When Quaker abolitionist Sarah Grimké asked Douglass in 1837 about her personal experiences with racial discrimination, she poignantly recounted two specific instances in which she experienced moments of humiliation, anger, resentment, and finally pity. Sarah Douglass's mother, Grace Mapps, who found "the excellence" of Quaker principles convincing, did not join the Society, Douglass explained, because of the treatment she and her children received. Douglass remembered being forced into segregated seats at the Friends' Philadelphia Arch Street Meeting House, with a white church member sitting "at either end of the bench to prevent white persons from sitting there. And even when a child my soul was made sad with hearing five or six times during the course of one meeting this language of remonstrance addressed to those who were willing to sit by us. 'This bench is for the black people. . . . This bench is for the people of color.' I have not been in Arch Street meeting for four years, but my mother goes once a week and frequently she has the whole bench to herself."

Direct experiences with blatant Quaker racial prejudice persisted into Douglass's adulthood and were just as, if not more, unsettling. When teaching in New York, Douglass attended Friends' services for a month before anyone greeted her. When a member finally spoke, she immediately assumed Douglass was a menial laborer. Douglass was appalled and nearly cried. "Judge what were my feelings," she wrote to her friend Grimké, "a stranger in a strange land, think of the time, the place & this the first salutation I received in a house consecrated to Him. I wept during the whole of that mtg. & for many succeeding sabbaths & I believe they were not tears of wounded pride alone." Though strongly antislavery in the nineteenth century, Quakers revealed deep levels of racial prejudice in their treatment of black Americans at religious meetings and probably elsewhere. Had Quaker prejudice diminished over the years? Douglass responded "unhesitatingly . . . no." Clarissa C. Lawrence, vice president of the Salem Female Anti-Slavery Society, described the consistent and blatant racial experiences she and other antebellum free blacks encountered when she spoke to the Anti-Slavery Convention of American Women in 1839: "We meet the monster prejudice *everywhere.*"[1]

Racism, or the doctrine of innate, permanent, and indelible black inferiority that emerged in the antebellum era, severely tested black reformers' religious and political faith. They clung, sometimes by a thread, to the Christian ideal of individual and collective transformation. At the same time they insisted that America, their nation as much as whites,' live up to its Christian republican ideals. A Christian nation could not do otherwise. In this period, northern blacks confronted increased discrimination in almost every aspect of their lives, including popular and elite entertainment and literature that portrayed African Americans as inferior beings necessitating white control. Even more devastating, antebellum scientists and others buttressed discrimination and black enslavement with a thoroughgoing racial ideology that further secured slavery and white supremacy.[2] Northern black reformers responded with frustration, dismay, and disappointment. Most addressed the cause of racial discrimination, not the theory. A few developed racial theories of their own that contested the doctrine of black inferiority and simultaneously underscored their belief in primary aspects of Western civilization. Some black racial theorists framed ideas about race within the parameters of biological racism, implying the existence of a "black" or African essence. Furthermore, northern black racial theorists, like most activists, understood racism through the lens of evangelicalism.

African American reformers believed racism infected all of white America; it was central to life and culture. Reformers exhibited incredible prescience about the cultural, political/economic, and social functions of American racial ideology. Racism, argued fugitive slave and Presbyterian minister Samuel R. Ward, was the cornerstone of white American thought. According to the editors of the *Colored American,* white Americans, rich and poor, "the high and the low," came together "as equals to hate the colored man." Presbyterian minister Samuel Cornish believed that racism was the "national sin." Cornish and others, disappointed with the unwillingness of most white abolitionists to equate the battle for equal rights with the abolition of slavery, said that the real abolition movement was the abolition of prejudice. The "chains of prejudice" were as "galling" as the chains of slavery. The "remorseless hand of prejudice" waged "warfare" against all blacks. Ohio and Illinois activist H. Ford Douglas regarded racism as "the mean spirit of selfishness that makes almost everyone in the country look upon himself, his color, his race, as alone worthy of consideration." Reformers especially stressed that racism operated at the most critical and basic level: denial of employment.[3]

White ministers and the American Colonization Society, reformers charged, were primarily responsible for the perpetuation of racism, but complicity lay at the feet of almost all white Americans. In *A Treatise on the Intellectual Character, and Civil and Political Condition of the Colored People of the*

U. States; and the Prejudice Exercised Towards Them: With a Sermon on the Duty of the Church To Them, Hartford, Connecticut, Congregational minister Hosea Easton explained in 1837 that racial doctrine was an extremely useful and practical tool for controlling blacks and protecting white status in the South and North. It provided the manpower to control slaves and reduced or nearly eliminated black competition for jobs and housing. "It becomes the interest of all parties, not excepting the clergy, to sanction the premises, and draw the conclusions, and hence, teach the rising generation." Easton explained that the process of racial indoctrination began at birth. White parents maintained parental control and taught their children manners and moral values through negative stereotyping of black character. A mother who wanted her young child to sleep would threaten, if "you don't the old *nigger* will care [sic] you off; don't you cry—Hark; the old *niggers'* coming—how ugly you are, you are worse than a little *nigger.*" Young adults, Easton noted, were reminded not to be as ignorant or poor as a "nigger" and were placed in "*nigger-seats*" if they misbehaved. The racist values parents taught in the home were reinforced in the larger society. "Cuts and placards descriptive of the negroe's deformity, are everywhere displayed to the observation of the young, with corresponding broken lingo . . . [and] . . . popular book stores, in commercial towns and cities, have their show windows lined with them. The bar-rooms of the most popular public houses in the country, sometimes have their ceiling literally covered with them. This display of American civility," Easton noted, "is under the daily observation of every class of society, even in New England."[4]

As a clergyman, Easton particularly targeted white ministers for perpetuating racism. Ministers were leaders supposedly teaching and exemplifying moral virtues. White clergymen, instead, were involved in justifying greed and white dominance as much as the rest of white society. It was not surprising then that white parents taught their children manners and morals by denigrating black character since clergymen consistently condoned slavery and racism. Is it any wonder, Easton and other reformers asked, that blacks experienced continual political, economic, and social discrimination or that a racial theory asserting African inferiority developed just when some were challenging slavery? There existed a "systematized" and legalized purpose underlying racist theory and practice.

When not condemning white clergy, reformers usually placed responsibility for persistent racism squarely on the shoulders of the American Colonization Society. Colonizationists, several of whom reformers believed were misguided philanthropists corrupted by slave apologists and their own racist paternalistic attitudes, were constantly asked to end their campaign to remove free blacks to Liberia. The colonization campaign, reformers argued, only increased and excused white hostility.[5]

Black evangelical reformers thought colonizationists diverted attention from the real "design" of racism: racial prejudice prevented interrogation into the foundation of national wealth. Slavery was the root of racism. "The true cause of . . . prejudice is slavery," Easton argued, "for certainly, nothing short of every thing, that is bad on earth and in hell . . . could be capable of producing such prejudicial injuries, as those under which the colored people are doomed to suffer." The Atlantic slave trade and European "modern philosophy" proclaiming the inferiority of Africans evolved together, according to Easton. "The whole system is founded in avarice." And there "could be nothing more natural, than for a slaveholding nation to indulge in a train of thoughts and conclusions that favored their idol, slavery." "The love of money is the root of all evil," Easton added. Thus it was in the "interest of all parties . . . to sanction the premises, and draw the conclusions, and hence, to teach the rising generation. What could accord better with the objects of this nation in reference to blacks, than to teach their little ones that a negro is part monkey?" Racist propaganda was "disastrous upon the mind" of the white community.

According to Easton, whites could not imagine people of African descent in any other sphere than subordinate positions. "If he should chance to be found in any other sphere of action than that of a slave, he magnifies to a monster of wonderful dimensions, so large that they cannot be made to believe that he is a man and a brother." As a result, free blacks were denied access to public transportation, eating establishments, and lecture halls unless segregated seating existed. Likewise, skilled jobs and schoolrooms, Easton noted, were restricted to whites unless the black person was a slave. Then the black male body shrank and became invisible even to allow entrance into "ladies' parlors, and into small private carriages, and elsewhere, without being disgustful on account of his deformity, or without producing any other discomfiture. Thus prejudice seems to possess a magical power, by which it makes a being appear most odious one moment, and the next, beautiful—at one moment too large to be on board a steam-boat, the next, so small as to be convenient almost any where."

Easton believed racism was even more fatal than slavery because it permeated every aspect of American life, especially the white church, and thrived in the recesses of white minds. Racial prejudice was "slavery in disguise." "It possesses imperial dominion over its votaries and victims. It demands and receives homage from priests and people. It drinks up the spirit of the church, and gathers blackness, and darkness, and death, around her brow," poisoning and chilling "the life blood of her heart." Though he believed the full effect of slavery would not be known until "the great day of eternity," Easton described in detail the insidious impact of racism in education and skilled training upon free blacks, including himself. He ended his chapter in the *Treatise* on "The Nature of Prejudice" with a personification in prose of racial prejudice: "O Prejudice, I cannot let thee pass without telling thee and thy possessors, that thou art a compound of all evil—of all the corrupt passions of the heart. Yea, thou art a participant in all the purposes of the wicked one—thou art the very essence of hell."[6]

Other reformers more explicitly connected race with political power. Newspaper editor and writer Martin Delany was foremost among those who argued that the idea of "distinct races" was a political tool of oppression. It was not enough to deprive the black population of the North "of equal privileges . . . to succeed, the equality of these classes must be denied, and their inferiority by nature as distinct races, actually asserted. This policy is necessary to appease the opposition that might be interposed in their behalf. Where ever there is arbitrary rule, there must of necessity, on the part of the dominant classes, superiority be assumed . . . to premise [the oppressed's] incapacity for self-government."[7] Frederick Douglass noted that slaveholders admitted that "the whole argument in defense of slavery, becomes utterly worthless the moment the African is proved to be equally a man with the Anglo-Saxon." This was the motive behind "Southern pretenders to science" interest in reading "the Negro out of the human family" and the reason that they cast doubt on the scriptural account of the origin of mankind.[8]

If white political and economic interests were the underlying reasons for racial prejudice, northern free black "condition" and behavior played a definite role in its perpetuation and persistence, according to a number of reformers. Nearly overwhelmed by the persistence and virulence of racism, reformers repeatedly contradicted themselves in dialogue about reasons for racial prejudice and means to battle against it. Was slavery the cause of racism, meaning that whites viewed all blacks as they viewed slaves, as degraded beings barely or not quite human? Or, as Easton noted, did racism function to protect national and regional slaveholding economic interests? Many said yes, and then no. Was skin color the cause of racism? Activists knew of individuals deemed "negro" or "mulatto" in one region of the country who moved to another region and became white. Was black behavior the cause? If blacks exhibited temperance, industry, and piety, would racism dissolve? Many reformers persisted in their belief that black morality was at issue.

Consequently, writers, delegates to conventions, and clergymen all determined to improve African American status politically, economically, and socially. They consistently admonished the northern black poor majority to exemplify Christian character. Poor free black "condition" or status remained a reason for the persistence of racism among some activists into the Civil War era. At the same time as they delineated in newspapers and speeches devastating discriminatory policies against African Americans in jobs, training, and education, reformers told northern blacks that they should get jobs, skills, and educations, the very things they complained were nearly impossible to obtain. Some suggested farming as a panacea. Settle in the country, several state convention delegates told young men, and become independent farmers. They would escape "almost entirely that prejudice which operates so injuriously against us in the cities. It is a mistake to suppose that there is prejudice against mere color."[9] Besides farming, reformers urged youths to learn specific skills as a path to "political and civil elevation." Cornish repeatedly advised black parents to apprentice their children at an early age. A virtuous life, cultivated mind, industrious habits, and prudent conduct combined with a professional job, farming, or business were the means for "political and civil elevation." Simultaneously sounding hopeless and optimistic, reformers generally maintained hope in God, their own exertions, and the possibility that a significant portion of whites were not racists. Blacks should "discard" the idea that white Americans were so devoid of fairness that they were incapable of being just to blacks. Believing racism was restricted to the United States and Canada, Garnet told audiences: "We speak of prejudice against color, but in fact nothing of the kind exists. . . . The prejudice is against condition alone." Douglass and others told northern blacks to be a "temperance people" to help reduce racism.[10]

For many abolitionists, black and white, especially in the early years of the movement, references to African Americans' "condition" concerned not free black poverty and illiteracy but the fact of black enslavement. The existence of slavery in the South, according to this idea, negatively influenced northern white attitudes toward blacks. Former slave fugitive William Wells Brown told abolitionist audiences, "We find the degrading influences of slavery all about us. . . . Why is it that I can ride in the coach, or omnibus, or railcar, or steamboat, in Great Britain or on the continent, and enjoy the same privileges that any man enjoys, while I cannot do it here? It is not because of the colour of my skin, but because of the influence of slavery." Douglass also thought free blacks were discriminated against because of slavery. "We are then a persecuted people; not because we are *colored*, but simply because that color has for a series of years been coupled in the public mind with the degradation of slavery and servitude. In these conditions, we are thought to be in our place; and to aspire to anything above them, is to contradict the established views of the community—to get out of our sphere, and commit the provoking sin of *impudence*."[11]

Several believed racism was a matter of class, while others argued that skin color was the cause. Like reformers who thought free blacks could aid in the emancipation of slaves and gain equal rights through good conduct, several antebellum activists decided, along with white abolitionists, that middle-class status would help in the battle against slavery and racism. Educated blacks with jobs that provided financial stability for themselves and their families would eliminate white prejudice and thus contribute to abolition. These reformers seemingly took almost complete responsibility for white racism. In 1829 Samuel Cornish editorialized in his *Rights of All* that education and wealth would destroy racism. Education, wealth, and the accompanying manners were key. Let "our colored population once become as learned as refined, and as wealthy as other classes of the community, and prejudice will hide her face—the tyrant's spell will be broken."[12] Similarly, delegates at the 1853 Illinois state convention resolved that education, financial prosperity, and temperance would eliminate prejudice. The "cruel and unnatural prejudice which exists against the colored people of the United States is not against color, but condition, and that we must change that condition, by using economy, amassing riches, educating our children, and being temperate."[13]

Not surprisingly, middle- and upper-class activists who exhibited the traits reformers claimed would change the hearts and minds of racists knew otherwise. They drew upon personal experiences to counter the notion that prejudice was based on class or "condition." As historian Emma Jones Lapsansky shows, white violence increased when African Americans demonstrated that they had their own financial resources by constructing churches and other buildings.[14] Recognizing increased white antagonism, educated blacks with property and income thought some black reformers were falling into the ideological trap of racist apologists. Skin color, not class, was the barrier to black social, political, and economic rights according to several men and women. Wealthy Pennsylvania businessmen William Whipper and Robert Purvis, along with other delegates to the 1848 State Convention of the Coloured Citizens of Pennsylvania, believed black male disfranchisement had nothing to do with black poverty and ignorance as some whites charged. If that were true many whites would be disfranchised. Politicians wishing to appeal to a broad white male electorate dared not make economic status and education a standard for the white suffrage qualification. No such amendment, delegates noted, would have passed the state convention.

The reason for black disfranchisement, they argued, was skin color. They felt that black leaders using the illogical false argument that behavior and class caused discrimination must "discard" such ideas immediately; they were only aiding whites in discrimination and validating the false assertion of black inferiority. Delegates insisted that activists keep before the public the conviction that political, economic, and social proscriptions were founded in prejudice. It must be clear, delegates declared, "that it is not our impiety—our ignorance—our immorality, or our wicked customs and habits that places us without the pale of constitutional landmarks. But it is our *complexion alone* which furnishes the apology."[15] If blacks could, by some feat of nature, change their skin color, then they would have "full exercise of constitutional privileges." Besides, there were many blacks, particularly the recently deceased James Forten Sr., who had exhibited all the virtues whites purportedly admired yet were still denied the vote. "If we had colored men who could write like Paul, preach like Peter, pray like Aminadab, iron hearted prejudice would cry out he is *black*."[16]

Whipper, who, like most black reformers in the 1850s, had moved away from moral reformation as the means to end slavery and racism, still agreed with other reformers that black behavior and condition were factors in racism. Nevertheless, they all insisted that the moral revolution must begin more in "the white man's heart than on the colored man's mind."[17] In an 1854 letter to the editor of the *Frederick Douglass' Paper*, Whipper told abolitionists to stop blaming slavery for racial prejudice in the United States. No one in his right mind would believe for a second that all prejudice would end if by some miracle slavery was abolished "tomorrow." Douglass, who also thought virtuous free black behavior might help in the argument against slavery and racism, said that whites hated blacks who achieved more because they contradicted the doctrine of white superiority. Whites preferred blacks whom they could easily degrade.[18]

Several educated middle- and upper-class women were particularly weary of the mainly male argument that status affected white treatment of blacks. Writing under the pseudonym "Jane Rustic," abolitionist lecturer and writer Frances Ellen Watkins Harper suggested through one of the many characters in her column, "Chit Chat, or Fancy Sketches," that wealth as a means to "position" and "power" was bribery. Besides, when would black Americans have wealth enough to gain sufficient power "to be felt in the community"? In an essay also in the *Anglo-African Magazine*, "Our Greatest Want," written this time under her own name, Harper made clear that there were several wealthy blacks but public opinion remained unchanged. "We have money among us, but how much of it is spent to bring deliverance to our captive brethren? Are our wealthiest men the most liberal sustainers of the Anti-slavery enterprise? Or does the bare fact of their having money, really help mould public opinion and reverse its sentiments?"

Sarah Douglass was certain that education, wealth, and a virtuous character mattered little. Personal experience showed her that blacks with education and financial security were resented more. *"They despise us for our color,"* Douglass cried. Uniformly slandered as sexually promiscuous in American society, elite black women who exhibited all the dominant society's gender conventions of feminine respectability found their efforts to avoid discrimination were to no avail. The daughter of wealthy Philadelphia sail manufacturer James Forten, Sarah Forten believed that skin color and slavery caused racism. Prejudice "originates from dislike to the color of the skin, as much as from the degradation of Slavery. . . . I must own that *it* has often engendered feelings of discontent and mortification in my breast when I saw that many were preferred before me, who by education—birth—or worldly circumstances were no better than myself—*their* sole claim to notice depending on the superior advantage of being *white*." Forten, realizing that wealth protected some blacks from the more insidious forms of racism, gives insight into how urban African American elites navigated the antebellum racial terrain by living circumspect lives. Middle- and upper-class blacks kept as much as possible to themselves, developing social networks and outlets that would not subject them to blatant racism. They ventured outside their social circles only when it was safe or necessary. "For our own family—we have to thank a kind Providence for placing us in a situation that has hitherto prevented us from falling under the weight of this evil—we feel it—but in a slight degree compared with many others. We are not much dependant upon the *tender mercies* of our enemies—always having resources within ourselves to which we can apply. We are not disturbed in our social relations—we never travel far from home and seldom go to public places unless quite sure that admission [is] free to all—therefore we meet with none of these mortifications which might otherwise ensue."[19] When compared to the poor northern black majority, northern blacks with financial resources experienced racism differently.

Demonstrating the fact that people of color often had varying degrees of African, European, and Native American ancestry, Easton rejected the notion that skin color caused racism. If skin color caused prejudice, then it would follow that prejudice would decrease proportionately to the variation in skin color among black Americans. He believed prejudice was just as strong toward those who were whiter than a white American "as against one who is as black as jet, if they are identified as belonging to that race of people who are the injured party." Color was not the cause of the "malignant prejudice of the whites against the blacks." It was only the chosen target of discrimination, the diversion, the symptom for the evil of slavery.[20]

Reformers also addressed white opposition to marriages between blacks and whites. It was merely a red herring, diverting attention from unfair political-economic practices and engendering emotional furor over the practice of a tiny minority in both groups. When it was rumored, for example, that New York City Episcopalian clergyman Peter Williams performed a marriage ceremony between a black and white couple, a white mob destroyed his church and rectory. In its early days of publication, the *Liberator* launched a campaign to repeal the Massachusetts law prohibiting marriage between blacks and whites. Garrison and other abolitionists consistently argued that the state undermined its antislavery tradition by giving credence to ideas of black inferiority, that African Americans should be denied certain rights and privileges. Mainly, reformers noted, the constant reference to potential black and white sexual liaisons reinforced racist charges of black male licentiousness. Cornish editorialized that African Americans were tired of colonizationists using the threat of "amalgamation" as their last resort in recruiting new members. If they were so concerned about black and white sexual unions, they would condemn it in the South, where a fast-growing "mulatto" population existed.[21] The real amalgamators, he and others argued, were not blacks but slaveholders who raped enslaved women. Ministers, editors, and others also pointed to brothels frequented by blacks and whites. Predictably, Whipper, who paid closer attention to language than many, noted that "amalgamation" did not apply to humans but only to lower animals. There was no evidence, he and others repeated constantly, that "there are different species and races in the human family."[22]

Ministers were especially concerned that state laws against interracial marriages encouraged living "in sin." Congregationalist minister and *Colored American* editor Charles B. Ray noted it was an "oppressive" law passed by men who preferred "concubinage . . . to a lawful holy union."[23] Some reformers suggested black prejudice against whites would prevent a rise in interracial marriages. "There is sufficient amount of prejudice retained in the breasts of colored people to forbid it," Whipper noted. Believing most white male interest in black women was debased, he added that the virtue and intelligence of northern black women formed an "impregnable barrier" to the dishonorable advances of white men.[24]

If ministers and others were concerned about the legalization of marriages between blacks and whites, others resented the fact of its existence. Substantial evidence suggests that marriages between blacks and whites was frowned upon by many in the antebellum northern African American communities. David Walker deviated from his *APPEAL* to comment that any black man, "or man of colour, who will leave his own colour . . . to marry a white woman . . . ought to be treated by her as he surely will be, viz: as a NIGGER!!!!" Cornish complained that whites readily accepted into white society wealthy Afro-Europeans who married whites. It would be better, he said, that they married blacks and contributed to the welfare of black communities.[25]

In alliance with white abolitionists, reformers were successful in challenging specific racially discriminatory legislation, mostly in Massachusetts and in a few, very few, other cities and states. Reformers' campaign to repeal the Massachusetts law against marriages between blacks and whites, for example, was successful in 1843, after a decade of petitions, editorials, and other forms of agitation. Even more important to reformers was greater access to education for black children. By 1845, black children could attend public schools in five Massachusetts towns or villages, but not in Boston. In that year, reformers aggressively demanded the desegregation of Boston public schools. After a lengthy process of legal and political maneuvering, Boston public schools were desegregated by the state legislature in 1855. Other large cities and northern states rejected desegregation in spite of strong abolitionist challenges. Northern courts upheld segregation for reasons similar to those stated by Ohio courts in 1850 and 1859, that whites still held an "almost invincible repugnance" against black children attending school with white children. Yet, a tiny minority of African Americans, twenty-eight, had been admitted to colleges in the North by 1860.[26]

As occurred with desegregation in the next century, admission did not mean equality in the classroom or positive interaction between black and white students on any educational level. Charlotte Forten, daughter of abolitionist Robert Forten and granddaughter of sailmaker James Forten, was incredibly lonely at the Salem, Massachusetts, Higginson Grammar School, where her father took her because of the segregated schools in Philadelphia. In her journal entry for September 1855 she expressed her belief that there was only one girl, "and only one," who "has no prejudice against color." "I wonder that every colored person is not a misanthrope. Surely we have everything to make us hate mankind. I have met girls in the schoolroom—they have been thoroughly kind and cordial to me—perhaps the next day met them in the street—they feared to recognize me."[27]

Of the five free states that prohibited black court testimony in cases where a white person was a party (Ohio, Illinois, California, Indiana, and Iowa), Ohio repealed the law, though in the southern part of the state, where most blacks lived, the courts ignored the repeal. By 1860 two black men served as jurors in Massachusetts after persistent activism. No other state had done so before the Civil War. And though attorney and activist John Mercer Langston thought the 1842 Ohio decision giving individuals with more than one-half European ancestry rights to suffrage and full citizenship was a step toward full citizenship for all black males, many other reformers thought the law actually protected discrimination.[28] Creating strong, viable free black communities that would become an equal part of American society was still at the top of the agenda for antebellum black evangelical reformers.

While most reformers concentrated on understanding the cause and removing the effects of racism, a few responded directly to particular elements of the emerging scientific theory of innate and permanent black inferiority. They relied on history, science, and most of all their Christian faith to understand a belief system that not only placed them outside American society but, for ethnologists, outside the human family. From the Revolutionary era to the Civil War era, northern black writers, ministers, editors, and others who addressed evolving racism consistently asserted a common humanity and equality under God. Late eighteenth-century writers like Phillis Wheatley and Lemuel Haynes reflected the Christian belief in humanity's being distinct from the animal world, the peak of divine creation. Influenced by the Enlightenment like other Americans, Wheatley and other black Christian writers believed the essential human traits were reason and faith.[29]

In response to the idea that people of African descent were inferior, naturally or because of God's curse, antebellum black editors, ministers, teachers, and writers consistently drew upon the creation story of the Bible. All humans were the same, descendants of Adam and Eve. Skin color was not a sign of distinct species but merely God's interest in variation as exhibited in the flora and fauna, the physical geography, climate, soil, and so on, nothing more. "The variety of color, in the human species," Easton wrote, "is the result of the same laws which variegate the whole creation. The same species of flowers is the same, possessing the same general qualities, undergoing no intrinsic change, from these accidental causes." There were no distinct races of humankind.

According to biblical proof, all humans shared common ancestors; any attempt to alter Scripture was a sin. New York City blacks in 1831 echoed a late eighteenth-century slave petitioner, summarizing the attitude of many African Americans in their dismissal of the evolving theory of polygenesis. "There are different *colors* among all species of animated creation. A difference of color is not a difference of species."[30] Easton repeated the sentiments of New York reformers and others: "I conclude it is a settled point with the wisest of the age, that no constitutional difference exists in the children of men, which can be said to be established by hereditary laws . . . that whatever differences exist, are casual or accidental." Garnet succinctly summarized black evangelicals' belief from the Revolution to the Civil War when he insisted in 1848 that "there is but one race, as there was but one Adam." Reformers constantly invoked Acts 17:26 of the Bible for proof of common human ancestry, common "blood." "God hath made of one blood all nations of men for to dwell upon all the face of the earth." This verse more than any other provided proof of human equality in northern black evangelical thought.[31]

But the scriptural "one blood" reference proved inadequate to quell the tide of religious proslavery theory that provided justification for African enslavement. White Christians continued to presume black inferiority, and they too relied on scriptural evidence. The curse of Ham from Genesis 9:20–27 in which Noah cursed his son Ham's younger son Canaan had historically provided justification for Christians involved in various types of subordination of non-Christians. Black clerics, in particular, challenged the belief that Africans and their descendants were slaves and intellectually and morally inferior because of a divine curse. Although they generally agreed with biblical genealogists that Africans were descendants of Ham, they believed black Americans were descendants of Cush and Mizraim, not Canaan, the youngest brother. In 1828 the *Freedom's Journal* reprinted a Maryland congressman's speech in the House of Representatives in which he claimed, "Slavery was the decree of Heaven" because of Canaan's curse. The editors wanted to know what business Noah had getting drunk and setting a poor example for his sons. Presbyterian minister J.W.C. Pennington denied that Noah's curse led to African bondage. In fact, he said, there was no evidence that Noah's curse extended to Canaan's posterity nor that God cursed Ham personally. Ham was blessed along with Noah's other sons coming out of the ark.[32] Pennington and others expressed outrage that white clergymen in particular used the patriarchal cursing and blessing so common in Scripture as justification for slavery. This was the height of deception and arrogance. "The depravity of the human heart is often seen in men's fondness for theory to justify their sins."[33]

Reformers not only vigorously denied biblical justification for black enslavement but used white justifications as an opportunity to condemn slaveholding clergymen. In the 1859 August issue of the *Anglo-African Magazine*, a contributor, "S. S. N.," blended history and biblical genealogy to question Noah's credentials as a prophet with the ability to curse anyone effectively. "We know it is customary to quote the curse of Canaan against us, to prove *our blood contaminated*. But Noah's curse could not have amounted to much." The writer wanted to know what curse condemned whites who had also been slaves for generations in the not too distant past. Besides, he wrote, the curse on a grandson for what a son had done was "very doubtful justice, to say the least . . . and if the curse took effect, which we don't believe (for it is conceded that Noah was no prophet, and had no right, after a drunken carousal, to curse anything, except the wine that had fuddled him,). . . ."[34]

According to historian George Fredrickson, orthodox Christianity's belief in the unity of mankind based on the biblical story of Adam and Eve as progenitors of all humans delayed the development of a "coherent and persuasive ideological racism." Most Christians and even nominal Christians believed all humans originated from the same parents and shared the "same basic psychology, possessed identical moral capabilities and were likely to react in similar ways to common conditions." Climate and other environmental factors contributed to differences among individuals and/or groups according to monogenetic theory. But the environment could be so influential that individuals or groups might experience irreparable damage. Slavery was just one of those major influences that many late eighteenth- and early nineteenth-century European and European American intellectuals and colonizationists pointed to as creating a permanently inferior "race," making it impossible for emancipated slaves, as Thomas Jefferson wrote, to become part of the body politic. By the 1840s, biblical literalism had declined and American ethnologists had successfully replaced the theory of environmentalism in the white intellectual community with polygenetic theory, claiming three separately created and unequal species.[35]

But polygenetic theory was already making inroads in the late eighteenth century, so much so that black and white writers felt the need to challenge the notion of innate black inferiority and the creation of a subhuman black species. In a 1789 petition, a former slave asked the question northern blacks would ask throughout the next several decades. He wanted to know how a "difference of colour" could mean "a difference in species." What made blacks somehow distinct? Blacks shared with whites the same human traits. "What inferiority of art in the fashioning of our bodies? what imperfection in the faculties of our minds?—has not a negro eyes? has not a negro hands, organs, dimensions, senses, affections, passions?" As Christians, northern black writers, like most Americans, persisted in their belief of shared common human origins.

Douglass, in his address "The Claims of the Negro Ethnologically Considered," a speech delivered at Western Reserve College in 1854, admitted that monogenesis could not be proved "apart from the authority of the Bible, neither the unity, nor diversity of origin of the human family, can be demonstrated." The argument for polygenetic theory was an old one with current manifestations. The question of "what are technically called the Negro race, are a part of the human family, and are descended from a common ancestry, with the rest of mankind," Douglass said, was one that had "eternal as well as . . . terrestrial interests. It covers the earth and reaches heaven. The unity of the human race—the brotherhood of man—the reciprocal duties of all to each, and of each to all, are too plainly taught in the Bible to admit of cavil.— The credit of the Bible is at stake" and the authority of that "sacred Book—as a record of the early history of mankind—must be materially affected." It was an issue as old as human history, a struggle between the selfish and the "philanthropic part of mankind" and manifested in his day between slaveholders and abolitionists. And, Douglass asserted, "precisely in proportion as the truth of human brotherhood gets recognition, will be the freedom and elevation, in this country, of persons of African descent. In truth, this question is at the bottom of the whole controversy." The larger question had to do with "whether the rights, privileges, and immunities enjoyed by some ought not to be shared and enjoyed by all." "For, let it be once granted that the human race are of multitudinous origin, naturally different in their moral, physical, and intellectual capacities, and at once you make plausible a demand for classes, grades and conditions, for different methods of culture, different moral, political, and religious institutions, and a chance is left for slavery, as a necessary institution." Douglass needed one authority: the Bible. "For myself I can say, my reason (not less than my feeling, and my faith) welcomes with joy, the declaration of the Inspired Apostle." Calling the new racial science "scientific moonshine," Douglass invoked Acts 17:26, "God has made of one blood all the nations of men for to dwell upon the face of the earth."[36]

Similar to the contributor to the *Anglo-African Magazine* who wondered if the Hamite curse should be applied to whites because of their past enslavement, Delany and Douglass repeatedly cited history to challenge the idea that oppression was "natural" and unique to blacks. Countering the racial science that sub-Saharan Africans were somehow historically and providentially suited to serve European and European American economic interests, the two reformers detailed the ubiquity of subjugation. Delany illustrated instances of peoples throughout the world who were "without rights nor privileges," the "Gypsies in Italy and Greece . . . Croats in the Germanic states . . . and the Irish among the British."[37] Douglass argued that oppressors conveniently blamed the victims of oppression for their own subjugation. "The evils most fostered by slavery and oppression, are precisely those which slaveholders and oppressors would transfer from their system to the inherent character of their victims. Thus the very crimes of slavery become slavery's best defense. By making the enslaved a character fit only for slavery they excuse themselves for refusing to make the slave a free man."[38]

Reformers knew that a distinct skin color was beneficial for protecting American slavery. Oppression was easier, Delany said, when the oppressed were "distinguished by any peculiar or general characteristics." Yet there were those, even among slaveholders, who did not assert a racial justification for slavery. Former president and slaveholder Andrew Jackson viewed blacks, according to Delany, as laborers and "would just as readily have held a white man." Still, Delany knew that the visibility of persons of West or West Central African ancestry greatly facilitated their oppression.[39]

Black evangelical reformers were especially incensed about the pervasive idea of inferior black intellectual capabilities. It not only justified slavery but also denied free blacks access to education and jobs, keeping nearly all blacks in perpetual poverty. Mainly they noted the absurdity of the insistence of a superior white intellect. The fallacy of such a theory was particularly evident in the ways in which theorists, including Jefferson, compared exceptional whites with uneducated, usually enslaved blacks. Eighteenth- and early nineteenth-century reformers generally viewed the sins of slavery and discrimination as sufficient explanation for differences in black and white intellectual attainment and social circumstances. Richard Allen and Absalom Jones gave an early response to proponents of inferior black intellect in the 1794 open address to "Those Who Keep Slaves and Approve the Practice." They challenged white theorists to prove their thesis of intellectual superiority by providing a level playing field. "We believe if you would try the experiment of taking a few black children, and cultivate their minds with the same care and let them have the same prospect in view as to living in the world, as you would wish for your own children, you would find upon the trial, they were not inferior in mental endowments."[40]

When debate about black inferiority intensified and eventually developed into a thoroughgoing racial ideology that justified slavery and racial discrimination scientifically, African American reformers responded even more vociferously to theories of innate black inferiority. By then scientific racism had become increasingly popularized in entertainment, especially minstrelsy, by broadsides and literature, and legitimized in federal and state laws and customs. Switching from early nineteenth-century reformers' history of a romanticized sub-Saharan past, claims of Egyptian and Ethiopian ancestry became common for proof of black intellectual capability. Some black reformers now claimed direct descent from the two African nations Europeans admired, thus falling even more into the trap of allowing racist science and propaganda to frame the debate. A coeditor of *Freedom's Journal*, John Russwurm, noted that though Egyptians were recognized for introducing the "arts and sciences," no one was willing to acknowledge that Egyptians resembled "the present race of Africans: though Herodotus . . . declared that the Egyptians had black skins and frizzled hair." Both nations, several argued, were populated by peoples of brown or black skin color and many had "wooly" hair. Activists who challenged theories of black inferiority consistently contrasted the culturally advanced civilizations of the two nations with the "barbarism" of Europe.[41] Thus, for some antebellum reformers, Egypt became part of the black American past, at least in public discourse, and displaced West Africa in much of the rhetoric as the ancestral homeland.

For most black evangelicals, the Bible provided unquestioned proof of Egyptian and Ethiopian ancestry. According to Easton and many, many others, "Ham was the son of Noah, and founder of the African race." Ham became the founder of Egypt, the "mighty empire," that developed "many of the arts, both of elegance and ability—handed down in an uninterrupted chain, to modern nations of Europe." Garnet believed his sense of ancient history followed conventional biblical wisdom. In his 1848 speech to the Female Benevolent Society of Troy, New York, Garnet explained that there existed "three grand divisions of the earth," namely Asia, Africa, and Europe, colonized by Noah's three sons, Shem, "the father of the Asiatics," Ham, father of the Africans, and Japheth, "the progenitor of the Europeans."[42]

Defining civilization, as did white theorists, with the development of written language, institutions of higher learning, and complex political, economic, and social systems, editors, ministers, teachers, and others hoped Egypt and Ethiopia would be the foil for assertions of innate black intellectual inferiority.[43] After all, there were sources other than the Bible that supported them, from well-respected historians like Herodotus in antiquity to more recent or current scholars, including French abolitionist Abbé Henri Grégoire. They had to explain, though, why both black nations were no longer superior. After praising the glories of ancient Egypt and claiming it as a black nation, articles in the *Freedom's Journal* titled "The Mutability of Human Affairs" expressly delineated ancient Egyptian and Ethiopian cultural degradation from highly enlightened civilized states. Borrowing from eighteenth-century French philosopher Constantin Francois Volney's meditation on the rise and fall of empires, the writer, probably John Russwurm, explained that empires rise and fall with the times. Change was inevitable in all nations, though greed and vanity were definitely factors in the fall of Egypt. Pennington blamed polytheism for Egyptian and Ethiopian declension. According to him, the two countries were advanced in politics, literature, and social affairs, but religious practice degraded them. "Our ancestors had sublime systems of religion; but the basis of it was false."[44] Unlike several northern blacks, Douglass was not sure if "Egyptians were Negroes," but he believed both groups shared an "affinity." While "it may not be claimed that the ancient Egyptians were Negroes,—viz:—answering in all respects, to the nations and tribes ranged under the general appellation, Negro; still, it may safely be affirmed, that a strong affinity and a direct relationship may be claimed by the Negro race, to *that grandest of all the nations of antiquity, the builders of the pyramids.*[45]

In the 1840s, reformers' claims of ancestral consanguinity with Egypt received a deathblow. Ethnologist Samuel G. Morton eventually convinced most Americans through his research on human skulls that Egyptians were white or "Caucasian," the term German anatomist Johann Frederich Blumenbach had coined for the European "race" in the last century. Morton's claim that blacks were permanently inferior to whites was followed with his argument that blacks had been separately created to inhabit tropical Africa. According to Morton, Caucasians were the true descendants of Adam. In charging ethnologists with using unscientific research, Douglass noted that they revealed the true nature of their "science" by separating sub-Saharan Africans from North Africa. It removed the difficulty of drawing biased conclusions.[46]

Countering charges of inferior black intellect shifted by the 1850s from a focus on Egypt as evidence of African intellectual capabilities to accomplishments among individuals of African ancestry in the diaspora. Alexandre Dumas, Alexander Pushkin, and others, including physician James McCune Smith and Frederick Douglass closer to home, were cited as evidence of black intellectual capacity. Garnet noted in the 1840s that "the old doctrine of natural inferiority of the colored race, propagated by Mr. Thomas Jefferson," had been refuted. He cited a prominent scholar who had disproved racial inferiority and numerous "respectable witnesses from among the slandered, both living and dead: Pushkin in Russia, Dumas in France, Toussaint in Haiti, Banaker, Theodore Sedgwick Wright, and a host in America, and a brilliant galaxy in Ancient History." Thomas Hamilton, the editor of the *Anglo-African Magazine,* placed an engraving of Dumas on the frontispiece of the first issue of the magazine, and a biography of Dumas was the magazine's first essay, after the editor's prospectus: "Whatever claims the American School of Ethnology may lay to Sappho, Euclid, St. Cyprian, or Terentius, they must yield to the negro an undoubted share in Pushkin, the Negro-Russian poet, in Placido the Negro-Spanish poet, and in Dumas the Negro-Celtic Historian, Dramatist and Romancer."

Douglass told his readers that the accomplishment of Dr. James McCune Smith "has, in a large measure, taken away our reproach. He has demonstrated the possibility of education for colored men, and has, by the force of his genius, thrown back the bolts of those iron gates which excluded the man of color in this country from the learned professions." A year later, Douglass proudly announced Smith's new membership in the American Geographical Society under the presidency of historian George Bancroft. In turn, Smith praised Douglass in his introduction to Douglass's second autobiography, *My Bondage and My Freedom,* for raising himself from "the lowest condition in society to the highest." As a former slave and now the editor of a successful newspaper, a lecturer, and a writer of two books, Douglass the reformer was the "burning and shining light on which the aged may look with gladness, the young with hope, and the down-trodden, as a representative of what they may themselves become."[47]

As reformers continued to allow racist theorists to establish the terms of the discourse, their debates about black intellectual capacity led to questions of cultural development or "civilization." A few reformers used environmental theory to understand cultural development among varying human populations. Physician James McCune Smith applied environmental theory to explain what he believed was the superior cultural development of the Western world. He thought cultural development depended on climate, geography, and exposure to Christianity, not innate human characteristics. Incorporating and expanding seventeenth- and eighteenth-century environmental theories of human diversity, Smith believed extreme climate limited intellectual development because it caused poor health, short life expectancy, and insufficient oxygen, all elements necessary for maintaining even body temperatures. Only in "temperate zones" were men able to develop the physical health that enabled mental development. Accordingly, the geographic position of a country contributed to the level of civilization. Smith believed geography affected the degree of interaction with other cultures and therefore opportunities for exposure to new ideas. He and Easton said that intercultural contact increased human knowledge, and that countries with topography allowing for communication from coastlines into the interior enabled the development of advanced civilizations. Easton believed temperate climate and geography created the appropriate environment for Christianization. Tropical people and those in cold climates were not receptive to Christianity because of their poor health. The physical vigor of those in temperate zones enabled a receptive mind, which resulted in a civilization more advanced than any other in the world.[48]

Like most Americans, black evangelicals often used civilization and Christianity synonymously; nations, they argued, would rise or fall according to their religious beliefs. When Samuel Cornish wrote about a group of Canadian Indians "daily improving in civilization," he meant they had become

Christians.[49] Christianity was a primary standard of civilization, though as we see in identification with ancient Egypt and Ethiopia, not the only standard. Reformers placed themselves at a disadvantage when they shared with promoters of scientific racism a nearly similar standard of civilization and a restricted application of Christianity. They were limited in their ability to substantially critique racial ideology and instead underscored the dominant belief in the superiority of Western civilization and implicitly white superiority, though, admittedly, not innate. At the same time, in keeping with their Judeo-Christian beliefs, some reformers hinted at another standard of civilization. In his *APPEAL*, David Walker implied that the standard of Christian civilization was how humans treat one another, or what reformers would have called the Golden Rule.[50]

Although those few activists who theorized about cultural differences relied mainly on what were considered the culturally advanced African civilizations of ancient Egypt and Ethiopia to disprove innate black intellectual inferiority, a few pointed to advanced civilizations in sub-Saharan Africa. Relying on travelers' accounts and histories of Africa as they became available, Douglass and Delany, for example, stressed intellectual and technological accomplishments of West and West Central Africans. Douglass noted the written language of the Mandingo. Delany, explaining why people of the African continent were enslaved, suggested that Europeans enslaved Africans because of their superior skills in farming, artisanry, and physical endurance. It was "for this cause and this alone, were they selected in preference to any other race of men, to do the labor of the New World."[51] Moreover, Delany believed scholarly evidence showed that sub-Saharan agricultural knowledge and labor developed northern Africa.[52] The romanticization of sub-Saharan African peoples and cultures was being replaced in the 1850s with a more informative assessment.

Skin color, however, was the defining trait for most European and European American naturalists and others in the eighteenth century engaged in classifying, categorizing, and ranking humans on a scale from the lowest to the highest degrée of intellectual and cultural development or civilization. Europeans, considered at the top of the human scale in intellect, morals, beauty, and skin color, according to these racial theorists, were the standard to which all other human populations were compared. Jefferson's reference in *Notes on the State of Virginia* to the skin color of blacks as "unfortunate" was particularly galling to David Walker. "They think that because they hold us in their infernal chains of slavery that we wish to be white, or of their color—but they are dreadfully deceived—we wish to be just as it pleased our Creator to have made us."[53]

Like most eighteenth-century Christians, most black theorists in the antebellum period explained human variation as one of God's mysteries. The idea that the first human parents produced varying skin colors and other differing human traits was inexplicable. Easton said that variety was a fact of nature. "The variety of color, in the human species, is the result of the same laws which variegate the whole creation. . . . The hair is subject to same laws of variety with the skin, though it may be considered in a somewhat different light. Were I asked why my hair is curled, my answer would be, because God gave nature the gift of producing variety. . . . This would be the best answer I could give; for it is impossible for man to comprehend nature or her works. . . . All must confess she possesses a mysterious power to produce variety." Garnet told an audience that because the sons of Noah had the same father, they were self-evidently the same skin color, "for we cannot through the medium of any law of nature or reason, come to the conclusion, that one was black, another was copper-colored, and the other was white." Since "Adam was a red man," he continued, how his descendants were of varying colors remained a mystery. God varied the complexion of his children for his own purposes.[54]

A few blacks, like most whites, made skin color the determiner of human character and civilization. Skin color was not incidental. In his confusing and mystical work, *Light and Truth: Collected From the Bible and Ancient and Modern History Containing the Universal History of the Colored and the Indian Race from the Creation of the World to the Present Time* (1836), Robert Benjamin Lewis inverted the standard of the white human complexional normative. According to Lewis, Egyptians were Ethiopians and Indians were originally Israelites of Egypt. Also, Moses was "colored," as were prominent individuals of the recent past. All humans shared the same basic characteristics until God divided them at the biblical Tower of Babel. Whites are almost nonexistent in Lewis's account except in reference to white American traders who negatively influenced American Indians, causing the downfall of Indian Christianity. Lewis's replacement of black with white as the human complexional normative implied that color was more than accidental, it was critical for understanding cultural development and intellectual capacity. Lewis's work evidently resonated with several black New Englanders. A Boston "Committee of Colored Gentlemen" reprinted *Light and Truth* at least once, in 1844, and probably a second time, in 1854.[55]

Less fanciful than Lewis, most African Americans who engaged in theorizing about human diversity relied on eighteenth-century environmentalism blending religion with science. John Russwurm in his *Freedom's Journal* articles on the "Mutability of Human Affairs" and "On Varieties of Human Race" concluded that the original color of humankind was copper, and that black and white skin colors developed as a consequence of different climatic influences. Frederick Douglass thought the most convincing explanation for varying skin colors was climatic. "The Portuguese, white in Europe, is brown in Asia. The Jews, who are to be found in all countries, never intermarrying, are white in Europe, brown in Asia, and black in Africa. . . . It is the sun that paints the peach—and may it not be, that he paints the *man* as well?" Douglass brought an original and what has proved to be prescient idea to the debate when he suggested that diversity was inherent within each individual. "My reading, on this point, however, as well as my own observation, have convinced me, that from the beginning the Almighty, within certain limits, endowed mankind with organizations capable of countless variations in form, feature and color, without having it necessary to begin a new creation for every new variety.[56]

The evangelical reformer foremost in developing scientific reasons for human variety however, was New York City physician James McCune Smith. Relying on the environmentalism of the eighteenth century, Smith dismissed polygenetic theory step by step. As a student with Henry Highland Garnet, Alexander Crummell, and several others who would become notable reformers, professionals, and artists at the African Free School, Smith knew the effects of slavery and racial prejudice firsthand as the child of former slaves growing up in New York City and even more so when he was refused admission to American medical schools. With the help of black Episcopalian minister Peter Williams, Smith attended the University of Glasgow, where he received three academic degrees, including a doctorate of medicine. Upon his return to the United States in 1837, he established a successful medical practice and opened a pharmacy on West Broadway. Back in New York, Smith immediately became involved in the abolition of slavery, development of free black institutions, and the demand for equal rights.[57]

Like other reformers, Smith denounced the whole idea of separate and distinct races. In his trenchant analysis of Thomas Jefferson's Query XIV in *Notes on the State of Virginia* and of later works that supported Jefferson's views, Smith took apart Jefferson's logic point by point in an August *Anglo-African Magazine* essay. There was only one race, Smith argued, the human race. First, he questioned Jefferson's query about the ability of blacks to be "elevated" to the white standard. Smith wanted to know what standard Jefferson meant. There was no fixed standard and it was "hard to say" if the slaveholder "with a slave-whip in his hand" was more elevated than the Christian slave who prayed to "God to soften the heart of the accomplished torturer—who is the more elevated?" Then Smith, citing Jefferson's claims of "deep-rooted prejudices" on the part of whites and "ten-thousand recollections" of their experience in slavery on the part of blacks, noted that the real question was whether blacks and whites could live together in "harmony under American institutions, each contributing to the peace and prosperity of the country, and to the development of the problem of self-government?" If there were reasons why the two populations could not live together, Smith added, it must be found in either the institutions themselves or in the "nature of the people." Finding nothing wrong with democratic institutions, as represented by states of "progress," Maine, Massachusetts, and Rhode Island, "where the laws are made equal for all men" and where blacks and whites live in "peace and harmony," then the question must apply to "anything in the races themselves which constitutes such a prohibition?"

Smith repeated portions of Jefferson's Query XIV that referred to the physical, mental, and moral distinctions between blacks and whites, but said some parts of *Notes on the State of Virginia* were too "revolting to any mind which has the slightest regard for the decencies and proprieties of life." Including Jefferson's *Notes* with other writings that supported or elaborated upon the former president's racist views, Smith attacked the claims of physical differences between blacks and whites with regard to bone structure, musculature, hair texture, and skin color. Since all humans had the same number of bones and represented a variety of bone "forms" within each population, bone structure established only that while "there are the same individual varieties in each race, there are also the same general resemblances." Smith ridiculed the idea that a single "type" existed among blacks and whites. It was "illogical" as evidence of "permanent difference between these two races." The argument was so fallacious that one might as well select "all the white men in this city who have grey eyes, and to argue that because the color of their eyes differs from that of the remainder, therefore the two classes belong to different races."

The New York City physician and intellectual then addressed ethnologists' idea that the skulls of Africans were closer to the skull of apes and "recedes" from the skull of the "white or Caucasian race." Proof lay in the measurements of the facial angle of the two groups. Smith demonstrated that the faulty evidence was biased in the selection process. The skulls selected for blacks were exceptions and those for whites above the usual measurement. Bone structure and skull measurement were not determiners of race. One only need observe the profiles of "Henry Clay, General Lafayette, or most of the heads found on French and Spanish coins of the latter part of the last century" to know whether there were whites whose facial angle was "equally acute." Travelers' accounts provided further proof that the retreating forehead was "not the type but a variety in the heads of the native blacks."

Facial angle was important, Smith noted, for ethnologists assumed it was the "measurer of intellect." They based their theories on assumptions "not yet proven" that "intelligence bears some proportion to the development of the brain" and that the facial angle was a measure of the "quantity of brain in man." The facial angle had no relation, Smith explained, to the degree of intelligence. With fully cited and detailed scientific data, he summarized, the facial angle simply measured the "position of the upper jaw in regard to the orifices of the ear and edge of the orbit." Rather than proof of separate human species, the evidence showed incredible human uniformity, "proving that, from the bony structure of the human frame, there can be deduced the sublime argument of the unity of the human race." Smith added that research by the "best anatomists" had not found any differences in size and weight between blacks and whites.

Smith quickly dismissed the argument that blacks and whites had distinct muscular systems. "These earnest seekers after not the truth, but the differences" argued that blacks had less calf and it was higher up than whites. Again the evidence produced was the exception. A poor diet was the cause of rickets, which affected all humans. "Bandy legs" were found in masters as much as in slaves in the South. One would have to rule out "many who have white complexion" from "the circle of manhood" if this rule applied. Regarding hair texture, Smith referred directly to Josiah Nott, the southern proslavery physician/ethnologist who "enumerates" hair texture as "among the reasons which led him to believe that the two races are of a distinct species—as much so as the 'swan and the goose.'" In response to Nott and others, Smith cited several scientists who argued that varying hair textures existed among all human populations and that hair did not constitute a distinct species. Consistently the environmentalist, Smith believed culture and climatic temperatures determined hair texture: black northerners' hair was getting straighter. "This must be consolatory to those who have gazed upon this, to them, insurmountable difficulty in the way of incorporating the blacks into the State."

Finally, Smith assessed Jefferson and other racial theorists' objection to African American skin color, which "may be called the 'physical distinction' upon which the question is made to rest by the opponents of the black man in this Republic." Smith's preliminary comments about Jefferson's assertion that white Americans were naturally repulsed by black skin color involved noting that white travelers found sub-Saharan African skin color attractive and a sarcastic reference to Jefferson's sexual liaison with Sally Hemings. He pointed out that some of Jefferson's descendants were living in Liberia. Smith also cited a clergyman who invoked biblical authority, "for we are all His workmanship.—Esphes. 2:10." Referring to travelers' assessments and clerical admonition, Smith stated, "Such testimony is enough to show that there is nothing essentially hideous or distinctly deformed in a black complexion."

Yet, Smith not only allowed scientific racial theorists who supported innate black inferiority to frame much of the debate, but also fell into the trap of unwittingly reifying biological racial theory with his claims that distinct personality traits and physical attributes existed among populations who shared similar skin color. Preliminary comments aside, Smith then directly addressed the substance of his argument. Skin color did matter to some extent. The choice of particular colors for the diversity of humankind was arbitrary, he noted, but, borrowing from British ethnologist and Quaker James Cowles Prichard's broad classification, Smith asserted that there were "three great varieties to the human complexions, varieties under which all mankind may be classed," the leucos, xanthous, and melanocomous. In "physics" white meant "a combination of all colors—a reflection from the white object, of all the rays of color." Or white defined an absence of color, an absence of pigmentation in the hair, eyes, skin, and so on, a phenomenon not confined to humans. And white was often termed since "Lord Bacon's time . . . the color of *defect*." Referring to albinism, Smith stated that this congenital deficiency was "a deformed" variety of the human species. This type, the "leucos, or white class of men, are very few," yet they existed among all human populations. "Horace Greeley is nearly an albino" Smith added sarcastically, referring to the editor of the *New York Tribune* who had recently repeated Jefferson's assertion that whites and blacks could not coexist in the United States.

The second great variety of humans was a larger proportion of mankind than the leucos: the "xanthous variety," marked by yellow hair and light eyes.

Citing medical writers from Galen, the ancient Greek physician, to more recent times, Smith explained that this population from northern Europe, "including the Danes, the Belgians, a portion of the Germans, and the northeastern part of Asia—to wit, Eastern Siberia—and even some of the Highlands of Africa," all shared "a certain degree of irritability and delicacy of constitution." Their fair skin was "agreeably relieved by that ruddy tint which characterizes the sanguine temperament. . . . Persons of very fair complexion are often less robust than those of more swarthy hue."

The last, but not least, human variety in Smith's classification constituted the largest human population and was distinguished by "black hair, dark eyes, and a complexion varying from a bright brunette of the Italian to jet black of the negro." The "melanocomous, or dark-haired variety of the human race," also shared particular personalities and physical attributes. They had a "choleric or melancholic temperament, and have generally sounder and more vigorous constitutions, and are less susceptible of morbific impressions from external causes than the sanguine." "Melanic" populations lived in the "south of Europe, nearly all Asia, all Africa and Australia, with a large portion of the American Continent." Describing varying skin colors of populations, particularly those with "black complexion" from the California Indians to the Himalayas, Smith concluded: "Hence it appears that the black comprises no special variety of the human race, no distinctive species of mankind, but is part and parcel of the great original stock of humanity—of the rule, and not of the exception. He also belongs to that variety which is endowed with the most powerful constitutions."

Climate determined skin color. "The Ethiopian can change his skin," and, Smith suggests in other writings, his temperament, too. Smith's human "varieties" lacked innate qualities, but in grouping human beings into specific categories with innate personality and physical capacities, he embraced elements of racial ideology, the very belief system he tried to discredit. Regarding the "original complexion of mankind," Smith cited Prichard: the first humans were of the "dark or melanic complexion."[58]

James McCune Smith and other black intellectuals who were engaged in theorizing about race maintained a belief in monogenetic theory not only because of their Christian faith but also because polygenesis ranked the separate and distinct species from the superior "Caucasian" to the inferior "Negro." Once down the path of polygenesis, there was no way out for establishing the equality of human endowments. But as Smith shows, some black theorists

were not averse to claiming innate characteristics, or nearly so, that purportedly placed them in equal or superior positions with regard to particular
characteristics within the human race.

At the same time Smith discounted racial ideology, he unwittingly provided
further ammunition for ideological racism. The idea that the "dark-haired" variety of humankind was "choleric," or hot-tempered and given to unreasonable
or excessive anger, repeated racial ideology about blacks. Racists could easily
discount the idea that dark hair signified a distinct human type but readily
agree with their previously held beliefs that nonwhites, specifically persons
of African descent, lacked reason. There was something innate, in the "negro
blood," according to Smith and other racial theorists, that demonstrated African American intellectual capabilities. In reference to Frederick Douglass's
sagacious intellect, Smith attributed it to his slave mother. Though a former
slave with no formal schooling, Douglass's intellect compared favorably to
well-known and educated multitalented people of African descent. Douglass
was indebted, Smith said, "for his energy, perseverance, eloquence, invective,
sagacity, and wide sympathy . . . to his negro blood. The very marvel of . . .
how his mother learned to read. The versatility of talent which he wields, in
common with Dumas, Ira Aldridge, and Miss Greenfield, would seem to be the
result of the grafting of the Anglo-saxon on good original, negro stock." Smith
had moved far away from eighteenth- and early nineteenth-century African
American antiracists who were convinced that human diversity was merely
incidental, a part of God's interest in earthly variation. As historian Mia Bay
explains, nineteenth-century black intellectuals developed "a profoundly ambivalent discourse" in which they questioned racial ideology but "sometimes
reified the concept of race."[59]

Smith shows, too, how reformers by the 1850s found it harder and harder
to avoid using the language of race, increasingly using the term "race" in
reference to human populations. Several referred to the "Negro race" even
as they firmly believed in the existence of one race, the "human race." Race
in reformers' vocabularies, though, was generally, though not always, of the
pre–nineteenth century meaning. Like eighteenth-century philosophers and
historians speaking of human populations, Smith used race, stock, and class
interchangeably. The Mandigos and Fulahs were separate races, the Anglo-
Saxons were a race, and slaveholders were a "base race of cowards." Ridiculing
the notion of a Caucasian race, he reminded "friends of 'Caucasus'" that the
term "Caucasian" was being dropped by ethnologists because "the people about

Mount Caucasus, are, and have ever been, Mongols." Smith reiterated over and over again that there was only one race, the "human race," and mocked "the assumed superiority of certain so-called 'races' of mankind—the term races meaning, not merely a distinct breed, but even a separate and distinct creation of the genus *homo*."[60]

Even so, except in a few instances, antebellum black theorists allowed ethnologists to frame the parameters of the debate. They felt compelled to explain differences in human skin color, hair texture, and facial features, the particular features ethnologists asserted denoted African American inferiority. Reformers, of course, had utilized the particular features ethnologists pointed to as evidence of innate inferiority for collective and self-definition of what constituted populations of African ancestry. Skin color, hair texture, and facial features were signifiers, not just the experience of oppression, for those who qualified for inclusion in the black communities. Consequently, black reformers found themselves talking, writing, and acting as if skin color and hair texture mattered even more than they were willing to acknowledge. African American antiracists were moving toward the idea of distinct races of human kind, and some, as we have seen, suggested biological features were substantive.

In his use of scientific evidence to refute polygenetic theory, Smith was the exception. Several activists who became trapped in elements of racial ideology claimed or implied innate black moral superiority and the reverse: innate white depravity. Their reasoning was less science and more, like David Walker, religious, if not apocalyptic. At the beginning of the antebellum era, Walker had placed white oppression of blacks within a racial framework, asserting innate characteristics of populations according to geography and skin color. Using Christian morality as the highest standard of human development, he suggested the possibility that whites, all whites, might be naturally inferior. History showed that Europeans had always been an "unjust, jealous, unmerciful, avaricious set of beings . . . always seeking after power and authority." Whites wreaked havoc all over the world, "acting more like devils than accountable men." When they became Christian, whites were less—not more— humane. "In fact, take them as a body, they are ten times more cruel, avaricious and unmerciful than ever they were . . . while they were heathens."[61] Walker contrasted white depravity with black goodness. "I know that blacks, take them half enlightened and ignorant, are more humane and merciful than the most enlightened and refined European that can be found in all the earth."[62]

In countering Jefferson, Walker had a query of his own. He wondered if the inhumanity and barbarism European Americans exhibited were innate. Whites called blacks brutes, but they were the ones who exhibited a kind of "*barbarity*" unknown in human history. Even heathens never exhibited such brutality.[63] Walker wondered why, with all the advantages of education and Christianity, whites were still behaving like barbarians. Were whites naturally morally inferior to blacks? "I therefore, in the name and fear of the Lord God of Heaven and of earth, divested of prejudice either on the side of my colour or that of the whites, advance my suspicion of them, whether they are *as good by nature* as we are or not. Their actions, since they were known as a people, have been the reverse."[64]

Martin Delany also shows that some activists were guilty of endorsing what George Fredrickson has called "romantic racism." According to Delany, the "colored races are highly susceptible of religion; it is a constituent principle of their nature, and an excellent trait in their character."[65] Thus, a few black reformers in the antebellum North argued simultaneously for equality of human endowments and asserted African American natural religiosity.

In moving from universalism toward particularism for understanding humankind, Walker and the few others theorizing about race reflected rather than adequately challenged scientific racism. They unwittingly engaged in what philosopher Anthony Appiah has termed "racialism," or the belief that there are heritable characteristics possessed by members of a group who share specific traits and tendencies with each other that they do not share with members of any other human group. Racialists, according to this theory, are not racists, however. It is only when racialist beliefs become the basis for claiming special privileges for members of what they consider their own group that they can be considered racist.[66] Still, antebellum African American racial theory contained critical elements of racial ideology that undermined their challenge to the new science.

Even though some reformers like Walker suggested blacks were morally superior to whites and embraced European/European American notions of advanced civilizations and biblical interpretations of their ancestral origins, most readily dismissed phrenology as proof of black inferiority. This new and popular "scientific" method, they asserted, was just further false evidence of ethnologists. The shape and size of the cranium purportedly determined intellectual capacity. Scientists argued that white brain capacity was large and blacks' was small. Prominent Philadelphia businessman William Whipper wanted to know "what organs a man ought to have to render him a slave." James McCune Smith simply said phrenology was unscientific.[67]

Most northern blacks not only rejected the theory of innate and inferior black characteristics, they almost all consistently rejected the idea of innate white prejudice against blacks. While colonizationists and others took up Thomas Jefferson's refrain of black and white incompatibility, reformers pointed to personal experience and history as evidence of harmonious black and white interaction. In their 1831 *Address to the Citizens of New York,* New York City blacks responded directly to the New York Colonization Society's assertion that free blacks must be removed because of a natural white antagonism to blacks. "There does exist in the United States a prejudice against us, but is it unconquerable? Is it not in the power of these gentlemen to subdue it?"[68] Douglass was among those who used personal experience to disprove the charges. Douglass's closest childhood friends were white children who showed no evidence of innate hostility to a darker complexion.[69] Smith believed the New England states were examples in the 1850s of places where blacks and whites were learning to live in "peace and harmony."[70] James Forten Jr. simply said that for whites to excuse slavery and discrimination on the basis of natural repulsion of blacks was a "mean, pitiful, objection."[71] In their essay on prejudice and colonization, clergymen Samuel Cornish and Theodore Wright concluded that colonizationists based their theories supporting innate white prejudice on grounds that could not be disproved. All such theories, they declared, were "hopelessly stupid and besotted."[72]

Delany pointed to the early colonial period to address the question of innate white prejudice toward blacks. In one of the earliest historical discussions on the origins of slavery and racism in the United States, Delany came down on the side of slavery. He pointed to Native Americans as the first slaves of the Europeans in the Americas. European hatred of Africans followed their interest in exploiting black labor; skin color simply made oppression easier. Racism was directly related to proslavery interest in justifying slavery.[73] In spite of confusion, disagreement, and contradiction about the cause of racism and the means to end it, most blacks agreed that whites could and would overcome racism. They viewed attitudinal change in an evangelical context. Conversion, a main tenet of evangelical theology, emphasized the importance and possibility of human transformation.

As victims of racial oppression, northern blacks were sensitive to the way in which the racial constructs worked. Their knowledge of relatives, friends, and others who became "white" or "passed" underscored their belief in the fluidity, mutability, and fiction of race and racial "purity." Garnet argued that the American Colonization Society's goal to remove black people from the United States would include many individuals deemed white. He cited examples of prominent persons who, he implied, would be forced out; it was now (in the 1840s) "too late to make a successful attempt to separate the black and white people in the New World." If forced out, exiles would insist "upon taking all who have our generous and prolific blood in their veins." Others noted that there were blacks who were considered white in the North but were black in the South. Smith said of the one hundred students who attended the New York African Free School with him in 1826–1827, six were now white.[74]

A small number of activists rejected and embraced notions of racial purity simultaneously. Confronted with white theories of pure races and the onslaught of Anglo-Saxonism in the 1850s that argued for the preservation of the purity of "Anglo-Saxons," some activists asserted their own "pure blood." Martin Delany unhesitatingly self-identified as "of pure African blood or unmixed African blood," so much so that Frederick Douglass noted that he thanked God for making him simply a man, but Delany thanked God for making him a black man.[75] Activists claiming "pure blood," however, were not without their critics. Reflecting disgust over the growing white American glorification of the idea of a "pure Anglo-Saxon race" in the 1850s, a writer to the African American magazine the *Anglo-African* condemned blacks for claiming Anglo-Saxon identity. The English were a mixed people and so were the Germans. All people, in fact, including Africans, were mixed with a variety of physical attributes and personality traits. This "nonsense" about Anglo-Saxon purity, the writer noted, had become so prevalent that "almost every white writer or speaker" referred to it to gain popularity. It was just one more attempt to justify "their highest claim to be our masters and rulers." But, the writer added, black Americans were so influenced by the notion of racial purity that they, too, were insisting on the fallacious existence of a "pure African race," while others, like the magazine's editors, were trying to connect Africans and Europeans into a new racial type. How "have we become Anglo-Africans?"[76]

A close examination of claims of pure or unmixed African ancestry, however convoluted linguistically and theoretically, indicates that the influential figures who self-referred as pure Africans were responding to the racist doctrine that any addition of "white blood" improved black intellect. Delany's many self-references to his and others' racial purity were mainly attempts to counter this pervasive and insidious element of racial doctrine.[77] Thomas Jefferson had stated that the "improvement of the blacks in body and mind, in the first instance of their mixture with the whites, has been observed by every one, and proves that their inferiority is not the effect merely of their condition of life."[78] Several decades later the idea that black intellect improved with a degree of white parentage was prominent in popular literature. Harriet Beecher Stowe's *Uncle Tom's Cabin* provides the most well-known mid-nineteenth-century example. In language, looks, and deportment, Stowe's characters of mixed African and European ancestry were more intelligent and courageous.[79]

Ironically, Delany and Garnet, who liked to stress their pure African ancestry, also expressed concern about the potential for divisiveness among individuals of varying skin colors. Their hope, like that of early organizers of free black communities who wanted unity through a common African and African American identity, was that anyone with some degree of African ancestry would join in the cause against slavery and racial prejudice. Shared African origins and oppression were the means for a united front to fight persistent discrimination and southern slavery. Yet for some northern whites in the late antebellum era, individuals of mixed European and African ancestry with physical characteristics deemed closer to European were more acceptable and thus enjoyed limited rights and privileges denied those considered more African. In several cities, especially Cincinnati, many individuals of European and African ancestry were better educated than other blacks and disproportionately represented in professional and skilled occupations; many were entrepreneurs.[80]

Delany feared the possibility of a national custom or policy giving these "mixed" individuals more rights and privileges than the majority of blacks, a system existing in New Orleans and the Caribbean. In his 1852 book, *The Condition, Elevation, Emigration, and Destiny of the Colored People of the United States Politically Considered*, Delany provided a brief history of early black "attainments," noting with pride that many were of "pure and unmixed African blood." In an aside, he argued that the end of white oppression could not be piecemeal; those of African and European ancestry would never enjoy full equality until all people of the diaspora were included. "The elevation of the colored man can only be completed by the elevation of the pure descendants of Africa; because to deny his equality, is to deny in a like proportion, the equality of all those mixed with the African organization."[81]

Notwithstanding a confusing discourse about race, reformers all agreed that the ideology of distinct racial categories placed in a hierarchy of superior to inferior was merely justification for white oppression and without scientific merit. That there was only one race, the human race, remained the dominant view. Of course, given their subordinate status, whether countering racism or reifying it in particular ways through romantic racism or racialism within the parameters of biological racism, reformers and racial theorists had little impact on dominant American society's ongoing racial project. During the peak of nineteenth-century evangelical religiosity, antebellum white leaders, ministers, politicians, and intellectuals ensured that white Americans maintained power and control in almost all aspects of American life and culture. The few successes black and white reformers achieved in challenging discriminatory racial policy in New England and elsewhere had no effect in changing or even loosening scientific racism. In fact, racism among intellectuals and the larger American population would become not only more entrenched but even more virulent in the late nineteenth century.

Finally, viewing the rise of racism through an evangelical millennial lens, African American reformers believed racism as much as slavery threatened the republic and therefore the world. Garnet thought racism would decline because the United States would become like the rest of the Western Hemisphere, a nation of mixed races. Unlike the Indians in the United States, who were dying, the black populations in the Americas, Garnet believed, were increasing, becoming so mixed with the dominant race that differences in skin color would become moot in the Americas and eventually the world. "Our blood," he said, "is mixed with every tribe from Cape Horn to the Frozen Ocean." And slavery would end, it was inevitable. Reflecting foundational principles of black evangelicalism, Garnet, who in the late 1840s was still committed to the republic, said God's judgment was firm. He admonished the nation to tremble because of God's justice. "Tremble, guilty nation, for the God of Justice lives and reigns."[82]

Smith, too, trembled for the nation. He, like Walker, revealed the millennialist tendencies in black evangelicalism. Smith was certain that northern blacks could save the nation. Similar to other black evangelicals, both Garnet and Smith thought northern blacks were divinely ordained to protect the republic from itself. Garnet, like many reformers, believed northern blacks should persist in advancing intellectually, morally, and financially and most of all lead in the protest against slavery, the role God gave them. In other words, antebellum reformers reflected late eighteenth-century and early nineteenth-century leaders' desires for a virtuous northern black population. Blacks should "agitate, agitate, and agitate until the chains of the three million's are broken." In an 1855 speech to the National Council of Colored People, a separate black organization formed in 1853 under the leadership of Douglass and Smith, Smith said that northern blacks' destiny was to "uphold" the principles of "human brotherhood" and the "practicability of democratic institutions, their ability to overcome the last vestige of tyranny in the human heart, the vincibility of caste by Christianity, the power of the gospel, the disenthrallment of three millions of bleeding and crushed slaves." If northern blacks did not work to rid the nation of racism and slavery, racism would invade the entire world. "The influence of our land and its institutions reaches to the uttermost parts of the earth; and go where we may, we will find American prejudice, or at least the odor of it, to contend against. It is easiest, as well as manliest, to meet and contend with it here at the fountainhead."[83]

Smith's millennialist belief in northern blacks as divinely appointed instruments to save the republic was a twist on the dominant American evangelical credence in viewing the United States as the "redeemer nation." It was the country's mission, evangelicals believed, to bring order to a chaotic world through its superior political and religious institutions; once accomplished, the reign of peace would begin.[84] As a model to the world, black reformers were convinced that the chosen nation must be transformed from its focus on greed and expediency to one in which Christian morality dominated. Free blacks living in the North would lead in ridding the nation of the sin of slavery and racism and establish a new nation, a new people, a new order of things. The Revolution would be complete; the nation would be prepared for the millennium.

CHAPTER 6

We Love Our Country . . . But We Love Liberty More

EMIGRATIONISM, NATIONALISM, EVANGELICALISM, AND
THE BEGINNING OF THE CIVIL WAR

I for one, sir, am willing, dearly as I love my native land (a land which will not protect
me however,) to leave it, and go wherever I can be free. We have already drank too long
the cup of bitterness and woe.
—Quoted in Phillip S. Foner and George E. Walker, eds.,
Proceedings of the Black State Conventions, 1840–1865

On the eve of the Civil War, many African Americans living in the North
had all but given up hope for the abolition of slavery and equality with white
America. The 1850 Fugitive Slave Law and the Dred Scott decision in 1857
further protected slavery and put free black life in even greater jeopardy. In
spite of the abolitionist movement and antiracist struggles, little change occurred overall in access to jobs and housing. If anything, things were worse.
In addition, only a tiny black male minority exercised the suffrage. While
several reformers, such as James McCune Smith, Sarah Mapps Douglass, and
Frederick Douglass, remained committed to the United States, a large number entertained the idea of emigration to Canada or West Africa. Yet, even as
activists devised more desperate means to end slavery or emigrate outside the
United States, their reasoning remained within the ideological framework of
black evangelical Christianity. And when reformers turned to violence as the
solution for ending slavery, they did so convinced that God was on their side
and that they were in keeping with national principles.

In the two decades before the Civil War, many black reformers switched,
as did most American reformers, to relying less on moral suasion and more on
the political system and governmental agencies to reform American society.

The temperance movement had also become politicized, shifting its focus to the ballot box and establishing laws forbidding liquor in individual states or counties. Northern black men, determined to influence American law and policy, persistently demanded the vote. The 1843 National Convention reflected this growing sense that political—not moral—means would end slavery and racism. Though political activism was important, the national black convention of 1843, the first held in eight years, was known not so much for Presbyterian minister Henry Highland Garnet's determination and success in gaining reformers' support for political action as it was for his failed attempt to gain endorsement for advocating slave insurrection. In fact, this much more controversial proposal seems to have been as important to Garnet as political action. It may have been one of his main interests in calling for a national convention in the first place. He was involved in selecting the date and place of the convention as well as in establishing the convention's theme of united action.[1]

The selection of Buffalo as the site for the convention showed the growth and spread of the northern black population into the West and indicated reformers' interest, particularly Garnet's, in broadening and influencing the constituency. Situated near Lake Erie with efficient transportation available between western New York and the Northwest, the location meant westerners could attend. Delegates represented constituencies in Illinois, Michigan, and Ohio as well as the New England and Atlantic states, except Pennsylvania, where William Whipper and others still opposed to separate black meetings were influential. In contrast to the early conventions, when Philadelphians dominated, the largest number of delegates in 1843 was from western and eastern New York cities such as Albany, Schenectady, Geneva, and Utica.

Before the convention even began, the problem of representation arose. It seems Garnet intended to pack the convention so that his resolutions for Liberty party endorsement and slave insurrection would carry. To his dismay, several men from nearby cities arrived without appropriate delegate credentials but with expectations of participating in the proceedings. Some came from cities that had not sent delegates and others were from cities that already had designated delegates. Garnet immediately set about to achieve his goal of getting endorsement for his agenda by controlling convention debate. He wanted to prevent overrepresentation from one city or region of the North and West. But fellow New Yorker Charles B. Ray and New Englanders Amos Beman, Frederick Douglass, and Charles Lenox Remond joined forces for different reasons in support of giving delegate status for those men from cities without representation and the status of "corresponding members" for cities that had already sent delegates. Garnet's opposition intended to prevent his politics from interfering in the national meeting. In the early 1840s, Remond and Douglass were still insisting that moral suasion was the only effective means for abolition. Congregational ministers Ray and Beman, on the other hand, thought that black political endorsement was premature and detrimental to gaining black male enfranchisement. Actually Remond and Douglass, still very much Garrisonians in the early 1840s, were ambivalent about even attending a meeting exclusive to blacks.

Not coincidentally, neither side discussed support or opposition to political means for ending slavery. Those who wanted to include more delegates or corresponding members argued on democratic principles of the "largest liberty" that all persons attending should participate. Besides, most of those included would be honorary members who could not determine policy but might express their personal opinion on any measure before the assembly. Garnet and his supporters were less evasive but still indirect. They argued for exclusion of local men without delegate credentials on procedural grounds. Uncredentialed persons might introduce "discordant" views that would consume the limited time of the convention. And many of those without credentials would narrow the discussion to local issues. It was necessary to establish and follow clear rules of procedure.

Determining convention delegate eligibility was generally subjective and fraught with difficulties. Delegates were usually chosen from the membership of local societies and churches in each city and town. Even more to the point, delegate status depended upon one's financial ability to travel and leave a job for two or three days. Few black northerners could afford this type of luxury, so besides ensuring that an elite minority would participate in the meetings, it also meant representation was uncertain, sporadic, and disproportionately dominated by ministers and those who were self-employed. For this reason delegates living near the convention site always outnumbered those living out of state, and even several delegates living in the area were able to attend only a few meetings because of work and other financial obligations. Garnet's desire to establish firm rules of representation was pertinent but unrealistic. It was not his major interest at this 1843 convention.

Garnet did succeed in controlling the ballot, at least to some extent, by agreeing to a compromise. Those individuals from cities that already had representation would be honorary members without voting privileges. New Haven clergyman Amos Beman urged compromise for the "harmony and success" of the convention.

Garnet's political maneuvering included helping choose the opening day's speaker. He chose a minister who had given up on moral suasion and viewed slave insurrection as a viable alternative. Traditionally, the opening day's speaker, usually a local pastor, set the tone of the national and state conventions. The Reverend Samuel H. Davis of Buffalo did just that. He began within the agreed upon black evangelical ideals of the necessity of black unity and importance of Revolutionary principles. Davis underscored black reformers' sentiment in the 1840s that alliance with white abolitionists had not produced sufficient change nor adequately promoted black evangelicals' broader agenda of equal rights and community development. But Davis deviated significantly from earlier speeches, at least implicitly. Time had demonstrated that petitions were ineffective methods for achieving equal rights and abolition. Yet blacks must persist "by every means in our power, strive to persuade the white people to act with more confidence in their own principles of liberty—to make laws, just and equal for all people." White abolitionist activity involved "noble efforts," according to Davis, but success lay in black exertions.

Rather than look to white abolitionists and public officials, Davis continued, activists should follow the examples of contemporary democratic struggles abroad and the American Revolution. White American respect for the international armed struggles taking place in Europe was encouraging. This was the means by which Americans had gained independence, and blacks should do no less. Blacks in America experienced far more oppression than any American patriot or current European insurgent. "We must profit by the example of our oppressors. We must act on their principles in resisting tyranny. . . . Forbid it heaven! that we should longer stand in silence, hugging the delusive phantom of hope," when every sound from the South "bears on its wings . . . the dismal sound of slavery's chain . . . and we ourselves are aliens and outcasts in our native land." Foreign struggles should encourage blacks to lead in their own struggle against slavery and racism. Freedom-loving people would sympathize with black Americans' "wise, persevering, and determined measures" and assist in the effort. There was, Davis added, "no other hope . . . left us, but in our own exertions, and an appeal to the God of armies!"[2]

The convention warmly received Davis's blend of reasoned appeals for justice and allusions to armed struggles. The speech sparked no debate. What seemed like the delegation's receptivity encouraged Garnet to push for convention endorsement of slave rebellion the following day. As chairman of the Business Committee he had helped decide the agenda for the assembly and probably scheduled his address for the second day, assuming support for the measure was more likely then than later. He quickly learned, though, that many reformers were opposed even to the suggestion of violence as a way to end slavery and that one of his most vocal opponents, newcomer Frederick Douglass, was a force to be reckoned with.

Garnet's "An Address to the Slaves of the United States of America" was at once a sympathetic pastoral letter to the enslaved and a prescription for slave insurrection. As importantly, the "Address" was the epitome of black evangelicalism with its combination of the sacred/secular, religious/political dimensions. The Bible condemned slavery, according to black evangelicals, and supported freedom and human equality. In his sermonic letter, Garnet placed responsibility for abolition squarely on the shoulders of slaves. The twenty-eight-year-old Presbyterian minister chastised, encouraged, and simultaneously instructed enslaved men and women in the art of religious-political warfare. He repeated Davis's dismay that abolitionists' appeal to slaveholders' Christian principles had not worked. Slaveholders had rejected all attempts for peaceful abolition. Now it was time for slaves to act. They must do what abolitionists failed to accomplish. As Christians, they should explain to slaveholders the sinfulness of slavery, "of a future judgment, and of the righteous retributions of an indignant God." Then tell masters that they were "DETERMINED TO BE FREE." It was as sinful for slaves to submit to slavery, Garnet explained, as it was for slaveholders to hold them in bondage. "The forlorn condition in which you are placed does not destroy your moral obligation to God." The "divine commandments" applied to all persons no matter what their condition. God required absolute love *and* obedience. Slaves were obligated to observe the Sabbath, "search the Scriptures—and bring up your children with respect for his laws. . . . But slavery sets all these naught and hurls defiance in the face of Jehovah."

> The diabolical injustice by which your liberties are cloven down, NEITHER GOD, NOR ANGELS, OR JUST MEN, COMMAND YOU TO SUFFER FOR A SINGLE MOMENT. THEREFORE IT IS YOUR SOLEMN AND IMPERATIVE DUTY TO USE EVERY MEANS, BOTH MORAL, INTELLECTUAL, AND PHYSICAL, THAT PROMISE SUCCESS.[3]

Garnet knew slaveholders were not going to give up slaveholding so easily. His strategy was to place the onus of violence on slaveholders. Promise slaveholders "renewed diligence" in the field, Garnet explained, but demand wages equivalent for the work. Slaveholders were heavily dependent upon slave labor. The large slave population attested to this. Slaves, then, should exploit their numbers and force masters to consider the portent of continued reliance on an unwilling and threatening labor force. "Remember you are three millions," Garnet repeated over and over again. If, as seemed likely, masters ignored slaves' demands, then "they, not you, will be responsible for the consequences."

Enslaved men and women should let their models be the American Revolutionaries whose maxim "LIBERTY OR DEATH" should combine with slaves' motto "RESISTANCE! RESISTANCE! RESISTANCE!" But, Garnet added, there were those who decried "physical resistance" in the "holy cause of Freedom." The convention was "among those who do not." If the enslaved began their own struggle for liberty and equality, the reform-minded international community would come to the aid of American slaves. "You can plead your own cause, and do the work of emancipation better than any others. The nations of the old world are moving in the great cause of universal freedom, and some of them at least, will ere long, do you justice." The time was ripe. If slaves wanted to be free in their lifetime, they needed to act now; there was not much hope of emancipation "without the shedding of blood."[4]

Certain that race played a major role in white abolitionists' rejection of slave insurrection, Garnet consistently urged black abolitionists to think independently. The widespread white American approval of armed struggle abroad, even among some abolitionists, provided sufficient evidence for him that whites had a double standard when considering militant black action. "If the scale was turned and black men were the masters, and white men the slaves, every destructive agent and element would be employed to lay the oppressor low."[5]

Garnet's plan to control delegate votes and set the tone at the beginning of the meeting almost worked. He nearly got convention endorsement for slave insurrection, but Ray and Beman allied again with Remond and Douglass in leading opposition against violent means. The antiviolence coalition succeeded in referring the address to a select committee commissioned to remove "objectionable points." Garnet strongly protested; he wanted the address adopted in its entirety. Trying to keep his address from being altered, Garnet took the floor for nearly an hour and a half, repeating much of what he and Davis had said the previous days. According to convention minutes, he brought the entire convention to tears and ended "amidst great applause," a testimony to his eloquence. Then, convention rules were suspended while Garnet and Douglass debated whether they as abolitionists should support slave violence.[6]

What is interesting about the debate is not so much that Garnet was finally defeated, but that a significant number of black abolitionists in the early 1840s supported violent means to end slavery. The resolution for violent means was defeated by only a small margin. Further, the debate shows that most reformers opposed violence not on principle, but for strategic reasons. Mainly they were afraid of losing white abolitionist allies. Garnet and other militants were convinced that "slave resistance" would generate the respect, sympathy, and aid of the international liberal community. Both groups, of course, agreed northern white public opinion was crucial.

Douglass complained that there was "too much physical force" in Garnet's "Address." If the address reached the slaves, Douglass argued, it would cause an insurrection and "we were called upon to avoid such a catastrophy." He urged the convention "to try moral means a little longer." Remond concurred in spite of the fact that only three years before he had exuberantly expressed support for violence while traveling in Britain. Buffalo delegate William Wells Brown, who had escaped from slavery in Kentucky nine years before, agreed with moral suasionists Remond and Douglass. Other abolitionists, particularly Ohio delegates, had more practical and immediate reasons for rejecting the Garnet motion. It would, according to A. M. Summers of Cincinnati, jeopardize the lives of free blacks in the slave states and those "who lived on the borders of the free states." On the other hand, other Ohioans supported Garnet, believing, as Walker had argued more than a decade earlier, that problems for black Americans could not get worse; it was time for drastic action.[7]

Actually, violent resistance was more in keeping with traditional northern black abolitionists' sentiment than moral suasion. Reformers considered the use of force morally justifiable. It was consistent with pride in their role as soldiers in the Revolution and, just as importantly, pride in the Haitian Revolution. While they found it expedient to write and speak discreetly about U.S. slave rebellions, they threw caution to the wind when considering slave rebellions outside the United States. The Haitian Revolution was as important to northern blacks as the American Revolution was to whites. Activists wrote about, talked about, and, it seems, dreamed about the Haitian Revolution.

By invoking the Haitian Revolution, northern black writers reminded whites of the potential threat of an American slave insurrection. Upset about

South Carolina legislation denying education to free blacks and restricting black employment, African Methodist Episcopal minister William Paul Quinn told slaveholders in an 1834 public address that the Haitian Revolution could be repeated in the United States. "I do not prophecy; I caution and warn; . . . I studiously avoid . . . the prophetical language of divinity. May the inhabitants of your, and the neighboring states, take . . . warning."[8]

In the early years of activism, northern blacks consistently praised Haiti as the second independent democratic nation in the Western Hemisphere and pointed to Haitian revolutionaries as proof that all humankind desired liberty. The violence exhibited in Haiti, according to reformers, was merely slaves resisting violent and savage oppressors. France's oppressive policies compelled revolutionaries on a course of self-defense. Moreover, Haiti was the only true republic because, unlike the United States, Haitians lived by their principles. "The Haitians have adopted the republican form of government; and so firmly is it established that in no country are the rights and privileges of citizens and foreigners more respected, and crimes less frequent. They are," John Russwurm told his fellow graduating seniors at Bowdoin College, "a brave generous people."[9]

After the late 1820s, though, Haiti presented problems. The evangelical, reform-minded Protestant majority believed Haitian "papists" were in need of Christianization. But Catholicism was not the main problem; Haiti's political-economic instability made it difficult for reformers to point to the young nation as a model of republicanism from which to censure the United States. Despite Haiti's limitations, the country still provided evidence of universal and innate desire for freedom. As Frederick Douglass would write later, Haiti first proved "that the colored man is capable of . . . patriotism, that he can and will hazard safety and life itself for the sacred cause of country and freedom."[10]

More than anything else, Haiti countered the persistent racist propaganda that African Americans were "naturally" docile and dependent, that black men were less than men. Antebellum American nationalism concurrent with racial and gender ideology created a virtue out of war, conquest, and aggression that confirmed white masculinity as being almost synonymous with the new language of "Anglo-Saxonism." Thus, to many whites, the inferior political-economic status of black men was evidence of their lack of "manliness." In Quinn's 1834 pamphlet to American slaveholders, he explained that blacks were replete with the variety of human qualities, from kindness to hatred and revenge. "That the Africans are as capable of gratitude and revenge as any

other people in the world, does not admit of a dispute; and that they have
more political information than any of their colour in the West Indies might
easily be demonstrated. . . . The fate of St. Domingo is fresh in all their minds,
as well as in all our memories."[11] Boston dentist, lawyer, and physician John
Rock explained to a Boston audience commemorating the Boston Massacre in
1858 that despite white Americans' assertions that black people were enslaved
because they lacked the courage of "the Indians or the white man," Haiti
proved otherwise. "The black man is not a coward. The history of the bloody
struggles for freedom in Haiti, in which the blacks whipped the French and
the English and gained their independence . . . will be a lasting refutation of
the malicious aspersions of our enemies."[12]

Increasingly, black men proved their masculinity by countering stereotypes
of docility and puerility through asserting violent action. Lacking typical
human responses, black men, within the racial ideological paradigm, toler-
ated the most inhuman treatment without response even when their lives
and those of their wives and daughters were at stake or when the latter were
victims of rape. Apparently subscribing to the notion of slave men's docility
but rejecting that it was inherent, militants like Garnet and Walker told slave
men to disprove such racial theories by defending their wives and children
from licentious slaveholders. In language similar to Walker's, Garnet pleaded
with slave husbands and fathers to give evidence of manhood. "You act as
though you were made for the special use of these devils. You act as though
your daughters were born to pamper the lusts of your masters and overseers.
And worse than all, you tamely submit while your lords tear your wives from
your embraces, and defile them before your eyes. In the name of God we ask,
are you men?"[13]

Reduced to feminine (or dependent) status in political and economic affairs, northern black men consistently pointed to evidence of black masculinity. Slave narratives served as a supplement for the Haitian Revolution in this
regard. Douglass's *Narrative*, published in 1845, countered notions of black
male effeminacy in critical ways while graphically portraying the brutality of
American slavery. Douglass broadened the ideal American masculine type to
include black men who used brain and brawn when encountering danger.
Unwilling to be beaten by slave breaker Edward Covey, Douglass's resistance
established his "manhood." The struggle was a battle—a war that began when
he learned to read. When he explained that "the battle revived within me a
sense of my own manhood," Douglass was referring to a universal sense of

humanness, specifically African American humanity, and black male masculinity.[14]

Without doubt, reformers' acceptance of violence as a means to end slavery
was in keeping with antebellum American culture. Violence in various forms
was becoming one of the defining characteristics of antebellum American life.
The Jacksonian age stressed rugged individualism, independence, and self-
reliance, which were often translated into personal physical conflicts and mob
riots, usually against blacks, in the cities. As early as 1837 Abraham Lincoln
expressed dismay that violence was overtaking the country. Mob rule "in lieu
of the sober judgment of the courts" was quickly becoming commonplace.
Multiple riots in Philadelphia and New York City contributed to the profes-
sionalization of the American police system in the 1850s.[15]

Consistently faced with mob attacks, northern blacks resorted to arms to
defend their homes and families throughout the wave of antiblack riots. They
also established Committees of Vigilance in the 1830s to protect themselves
from kidnappers who sold free blacks into slavery. Certain that God was
on their side, vigilance committees, also designed to shield slave runaways
from the fugitive slave laws, were not always peaceful. In 1833, for instance,
a Detroit group assaulted a local sheriff for detaining accused fugitives. And
when a black person helped catch a fugitive slave, he was subjected to what
were called "trials," resulting in punishments that included whippings and
ostracism from black communities. Garnet, then a prominent minister, was
involved in an Ohio "trial" of a black slave catcher in the 1850s.[16] Garnet's
actions were consistent with reformers' willingness to use force in earlier
decades. Northern blacks invoked Christian principles in this area as in all
others. God sanctioned harboring fugitives and defending oneself or others
from enslavement. Reformers never entertained the notion that theirs was not
a holy cause. The religious was the militant/political.

Thus support for nonviolence was more a matter of strategy for most black
evangelical reformers than a firm commitment to nonviolence or "moral
suasion." Responding to tremendous condemnation of slave violence after
Walker's APPEAL and Nat Turner's revolt, black abolitionists assured potential
white abolitionist allies and others that they supported only "legal means" to
end slavery. At the same time, abolitionists consistently lauded the Haitian
Revolution.

Black abolitionists were especially careful about public support for violent action because William Lloyd Garrison, arguably the strongest advocate

for abolition and equal rights among white abolitionists, became a pacifist extremist in the late 1830s. He eventually condemned all violence on the basis of Christian principles and organized the Non-Resistance Society, which opposed all human governments because they were founded in force. Governments, according to nonresistants, were "Anti-Christ" and maintained solely by military power. Christians were not authorized "to combine together in order to lacerate, sue, imprison, or hang their enemies, nor as individuals to resort to physical force to break down the heart of an adversary." Several white abolitionists, including Quaker Angelina Grimké, were peace extremists along with Garrison.[17] Publicly, then, most black abolitionists supported moral suasion in the 1830s and 1840s.

In the late 1830s and early 1840s, antebellum slave revolts challenged all abolitionists' nonviolent principles and encouraged many black abolitionists to sanction slave rebellion publicly. The *Amistad* incident in 1839, in which fifty-three slaves revolted on a Spanish schooner, ending up on the northeastern coastline, created the paradox of antiviolent abolitionists raising funds for the rebels' legal defense. The *Amistad* captives, several abolitionists argued, had simply exercised their "right of self-defense." The same was true for the American slaves who revolted on the *Creole* in 1841 and entered British waters near the Bahaman Islands. Additionally, the spread of slavery into Texas and the West added to the idea that dependence on moral suasion alone was ineffective.

Still, up to 1848, at least publicly, many black abolitionists remained committed to nonviolence, hoping the abolition movement would succeed in influencing the nation to end slavery either through moral suasion or the political process. The majority of delegates at national conventions persistently rejected violent means throughout the 1840s. Largely under the influence of Frederick Douglass, the 1847 convention in Troy, New York, appointed a committee to determine the best means to abolish slavery. The committee's report, written by Douglass, was really the same response he made to Garnet's 1843 address at the Buffalo National Convention. The most effective way to end slavery, according to Douglass, was "a faithful, earnest and persevering enforcement of the great principles of justice and morality, religion and humanity." Several delegates, including Garnet, objected to Douglass's exclusion of other means, especially political action. The 1847 convention adopted nonviolent resolutions and voted to address slaveholders, not slaves, at the next year's convention. Douglass's influence in black evangelical reform had grown.

However, Garnet and other militants who attended the 1847 and 1848 conventions persisted. Unable to gain convention endorsement for slave insurrection, they tried to push through endorsement for military training of northern black men. Denied admission to the army and state militias, black men, according to militant convention delegates, needed "to use every means in their power to obtain that science, so as to enable them to measure arms with assailants *without* and invaders within." At the 1848 convention, the motion was postponed "indefinitely."[18]

Garnet tried another strategic move; he advocated distributing Bibles to slaves. Believing as Nat Turner and most black evangelicals did that the Bible was a revolutionary text, Garnet tried to get support for his idea. Douglass thought the idea was ludicrous; slaveholders would never allow it. But Garnet, Henry Bibb, and Samuel R. Ward (all fugitives, like Douglass) thought the idea had merit. Debating this and several other issues before black abolitionists' societies in the late 1840s, these men argued that Bible distribution among slaves was a Christian duty. But again, the duty was not limited to evangelism; like Walker and others advocating insurrection, they believed the Scriptures supported slave rebellion. Garnet had drawn from the Bible to support the slave's duty to "resist." He may also have planned to surreptitiously slip in his "Address" encouraging slaves to resist their enslavement, as Walker had done two decades earlier with his *APPEAL*. He was trying to get the American Bible Society, a mostly white organization, to change its opposition to his plan. Reportedly, the institution was reconsidering.[19]

Slave revolts, and the growing sentiment among black abolitionists that too many white abolitionists promoted a double standard in praising revolutions in Europe while demanding nonviolent means at home, contributed to reformers' general acceptance of violent means by 1850. As more and more abolitionists embraced political means, they and others were beginning to imagine slave insurrection as the only legitimate way to end slavery. When several white abolitionists became more ambivalent about how to get rid of the dreaded system and when the broader public, particularly slaveholders, supported international armed struggles, a growing number boldly advocated slave insurrection.[20] A passionate and gendered editorial in the *Ram's Horn*, a short-lived newspaper published by New York City black businessmen Willis A. Hodges and Thomas Van Rensellaer in the late 1840s, sarcastically advised slaves to resist. "Slaves of the South, Now Is Your Time! Strike for your freedom *now*, at the suggestion of your enslavers. . . . What have you to gain by procrastination in a manly struggle for liberty? . . . God is with you for liberty . . . . Men will respect you in proportion to the physical efforts you put forth in resisting tyranny and slavery."[21] Likewise, delegates to the 1849 conventions of Maine and New Hampshire debated whether it was northern blacks' duty to support a slave revolt if one occurred, and delegates at the 1849 Ohio state convention voted to distribute five hundred copies of Walker's *APPEAL* and Garnet's "Address."[22]

Things had definitely changed by the end of the decade. Former moral suasionists, even Douglass, advocated violence. Influenced by Garnet and other militants' assertion of a white double standard and free of Garrison's imposing influence, Douglass wanted to know why it was appropriate for oppressed Europeans to engage in armed struggle for freedom and not American slaves. When he spoke in the popular abolitionists' meeting place Faneuil Hall, Douglass told the Boston audience in 1849 that he would "welcome the intelligence tomorrow, should it come, that the slaves had risen in the South, and . . . were engaged in spreading death and devastation there." The South was in a state of war; slaveholders were waging war on the "oppressed." When many in the audience jeered, Douglass argued that slaves had as much right to resist their oppression as the oppressed in France. "Why you welcomed the intelligence from France, that Louis Philippe had been barricaded in Paris . . . you . . . joined heartily in the watchword of 'Liberty, Equality, Fraternity'—and should you not hail, with equal pleasure, the tidings from the South that the slaves had risen, and achieved for himself, against the iron-hearted slaveholder, what the republicans of France achieved against the royalists of France?"[23]

Political events of the 1850s contributed even more to the ambivalence of many white abolitionists about nonviolent principles and created nearly unanimous black support for slave rebellion. Indeed, the Fugitive Slave Law stimulated black consensus as never before. Passed in September of 1850, the law weighed so heavily in favor of slave catchers that abolitionists believed all northern blacks were threatened. Slaveholders, presenting an affidavit before federal commissioners, could claim a black person as their slave without trial for the accused or any provision for testimony on her/his behalf. Additionally, commissioners appeared to be rewarded if they decided in favor of the slaveholder; they received a $10 fee if they ruled the prisoner a slave but only $5 if they determined the prisoner was free.[24]

Northern black response to the Fugitive Slave Law was swift and militant. A late summer 1850 convention of fugitive slaves in central New York—

Frederick Douglass was elected president—proclaimed the inevitability of a slave revolt, encouraged slaves to escape, promising aid in the venture, and pledged northern black armed support if slaves chose to revolt. "When the insurrection of the Southern slaves shall take place, as take place it will unless speedily prevented by voluntary emancipation, the great majority of the colored men of the North . . . will be found by your side, with deep stored and long-accumulated revenge in their heart, and with death-dealing weapons in their hands." In their "Letter to the American Slaves from those who have fled from American Slavery," delegates, sounding like Garnet only seven years earlier, added that slaves were as justified as were the American Revolutionaries in "making blood to flow even unto the horse-bridles."[25]

Others, fugitives and nonfugitives, were less vitriolic but clearly as militant and evangelical as those attending the fugitives' convention. Several argued that a resort to violence was founded in Christian and republican principles. Indeed, resistance, including armed rebellion, became a Christian duty. Individual and collective armed defense became an imperative for all black Americans, North and South, free and slave. Soon after the Fugitive Slave Law passed in Congress, a mass meeting in Springfield, Massachusetts, declared "resistance to tyrants is obedience to God." In October 1850, New York Presbyterian minister Samuel Ringgold Ward (a cousin of Henry Highland Garnet) declared war on slave hunters and kidnappers. Referring to armed resistance, Ward urged blacks to practice "the natural and inalienable right of self-defence—self-protection" in an editorial in his short-lived newspaper *The Impartial Citizen*. Ward implied that the republic was threatened by the new law. All free blacks in America, according to Ward, should "teach Southern slavecrats, and Northern doughfaces, that to perpetuate the Union, they must beware how they expose *us* to slavery, and themselves to death and destruction, present and future, temporal and eternal!" Delegates, including Amos Beman, at the 1851 New York State Convention resolved: "That the fugitive slave law is the law of tyrants. . . . That disobedience to tyrants is obedience to God. . . . That we will obey God."[26]

Northern black militancy was no longer simply rhetorical or strategic. Committees of Vigilance expanded in the 1850s to take care of the added southern threat under the new law. Several white abolitionists contributed significant funds to these committees, and the Vigilant Committees, the Underground Railroad, and other organizations, along with private individuals effectively kept several alleged fugitives from bondage. Some of the rescuers

were armed. William Whipper was especially active in financially supporting
and hiding fugitive slaves, risking his Pennsylvania lumber business to aid
their flight to Canada. A few rescue campaigns were successful. Even though
the most famous, that of Anthony Burns, ended with the fugitive's reenslavement out of Boston, Ohio schoolteacher Charles Langston, lawyer John Mercer Langston's brother, led several black men and Oberlin College students
in the successful rescue of a fugitive slave whom they spirited off to Canada.
Black abolitionists insisted that violent resistance was sanctioned by the Bible.
Keeping within black evangelical principles, John Langston characterized the
rescue of fugitive slaves as a holy crusade, a Christian republican action.[27]
Hundreds of fugitives escaped to Canada in this decade.[28]

In contrast to pronouncements of "peaceful and legal means" in the 1830s,
carrying arms, gaining military training, and advocating slave rebellion became
prominent public resolves among black reformers in the 1850s. Sixty-five black
American men petitioned the Massachusetts Legislative Committee on the
Militia for the creation of an all black Independent Military Company in 1853.
Their reasoning for a separate company was based on their exclusion from
the General Militia and the fact that a grant was recently given to a "company
of white citizens." Also, they deserved their right to form a militia company
as men who were "law-abiding, tax-paying, liberty-loving, NATIVE-BORN,
AMERICAN CITIZENS" and descendants of Revolutionary War soldiers. "We
are men, and we wish to be treated as men."[29]

Black unity nearly came to fruition in the last decade before the Civil War,
a goal almost all reformers believed essential for effective change. By then
most, including William Whipper and Frederick Douglass, accepted the idea
of separate institutions strategically, as a means to achieve equality and the
abolition of slavery. They also embraced political action. Most reformers by
then agreed, too, that the Constitution was an antislavery document. Signal-
ing that Garrison had lost significant influence by the 1850s among the vast
majority of black abolitionists, delegates at the 1855 National Convention held
in Philadelphia voted to adopt "An Address to the People of the United States,"
prepared by New York City physician James McCune Smith. The "Address"
outlined African American rights under the Constitution. Blacks were held in
slavery "in violation of the Constitution" and Congress had the power under
the Constitution to abolish slavery in the slave states under the Constitution's
general welfare clause. Slavery "inhibits, obstructs and threatens to destroy the
'general welfare' and is therefore an institution which Congress is competent

and in duty bound, to abolish everywhere where it may cause such obstruction." Frederick Douglass motioned to adopt the address. Charles Remond and Robert Purvis were in the minority, holding to the Garrisonian belief that the Constitution was proslavery.[30]

Having broken away from the Garrisonians in the late 1840s and thinking more independently generally, Douglass became intensely involved in northern black evangelical reform in the next decade. Beginning with the publication of his newspaper *The North Star,* coedited at times with Martin Delany and with James McCune Smith contributing many articles, Douglass embraced the efficacy of separate action for achieving collective goals. He attempted to establish a National League of Colored People in 1849 and he, along with Smith, successfully organized the National Council of Colored People at the National Convention in 1853. The goals and means of both organizations were similar to those of the 1830 and 1831 national conventions, abolition, equal rights, and community development, which in these later years stressed even more the necessity of blacks' access to education. Also in the late 1840s and 1850s, William Whipper became active in black conventions. Before this latter decade Whipper persisted in his denunciation of distinct terms of identity and may have influenced the 1848 black Pennsylvania State Convention to avoid a distinct name for the political organization created to obtain "for the colored people of Pennsylvania all the Rights and Immunities of Citizenship." The Citizens' Union of the Commonwealth of Pennsylvania welcomed all concerned persons over eighteen years of age.[31]

In spite of the more militant and vociferous activity, reformers in the 1840s and early 1850s remained optimistic about forthcoming inevitable change through their hard work. They were still committed to American principles and American nationality, despite the continuing debates over distinct terms of identity. Viewing violence through the prism of black evangelicalism, support for slave rebellion was not support for anarchy. Northern black editors, teachers, lawyers, and others invoked republican Christian principles in their appeals to slaves. They, not most whites, were expressing true "republicanism." They were the true Americans. Rather than a desire to overthrow the government, northern blacks who participated in the movement to end slavery and gain equal rights indicated determination to be an integral part of the nation they called their own. As evangelical reformers, their goal was to make the United States better; they expected white America to practice the Christian Revolutionary principles it claimed to hold dear.

The Dred Scott decision, which denied that free blacks had rights, and then John Brown's failed plans in his raid at Harper's Ferry stimulated even more support for violent means. Douglass and James McCune Smith apparently endorsed supporting slave insurrections as part of the Radical Abolitionist party agenda. Others, like John Rock, expressed support for violence as a badge of honor. In an 1859 speech, Rock praised peaceful and violent means. He was unsure in 1859 if slavery would end peaceably or violently, but he was certain that abolition would win. "Our cause is a cause of God and cannot be overthrown."[32] Perhaps African American insurgent John A. Copeland Jr. best summarized reformers' evangelical belief that violence was part of God's plan to eradicate the evil of slavery. In his letter to his parents before being executed on December 16, 1859, for fighting alongside John Brown at Harper's Ferry, Copeland assured his parents that he was dying for a cause larger than one man. "Dear Parents, my fate so far as man can seal it, is sealed, but let not this fact occasion you any misery; for remember the *cause* in which I was engaged; *remember it was a holy cause*, one in which men in every way better than I am, have suffered & died."[33]

In a December 1860 speech on John Brown at Tremont Temple in Boston, Douglass explained at length why moral suasion was unrealistic. He argued that most white Americans had become oblivious to the principles of "justice and liberty." There was nothing left, he explained, but to make slaveholders fear for their lives, and slaves were the ones to do this. They "must make these slaveholders feel that there is something uncomfortable about slavery—must make them feel that it is not so pleasant, after all, to go to bed with bowie-knives, and revolvers, and pistols, as they must." Douglass reminded his audience that he believed in "agitation," but it had not made "slaveholders feel the injustice of their course." While the "hope of a general insurrection" was in vain, Douglass thought that slaveholders needed to be constantly reminded by multiple slave uprisings throughout the South and constant slave escapes that slavery was a constant threat to them and their families. "We must make him feel that there is death in the air about him, that there is death in the pot before him, that there is death all around him. . . . We need not only to appeal to the moral sense of these slaveholders; we have need, and a right, to appeal to their fears."[34] Moral means were good but not enough. Their cause, whether through moral or violent methods, was in the right.

Black evangelicalism had hardly changed since the early years of more aggressive abolitionism. Even though they now advocated political and violent means, reformers consistently committed themselves to the idea of national transformation. They would persist in playing the role of catalysts moving the republic toward God's plans for the nation and for the world. As Christians and as Americans, they could do nothing less.

While the majority expressed optimism about the nation's eventual transformation in the early to mid-1850s, a growing activist minority became increasingly pessimistic about the future of African Americans in the United States. Slowly and steadily many African Americans living in the North considered emigration a viable alternative. Besides the 1850 Fugitive Slave Law that imperiled the status of all free blacks, the Kansas-Nebraska Act, passed in May 1854, repealed the 1820 Missouri Compromise that had limited slavery to the 36°30' parallel. Through "popular sovereignty," the new law provided that settlers in the Kansas and Nebraska territories could decide whether the new states created would be slave or free. The Dred Scott decision, arguing the constitutional right of slavery expansion into western territories and definitively excluding free blacks from the provisions of the Declaration of Independence and Constitution, signaled to many the necessity for considering an alternate homeland. When the Constitution was adopted, Chief Justice Roger Taney said that people of African ancestry in the new republic were "regarded as beings of an inferior order . . . so far inferior, that they had no rights which the white man was bound to respect."[35] Effectively placing African American status on the same level, legally, as domestic animals, the Supreme Court's decision dealt a harsh blow to optimistic and patriotic northern black evangelical Christians.

But the idea of emigration was one thing; the support for emigrating outside the United States was fraught with ideological complications. The American Colonization Society linked emigration with the theory of innate black inferiority. From the inception of the organization in 1816, black reformers consistently distinguished between emigration as one of several alternatives available to all Americans, including black Americans, and colonizationists' free black removal policy. Newspaper editors informed black readers of the advantages and disadvantages of living in places like Canada, Haiti, and other places in the Caribbean. They also consistently challenged colonizationists' notion that blacks could never become equal members of American society.[36]

The problem for anti-emigrationists was that a free black minority in the North and Upper South continued to emigrate to islands in the Caribbean, Canada, and Liberia, the American Colonization Society's colony. Of course, reformers always understood that slaves would choose Liberia over bondage, but most publicly condemned free black emigration to Liberia and elsewhere even as they argued that blacks had a right to emigrate as individuals wherever they chose. In his editorial for the *Colored American* in 1840, editor Charles Ray explained to northern blacks considering Trinidad or British Guiana as a place of refuge that Caribbean planters were recruiting black Americans because newly freed slaves were unwilling to accept near slave wages. Emigrants would work in the fields for wages so low that economic independence would remain a dream. If emigrants believed they could do no better in the North, Ray editorialized, then they should go. A few months later, though, he insisted that all free blacks remain in the United States.[37] Several Philadelphia women weighed in on the question of emigration in the pages of the *Liberator* after an article published in that paper by "A Colored Female" advocated emigration to Mexico. The United States, according to one writer who was most likely a member of the elite Female Literary Association of Philadelphia, was her home. No other country offered such advantages.[38]

Even more disturbing to anti-emigrationists was that ordinary free blacks were not the only ones supporting emigration. Now several prominent reformers advocated emigration outside the United States. Their numbers grew in the 1840s and 1850s. Emigrationists were influenced mainly by increasingly repressive racist policies, nationally and locally, and the inability of blacks to compete for jobs with the large European immigrant population crowding into the cities. Immigrants, mainly Irish, competed with urban blacks for menial jobs that blacks had held during slavery and after. According to John Rock, a Catholic priest advised immigrants to do any job no matter how degrading "and do it for less than they [American-born blacks and whites] can afford to do it. . . . The Irish adopted this plan; they lived on less than the Americans could live upon, and worked for less, and the result is that nearly all the menial employments are monopolized by the Irish, who now get as good prices as anybody."[39]

In January 1849, Garnet, energized like other reformers by the successful black farming settlements in Ohio and Indiana, repeated the admonition that northern blacks should move to the countryside rather than congregate in cities, where economic opportunities were negligible. He added, though, that urging migration to the country was too restrictive; blacks should migrate to U.S. territories so that they might influence territorial policy. They should not feel, however, restricted to North America. Emigration had ever proven successful in improving the status of mankind, and blacks should seize these same opportunities for socioeconomic betterment. Garnet then distanced himself even farther outside the anticolonization black evangelical reformer majority camp in suggesting Liberia as a viable alternative now that it was independent in spite of disagreements with colonizationists. In a letter to the editor of *The North Star*, Garnet explained his new position to Douglass and his readership. "I hesitate not to say, that my mind, of late, has greatly changed in regard to the American Colonization scheme. So far as it benefits the land of my fathers, I bid it Godspeed, but so far as it denies the possibilities of our elevation here, I oppose it. I would rather see a man free in Liberia, than a slave in the United States."[40]

Increasingly, emigrationist activists departed from black evangelical ideals. Rather than persist in their vision for national transformation, America's becoming a model of Christian republicanism in which freedom, equality, and justice reigned, emigrationists began viewing the United States as hopelessly corrupted by slavery and racial prejudice.

At the Ohio 1849 State Convention, attorney John Mercer Langston declared, "I for one, sir, am willing, dearly as I love my native land (a land which will not protect me however,) to leave it, and go wherever I can be free. We have already drank too long the cup of bitterness and woe, and do [we] gentlemen want to drink it any longer?"[41]

In 1850 Garnet left for England and, after a lengthy speaking tour in which he helped increase the membership of the abolitionist movement and free produce movement in Britain, became a missionary for the United Presbyterian Church in Jamaica.[42] In his absence emigrationism grew more vocal and influential, especially when physician/editor Martin Robison Delany became one of the main leaders of the movement.

Delany's emigrationism, it seems, was as much influenced by personal experience as with the passage of the Fugitive Slave Law and intensified racism. As a reformer, Delany was fully committed to living in the United States before the 1850s. Born in Charlestown, Virginia, in 1812, the son of a free mother and slave father, Delany grew up in Chambersburg, Pennsylvania, and later moved to Pittsburgh at age nineteen, where he attended black abolitionist and AME cleric Lewis Woodson's African Educational Society School. After he apprenticed to a local physician for three years, Delany practiced medicine. From 1843 to 1848, Delany edited and published a newspaper, the *Mystery*, an antislavery journal that also addressed local issues of concern to the Pittsburgh African American community. He gave up ownership of the paper due to financial problems and worked with Frederick Douglass on the newly established *North Star* in the late 1840s. Delany believed strongly that personal striving, involving hard work, frugality, and sobriety, would help remove economic, political, and social barriers against African Americans in the North. These virtues, combined with persistent agitation, would culminate in the exercise of the rights of American citizenship for black Americans.[43]

Delany, never as strong an evangelical reformer as other abolitionists, remained committed to these ideals until he found it impossible to contend any longer with northern racism. When he had finally achieved his goal to attend Harvard Medical School, Delany quickly learned that though he had become the model American, living up to its purported ideals of industry, frugality, sobriety, and Christianity, his status as a black person mattered far more than anything else. In the wake of student pressure, the dean asked Delany to leave the program. It was this experience, it seems, that pushed Delany over the edge. Delany decided emigration was the only viable solution for the black struggle. Soon after his forced departure from Harvard, Delany attended a Toronto emigration convention that admonished free blacks to emigrate to Canada. And though he was part of a delegation that disapproved of the convention's emigrationist resolution, within a year he had worked out a much stronger emigrationist position that involved a complex analysis of the role of race and class in human societies.

In the early 1850s, Delany rejected the assertion of a dual Colored American identity and instead stressed African identity. In 1852 he published *The Condition, Elevation, Emigration and Destiny of the Colored People of the United States Politically Considered* with themes that signaled a clear departure from northern black political evangelical thought. Rather than base his principles in the Bible that supported liberty and equality, he relied on history and an incipient political theory for understanding the future of people of color in the United States. According to Delany, social-political equality was impossible. History demonstrated that every society had a well-defined class structure, especially those "laying the greatest claim to civilization and enlightenment." Because these societies considered themselves enlightened, inequality was justified on the basis of group or racial inferiority. If the subordinate class had physical or cultural characteristics distinguishing them from the "ruling class," it was easier to relegate them to an inferior status.

This, Delany explained, was the situation in the United States. The American republic was founded in freedom and equality for whites only. The Fugitive Slave Law was just the prelude to a more definitive national policy of white control. Delany wrote in his book and repeatedly told black audiences in the early 1850s that the Fugitive Slave Law was essential for preserving the American political economic system. It was to be expected. Sounding more like early twenty-first-century American political theorists who argue that race/racism was central to founding principles, Delany asserted that the inequalities within American political structure were systemic, the basis of national organization. They would not change. Black Americans must recognize that subordinate black status, slave and free, was intrinsic to the viability of white American society. Truly the first and most notable American black nationalist, Delany explained, "we are slaves in the midst of freedom." To succeed, blacks must create their own nation or help develop a black nation already in existence in Central America or the Caribbean.[44]

Although the most prominent then and now, Delany's nationalistic ideas were not original. Others leaned in this direction in the 1830s, and the 1849 and 1852 Ohio Convention emigration committee reports had included support for Black Nationalism. Committee members suggested "voluntary emigration" to an area on the North American continent where black Americans could establish a separate nation. They advised that a national convention consider the subject and appoint an agent to scout out "the most suitable point for the settlement of our people." One emigrationist at the 1849 Ohio Convention argued that "we must have [a] nationality. I am for going any where, so we can be an independent people."[45]

In August 1853, Delany called for a National Emigration Convention to plan black emigration within the Western Hemisphere. Predictably, activists engaged in bitter debate. The controversy was similar to the problem of publicly supporting slave rebellion: were blacks going to think independently of whites, emigrationists asked, or were they always going to limit policies in reaction to white behavior and law. Also not surprising, diverse opinions among emigrationists developed. Mainly they could not agree upon a destination and almost all rejected West Africa, at first.

Northern freeborn Mary Ann Shadd became one of the strongest proponents of black emigration to Canada. Shadd, born in 1823 to an African-European Delaware family of artisans and property holders who had been free long before the Revolution, was the daughter of abolitionist shoemaker Abraham Shadd, one of the founders of the national convention movement in the 1830s.

Like many middle-class girls, Mary Ann gained an education through private tutors, which prepared her for a career in teaching. She taught in black schools in Delaware, New Jersey, Pennsylvania, and New York City. After attending the Toronto Anti-Slavery Convention in 1851 where emigrationist fugitive slave Henry Bibb and James T. Holly explained the virtues of Canadian emigration, twenty-eight-year-old Shadd moved to a small black community in Windsor, Canada West, located near the Detroit River, across the Michigan border. There she opened a school for children consisting mostly of fugitive slaves. Shadd quickly became the leading and most vociferous advocate of black emigration to Canada. Nine months after arriving in her adopted country, she published *A Plea for Emigration: or Notes of Canada West in its Moral, Social, and Political Aspect with Suggestions Respecting Mexico, W. Indies and Vancouver Island for the Information of Colored Emigrants* to encourage Canadian emigration and provide information about Canadian society, climate, topography, geography, and job opportunities for potential emigrants. Referring to the 1850 Fugitive Slave Law, Shadd noted that life in the United States for blacks was increasingly precarious and the American Colonization Society "in the garb of Christianity and Philanthropy" was making life harder.

Africa, according to Shadd, remained a disease-ridden place, and since neither a home in Africa nor the United States was beneficial, blacks in America should know as much as possible about Canada. Canada had plenty of land and a high demand for labor. Blacks and whites were equal, she noted, there was no degraded class. A person's work was judged on merit, not skin color, and the climate was "the most desirable known in so high a latitude, for emigrants generally, and colored people particularly." Entrepreneurial possibilities were limited only by the emigrant's imagination and pocketbook. Shadd admitted that blacks confronted some prejudice and bigotry in Canada, but argued it was much more suitable than "scampering from state to state, in a vain endeavor to gather the crumbs of freedom that a proslavery [broom] might sweep away at any moment."[46]

When she became founder and editor of the *Provincial Freeman* in March 1853 with Samuel Ringgold Ward, Shadd's emigrationist message had a forum. The *Provincial Freeman* was really Shadd's newspaper from the beginning. She turned it into a regularly published weekly, becoming the first African American woman newspaper editor. Shadd, similar to Maria Stewart of an earlier generation, wrote and spoke forcefully, unhesitatingly criticizing Canadian blacks for segregating themselves in separate institutions. She condemned sympathetic white Americans for sending their cast-off goods to Canadian fugitives while congratulating themselves on their selflessness. Shadd also lectured widely on the benefits of Canadian emigration in Pennsylvania and other northern states, distributing her *Notes of Canada West* throughout her travels. Not surprisingly, also like Maria Stewart, Shadd, who married Toronto businessman Thomas J. Cary in 1856, offended many black male activists' masculine sensibilities in her excoriating statements about the inadequacies of black male leadership.[47]

At first, Delany disagreed with Shadd's promotion of Canadian emigration because he thought, as did many Americans, that Canada would eventually become part of the United States. At the same time, Shadd rejected Delany's Black Nationalism. She and several black Canadian immigrants believed blacks should, as British subjects, become integrated into Canadian society, not form separate institutions and settlements. In 1856 Delany moved to Canada and remained active in the emigration movement, using his new residence in Chatham, Canada, as headquarters for his nationalist program. Anti-emigrationist reformers were appalled by Delany's new views, but even more so by his reasons. His public assertion that blacks would never achieve parity in the United States was the same propaganda of colonizationists. Delany was not only challenging northern black American identity, he was rejecting their evangelical vision of a true American republic.[48]

While Shadd, Delany, and others were advocating Canada, interest in Haiti grew in spite of the aborted plans of the early 1820s. Episcopalian priest James Theodore Holly became the prime mover behind support for Haitian emigration. Growing up in Washington, D.C., the son of a free black shoemaker, Holly lived and worked in New York as a clerk in the New York American Missionary Association offices and later in Vermont, operating a boot making business with his brother. As a young man, Holly, a baptized Catholic, first expressed interest in emigrating to Liberia, but when the American Colonization Society rejected his request for getting medical training before settling in West Africa, he turned to Canada. By the mid-1850s, Holly had shifted focus again, this time to Haiti. Haiti offered citizenship and full equality to black Americans, according to Holly. Blacks in America would never gain political and economic rights in the United States. After having converted to the Episcopalian faith, Holly then added religious motives to political-economic reasons for northern black emigration to the new republic. He argued that free black Protestants would help evangelize Catholic Haiti. With or without the blessing of organizations, several free blacks interested in leaving the East and Midwest simply emigrated individually or in groups to places as far as Kansas, California, and even Australia in the mid- to late 1850s. Philadelphian George Goines and several other northern blacks emigrated together, for example, to work in the gold mines of Australia.[49]

At the 1856 emigration convention, Holly's religious/political-economic agenda for free black emigration to Haiti dominated debate. But within two years, Delany and Henry Highland Garnet had turned their sights toward Africa. National Emigration Conventions in language and word had assiduously separated their project from that of the American Colonization Society. The 1853 "Call for a National Emigration Convention of Colored Men" distinguished between black emigration and colonization; the difference was Africa. "No person will be admitted to a seat to the Convention, who would introduce the subject of emigration to the Eastern Hemisphere . . . either to Asia, Africa, or Europe—as our object and determination is to consider our claims to the West Indies, Central and South America, and the Canadas." When Delany and Garnet, who had returned to the United States in 1856, came out publicly in favor of emigration to West Africa, Frederick Douglass and other reformers were outraged.

But Africa beckoned. Delany and others had become interested in West Africa through the writings of English traveler David Livingstone and Thomas J. Bowen, a Southern Baptist missionary to Yoruba. While Holly was still organizing his Haitian program, Delany began coordinating plans for an expedition to the West African interior and Garnet helped establish the African Civilization Society, an organization committed to the "civilization and christianization of Africa." No longer keeping their distance from the American Colonization Society by urging emigration anywhere but Africa, both Delany and Garnet raised funds for free black emigration to some part of West Africa. To make matters worse, in the minds of anti-emigrationists, part of the funds that supported Garnet's African Civilization Society came from the American Colonization Society.[50]

Although emigrationists' disagreements over destinations continued, they eventually agreed more than they disagreed. Mainly, they all rejected the optimism of reformers who were still convinced that abolition of slavery and equal rights for African Americans were forthcoming in the United States. Most emigrationists were willing to give up their American identity and seek a black nationality outside the United States. They believed that blacks must have primary control over their own political and economic development, either as part of another black nation, like Haiti, or as a separate and distinct nation of American exiles. Even Mary Ann Shadd Cary, who remained committed to Canada, eventually supported limited emigration to Africa, and her father and brother Isaac were on the General Board of Commissioners for Delany's Niger Valley exploration in 1859.[51]

Even so, while most emigrationists were willing to give up their claims to an American national identity, they retained their commitment to evangelical Protestantism and American republican principles. Believing American religious, economic, and political ideals were superior, they would transplant their republican Protestant American ethos, or as Garnet explained, a "Christian nationality," to their new country. American evangelicalism would spread to other parts of the world via northern black emigration and settlement. The African Civilization Society's constitution reveals the evangelistic goal of its membership. "[W]e can no longer mistake the intention of the Divine Mind towards Africa. It is evident that the prophecy that 'Ethiopia shall soon stretch out her hands unto God,' is on the point of fulfillment, and that the work, when commenced, shall be 'soon' accomplished. . . . In order, therefore, to aid in this great work, and promote the civilization and Christianization of Africa . . . we have formed ourselves into an Association."[52]

Likewise, Delany's project of black emigration to a purchased territory in West Africa involved a mixture of political, religious, and economic motivations. In his report on his West African travels from May 1859 to April 1860, Delany explained his goal for establishing a black American nation in West Africa: "I had but one object in view—the Moral, Social, and Political Elevation of Ourselves, and the Regeneration of Africa."[53] Delany's plan involved not mass black emigration but a "select and intelligent people of high moral as well as religious character" to create a nation with a thriving economy and republican government that would civilize and Christianize the native populations.

Although political and economic interests were primary in Delany's West African project, religion was still a part. White missionaries, Delany believed, had taken the "gospel" to Africans but because of prejudice had little or no expectations that Africans could create political and economic systems that rivaled Europe or America. It was time for them to go. "Religion has done its work, and now requires temporal and secular aid to give it another impulse." Black American emigrants would, according to Delany, raise Christianity to a higher level, complementing government and laws. "Christianity certainly is the most advanced civilization that man ever attained to, and wherever propagated in its purity, to be effective, law and government must be brought in harmony with it—otherwise it becomes corrupted, and a corresponding degeneracy ensues, placing its votaries even in a worse condition than the primitive." Protestant missionaries, Delany thought, had taken Africans to a "purer and higher civilization." Missionaries provided education and imparted the arts, sciences, manners, and customs, "more or less of civilized life." There was simply more to do.

Civilization and Christianity went hand in hand. He advised missionaries and others to go further in teaching West Africans specific western European manners and customs. "If all persons who settle among the natives would, as far as it is in their power and comes with their province, induce, by making it a rule of their house or family, every native servant to sit on a stool or chair: eat at a table instead of on the ground; eat with a knife and fork (or begin with a spoon) instead of with their fingers; eat in the house . . . sleep on a bed . . . and have them wear some sort of garment to cover the entire person above the knees . . . I am certain that it would go far toward impressing them with some of the habits of civilized life." On the other hand, Delany was not completely devoid of sensitivity to important aspects of cultures different from his own. He resented missionaries' custom of Anglicizing or completely changing West African names upon conversion to Christianity. He could not "see the utility" of changing the names of new converts. African names were "much more significant . . . than the Saxon, Gaelic, or Celtic" names. The missionaries should stop because they were impressing upon converts that the Christian faith implied "a loss of name, and . . . loss of identity."[54]

Moreover, emigrationists would transplant American capitalism, minus slavery. Activists' critique of capitalism remained restricted to its excesses, namely slavery, not the system itself. Similar to the earlier emigration project under Paul Cuffe, Delany, in particular, encouraged the development of an entrepreneurial spirit. National and international trade would be critical for the success of the black nation. A fourth C, cotton, could have been added to Delany's three C's of colonization: Christianity, Commerce, and Civilization. He intended his new nation to serve as a "reflex influence" to compete successfully with cotton cultivation in the South and help bring slavery to an end. Delany also hoped to develop trade in beeswax, ivory, and coffee. Black commercialism, Delany, Garnet, and others argued, would be the primary means of abolishing slavery in the United States and ending the international slave trade. Transplanted black Americans would participate as equals in the international market and in turn would enhance the political status of blacks still in the United States.[55]

By 1861, a large number, probably the northern black majority, supported emigration generally and many activists were considering leaving the United States for good. Even William Whipper, arguably the most patriotic of evangelical reformers in the 1830s and 1840s, supported the idea of emigration. Active in helping fugitive slaves migrate to Canada through his southern Pennsylvania property via the Underground Railroad, Whipper purchased property in Dresden, Ontario, in the early 1850s where he built several buildings. In 1856 Whipper questioned white New York abolitionist and philanthropist Gerrit Smith's condemnation of black emigration. He told Smith that if he were referring solely to colonizationist-sponsored emigration then he agreed, but if he rejected all black emigration, then he wanted an explanation.

Whipper could not conceive how Gerrit Smith's liberal mind could justify such denunciations, since historically emigration had always been the means of "progress and development" of the oppressed. Like other activists, Whipper asked why the interest in emigrating to places with greater opportunities should be denied to black Americans. Besides, black emigrants were contributing to abolition and equal rights by demonstrating black capacity "to enter into and pursue acts of civilized life." Whipper, who planned to emigrate to Canada in 1861, agreed with Garnet's African civilization project and Delany's emigrationist programs for West Africa. Black Americans could play a role, Whipper concluded, in the economic development of West Africa. But for the Civil War, Whipper would have ended his days in Dresden, Ontario.[56]

And Douglass, one of the most adamant opponents of emigration, considered the feasibility of limited black emigration to Haiti in the early months of 1861. "If we go anywhere, let us go to Hayti," he wrote. As a refuge for southern free blacks who were being threatened with enslavement if they did not leave their state and for northern free blacks whose lives were "becoming more narrow every year," Haiti promised the possibility of "a place of retreat, an asylum." And, too, Douglass wanted to disprove the American press's negative reports about Haiti which had "long made Haiti the bug bear and scarecrow of the cause of freedom." He noted that the press and other writers were either ignorant of Haitian culture and society or "willfully blind to her obvious virtues. . . . The fact is, white Americans find it hard to tell the truth about colored people. They see us with a dollar in their eyes." Douglass did not leave the

United States at that point, however. He explained to his readers that after his article about plans to travel to Haiti in late April to investigate whether or not the island was suitable for black emigration was printed, the "circumstances" in the United States promised "a tremendous revolution" for the future. Refer-ring to the Confederate firing on Fort Sumter, Douglass added, "We shall stay here and watch the current of events. . . . When the Northern people have been made to experience a little more of the savage barbarism of slavery, they may be willing to make war upon it, and in that case we stand ready to lend a hand in any way we can be of service. At any rate, this is no time for us to leave the country." Douglass returned to his original antagonism to emigration and, more telling, his evangelical optimism. Still, up to the early months of 1861, the majority of activists supported emigration of some kind.[57]

Unlike Douglass, party politics and the events of the late 1850s and early 1860s offered little comfort to some reformers. The Republican party did not reflect black evangelical ideals. These reformers thought that blacks who sup-ported Republican candidates compromised their abolition principles in sup-port of a party that opposed only the spread of slavery, supported the Fugitive Slave Law, and, in essence, positioned itself as representatives of northern white interests. Garnet and a few other delegates found themselves in the tiny minority in their opposition to the majority's resolution to support the New York Republican gubernatorial candidate over the Radical Abolitionist party's candidate, Gerrit Smith, at the 1858 Colored Men's State Suffrage Convention held in Troy.[58] Editor Thomas Hamilton explained in his *Weekly Anglo-African* editorial that the Democratic and Republican parties in 1860 were two sides of the same coin. Both parties were willing to sacrifice black American lives to "save themselves and the country—to save the country intact for the white race." Hamilton thought that while the Republicans were the more intelligent of the two parties, it was the "more dangerous enemy" because the party acted under the "guise of humanity" in its opposition to the reopening of the Atlan-tic slave trade and the spread of slavery into the territories while in truth the Republicans consistently raised the specter of the "threatening" black man. "Their opposition to slavery means opposition to the black man—nothing else."[59]

Ohio activist H. Ford Douglas had hope for the Republicans but viewed the party with almost as much suspicion as Hamilton. In September 1860 he believed the party was still mired in compromise, duplicity, and racism. Like black evangelicals from the late eighteenth century, Ford Douglas argued that all Americans, white and black, were negatively impacted by slavery. If it was acceptable to enslave one person, then no one was exempt. The Republican party should educate Americans about the Christian republican principles of the nation to "make them recognize the white man, the black man, the red man, *all* men, to all the rights of manhood." While he hoped the Republicans would succeed, contrary to an earlier statement, Ford Douglas believed that the party was little different from the Democrats but in its potential to become great. In "its pres[ent] position it can do nothing for the salvation of the nation, notwithstanding the noble anti-slavery men who are in it. For God has made it certain that the truth cannot be advanced by the telling of lies. I believe that in giving the enemy the one half, you cannot save the other."[60]

For the majority, however, the Republican party offered a glimmer of hope. Like Frederick Douglass, most thought the rise of the Republican party in the mid-1850s and Abraham Lincoln's election in 1860 could mean the beginning of the end of slavery, and they hoped the end of racial discrimination as well. Many black Republican party supporters embraced a type of political pragmatism, one that involved compromise and determination to work within and outside the party to create change. The pragmatists, like those at the 1858 Colored Men's State Suffrage Convention in New York, found themselves having to choose between the lesser of two evils. In New York, if black men had voted their principles and supported Radical Abolitionist party candidate Gerrit Smith, who had no chance of being elected, the Democrat probably would have been elected. Antislavery lecturer William J. Watkins's political pragmatism was representative of many black Republican party supporters. In his defense for supporting the Republican candidate over Smith, Watkins argued that while he still maintained his "Rad. Abolition Principles" it was "a question of Policy, as well as of Principle; and I maintain that we may when a great end is sought to be attained, consult the genius of Expediency, without sacrificing one iota of moral Principle."[61]

As with support for the Republican party, reformers debated how to respond to Abraham Lincoln's contradictory actions as president and whether they should support the war, once it came. For most, the question of support for Lincoln and the war was not simply a matter of principle, but of whether their primary goals, freedom and equality, would be met. Black evangelicalism informed northern black activists' understanding of the events during the Civil War. From April 1861 throughout most of 1862, reformers simultaneously denounced Lincoln's actions while expecting and demanding full and complete emancipation, the first step toward true republicanism. Reenergized to act as guardians of the nation's founding principles—based, they believed, in the Bible—black reformers informed white Americans, including white abolitionists, that the goal of the war was not to save the union but emancipation. As James McCune Smith cautioned Gerrit Smith in his letter dated August 22, 1861, the Union "panic" after the battle at Bull Run in July provided the opportunity for a national debate about ending slavery; instead, even white abolitionists were countenancing unionism over emancipation. "The only salvation of this nation is *Immediate Emancipation*," Smith reminded his fellow abolitionist.[62] Another reformer, responding to the formation of black regiments in the spring of 1861, cautioned, "Our policy must be neutral, ever praying for the success of that party determined to initiate first the policy of justice and equal rights." But other reformers responded with tremendous hope. In early 1862 John Rock said he disagreed with those who saw no hope in the war. "There is nothing in it but hope." Rock noted that the government already had to consider slavery "while fighting for its own existence," and sooner or later the government "must choke her to death."[63]

Not surprisingly, reformers instantly condemned Lincoln's initial approval of generals who returned fugitives to their slaveholders or allowed slaveholders to cross Union lines to retrieve fugitive slaves in the very beginning of the war. Similarly, they were furious in the fall of 1861 and spring of 1862 when the president rejected Generals John C. Fremont's and David Hunter's emancipation of slaves in Missouri, a Union border state, and in the southern seacoast where the Union had gained control. Philip A. Bell, editor and publisher of the San Francisco newspaper *Pacific Appeal*, called Lincoln's rejection of Hunter's actions a "Pro-slavery Proclamation," contradictory to the Confiscation Act of August 6, 1861, a policy that freed slaves who had been used by the Confederacy for military purposes if they came under Union protection.

Likewise, Lincoln's colonization efforts to remove African Americans outside the United States in the late summer of 1862 were similarly condemned. Frederick Douglass, ever ready to advise and criticize Lincoln and other Republicans, sharply attacked the president in his newspaper, *Douglass' Monthly*. Douglass and other reformers were furious about Lincoln's claim that blacks and whites could not live peaceably together and his suggestion that the existence of African Americans in the United States had caused the war. The president was only fueling the pervasive mob attacks on free blacks throughout the North and revealing his true interests, not eliminating slavery but protecting whites, North and South, slaveholders and nonslaveholders alike. Douglass explained to his readers that "though elected as an anti-slavery man, Mr. Lincoln is quite a genuine representative of American prejudice and Negro hatred and far more concerned for the preservation of slavery, and the favor of the Border Slave States, than for any sentiment of magnanimity or principle of justice and humanity." Philadelphia reformer Isaiah Wears called Lincoln's colonization scheme "unreasonable and anti-Christian in the extreme."[64]

Reformer poet Frances Ellen Watkins Harper viewed Lincoln's colonization scheme as symptomatic of a larger problem: the nation existed in the throes of decay, rejecting the "glorious opportunities for standing as an example to the nations leading the van of the world's progress" unless some "leader, high and strong, and bold and brave . . . of great noble purposes" full of "hatred of oppression and a love of freedom" arose to save it from itself. Watkins saw no future for the country without such leadership. The nation's guilt was so great that she doubted that "God will spare her in her crimes . . . for the wrongs of the Indians or the outrages of the negro." Harper likened Lincoln and his plan to a man "almost dying with a loathsome cancer, and busying himself about having his hair trimmed according to the latest fashion."[65]

Lincoln's Emancipation Proclamation gave reformers renewed hope and a recommitment to their evangelical vision. The policy of January 1863 declaring free all enslaved persons in rebel states not in areas over which the Union controlled and accepting black men in the navy and army reenergized most reformers in spite of the proclamation's limitations. It is at this point that the Civil War, like the Revolutionary War, proved a defining moment in northern black thought. While some reformers described their dismay about the limitations of the Emancipation Proclamation, most celebrated the new policy and, rather than discuss emigration outside the United States, set about to ensure emancipation and equal rights for black Americans.[66]

Remaining cautiously optimistic, several activists returned from the despair of the early to late 1850s to the optimism of the 1830s and 1840s. They believed their efforts and the actions of slaves fleeing their oppressors, combined with divine aid, would bring about the transformation of the nation. California activist poet James Bell had suggested in his poem "What Shall We Do with the Contrabands?" written in May 1862, that slaves flocking to Union lines become part of the liberating army. Longtime reformer and Presbyterian minister Reverend James W. C. Pennington reflected the view of most reformers. God was guiding the direction of the war in spite of national leadership.

Pennington admonished African Americans to "remember that emancipation was resorted to as a purely military necessity imposed upon this government in the Providence of an all-wise God. The President has no alternative but to fall into the powerful current of events which God had put in motion."[67]

With God by their side, reformers addressed emancipation and equal rights on multiple fronts. Frederick Douglass, Henry Highland Garnet, Mary Ann Shadd Cary, William Wells Brown, Frances Ellen Watkins Harper, and many others became recruiters for the Union Army. Some men, or their sons, joined the army. Martin Delany and another fervent emigrationist, H. Ford Douglas, reversed course to become some of the few black commissioned officers. These reformers and many others strongly supported the war on the home front by collecting funds and clothes for fugitive slaves escaping to Union lines, becoming teachers and/or missionaries in the occupied South, and constantly agitating for equal rights, particularly the franchise for all black men. Activists' conviction that freedom without equal rights was only half-freedom persisted.[68]

Through their efforts and divine intervention, African American reformers imagined the United States a "true" republic. It would fulfill God's plan for the United States as a model nation, establishing the universal truths of freedom and equality that would take Christian republicanism to the world. As in the Revolutionary era, black evangelicalism combined the sacred and secular, Christianity and republicanism, for an understanding of African Americans' place in the post–Civil War republic.

Epilogue

In the late eighteenth and early nineteenth centuries, a significant portion of northern blacks were heavily influenced by the thoughts and values, political and religious, coming out of the Revolutionary era. As a consequence, many converted to evangelical Christianity and embraced the principles of republicanism. These men and women of African descent cast their lot with the new North American republic. In doing so, they created a Christianity that suited their own needs as enslaved Christians, individuals just emerging out of slavery, and those who either had been born free or had been free for some time.

Formerly enslaved, Richard Allen stands out as a primary leader who, along with many others, engaged in establishing viable urban free black communities in the North. These men and women utilized the "African" identity that many people of West and West Central African descent had been claiming as a means of uniting disparate populations living or migrating into the urban areas because of shared oppression and interest in challenging their noncitizen status. Ministers like Allen almost immediately worked toward providing the African identity with substance, a common history. A significant part of uniting people of African descent included evangelizing the growing urban black population, a proselytizing effort that involved moral and behavioral change or improvement. Yet black Christian evangelism, for late eighteenth- and early nineteenth-century clerics, involved reinterpreting Christianity to establish universal human equality and right to freedom based in the Bible. Ministers and others expected and demanded citizenship, full participation in the body politic. To achieve this end, most community leaders decided physical distance from white churches was essential. Whites did not share black ministers' interpretations of particular Old and New Testament stories, nor were white clerics willing to place emphasis on the very themes of freedom and human equality that black preachers and others believed essential. Thus, from the start, the constitutive elements of black evangelicalism were political and sacred.

With its emphasis on a loving God intimately involved in individual and collective lives, black evangelicalism contributed to the means for many Africans to understand their new world. For those who embraced the European American faith and then refashioned it, Christianity met spiritual needs at a time of profound and persistent disruption. It helped enable a sense of personal value and purpose that contradicted and transcended their captors' definition of their place in human society. Christian spirituality gave sustenance and a moral compass to black American reformers for specific personal and political experiences. After a year-long illness and finally the death of their five-year-old daughter in 1849 on Christmas eve, Malvina and James McCune Smith were encouraged by the thought that they would meet their "dear little one where there will be no more sickness, nor pain nor parting forevermore."

In 1846 when he was afflicted with despair of another kind—the state of New York's rejection of equal suffrage due in large part to the Democratic party's exploitation of racial hatred among white workers—Smith sought his God. He drew near to God "for renewed faith and hope and encouragement" that black reformers would succeed in convincing whites of "the eternal equality of the Human Race—which is the first principle of Good Government—of Bible Politics."[1]

Evangelical Christianity met northern black political interest and purpose, enabling firm belief in national transformation in which equality and freedom reigned supreme: a nation ruled by law, not by race or ethnicity. Alternative visions, such as emigration and the creation of a black nation, ultimately failed for most on the altar of hope and conviction that they could, with God's help, persuade their fellow Americans to join them in enabling the nation to live up to its founding principles. They hoped to create a "true republic," not one based in hypocrisy, with freedom and rights for some.

In particular ways, black evangelicalism both enabled and thwarted most black reformers' ability to critique American liberalism. Black reformers were often so immersed in the culture that they could not substantively question whether inequality was built into the very structure of the nation. Even so, black evangelicalism was in itself a consistent critique of the failure of American Christian republicanism. Reformers would not accept the racial nationalism that quickly became part and parcel of the new republic in law and custom. Instead, black evangelical reformers served as the nation's conscience, calling the nation to its highest standards, often at great risk to themselves and their families in their persistent efforts to create an inclusive America. The consistent demands for establishing a "true republic" notwithstanding, reformers often despaired of white Christian hypocrisy and the general public's interest in restricting republican ideals to whites.

David Walker and Martin Delany were two men who despaired yet took different paths toward resolution. Walker, highly influenced by the evangelicalism of the early republic, chose reform in his condemnation of the nation for promoting and perpetuating the national sins of slavery and racism. His jeremiad, now legend, reflected not just the Puritan jeremiads of an earlier age, but anticipated the jeremiads that would become part of black evangelicalism then and to the present. Black ministers, including Samuel Cornish in the antebellum period and Martin Luther King Jr. in the last century, did not hesitate to expose the failures of American Christianity. Of course, politicians, businessmen, and others were similarly chastised for exploiting racism for their own ends. Martin Delany's path led him in the 1850s to support emigration outside the United States to establish a black nation completely under black control and power. Although Delany was reinvigorated by the Civil War and placed his hope in the future of the republic when he became a Union officer, emigration, usually fueled by despair, remained a viable alternative for many African Americans.

It was the Emancipation Proclamation that made the difference for mid-nineteenth-century African American support for the Civil War. During the war some reformers refocused on the millennium. In a March 1863 speech at New York's Cooper Institute, Douglass praised the Emancipation Proclamation as a document that will stand in the history of civilization alongside the Catholic Emancipation, British Reform Bill, and "with that noble act of Russian liberty" that freed 20 million serfs. Douglass added, "I believe in the millennium—the final perfection of the race [meaning the human race], and hail this Proclamation, though wrung out under the goading lash of a stern military necessity, as one reason of the hope that is in me. . . . To me it has a higher significance. It is a grand moral necessity."[2] Three months before, Abraham Lincoln in his Annual Message to Congress reflected black and white abolitionists' sense that God was divinely directing the outcome of the war to save the nation as the "Last Best Hope on Earth." And as every grammar school student should know, two years later Lincoln repeated his sense of not only divine leading but also divine judgment in his Second Inaugural Address, a speech that sounds as much like David Walker as it complements Frances Ellen Watkins Harper and Frederick Douglass: "Fondly do we hope—fervently do we pray—that this mighty scourge of war may speedily pass away. Yet, if God wills that it continue until all the wealth piled by the bondman's two hundred and fifty years of unrequited toil shall be sunk, and until every drop of blood drawn with the lash, shall be paid by another drawn with the sword, as was said three thousand years ago, so still it must be said, 'the judgments of the Lord are true and righteous altogether.'"[3]

After the war, reformers held out hope for true transformation in the nations' policies toward African Americans, especially with Congressional Reconstruction. Few imagined the unspeakable terror of lynching, disfranchisement, and legal segregation that would grip the entire country in the late nineteenth century and much of the twentieth century. Still many, if not most African Americans, remained committed to the ideal of what the United States could be. It would take a consistent struggle by many and varied reformers who risked their lives to bring down legal segregation and gain the franchise for African Americans.

Further study should address the ways in which black evangelicalism has shifted or changed in the last two centuries. Several lines of inquiry might be examined. One that seems critically important is whether black evangelicalism has broadened to become more inclusive in its stress on freedom and equality. How did ministers and others respond to the reservation policies toward Native Americans and proscriptions against the growing Mexican American and Asian American populations in the late nineteenth and twentieth centuries? Did black evangelical reformers support women's rights, especially the suffrage? Also, to what extent do ministers still believe in the necessity of physical distance for inculcating values of black humanity? Do most believe that separate churches and separate denominations are necessary because of white racism, lack of emphasis on universal human equality, and interpretation of key stories in the Old and New Testament that place African Americans at the center?

Though further study is needed to explain the greater complexity of African American religious thought in the centuries after the Civil War, black evangelicalism did continue as both a political and sacred Christianity that would influence millions into the twenty-first century. We know it played a role in engendering mass political action in the civil rights movement of the

1950s and 1960s. Black evangelical congregants benefited from the culmination of centuries of a belief system that asserted black equality and freedom as much as a need for spiritual growth. Black evangelicalism was just as evident during the 2008 presidential election when candidate Barack Obama, himself a black evangelical Christian, reflected the consistent determination of black evangelicals of the late eighteenth century to call upon the nation to live up to its principles, its "better" self, as a model to the world. In a speech to an Independence, Missouri, audience, Obama explained his definition of patriotism after his own was questioned over and over on the campaign trail. For me, he said, "patriotism is always more than just loyalty to a place on a map or a certain kind of people. . . . It is also loyalty to America's ideals—ideals for which anyone can sacrifice, or defend, or give their last full measure of devotion. I believe it is this loyalty that allows a country teeming with different races and ethnicities, religions and customs, to come together as one."[4] Obama added that America's children should be taught the nation's history, "teach them that America has been a force for good in the world, and that other nations and other people have looked to us as the last, best hope of Earth."

NOTES

INTRODUCTION

1. For a contrary interpretation, see Sterling Stuckey, *Slave Culture: Nationalist Theory and the Foundations of Black America* (New York: Oxford Univ. Press, 1987), and Eddie S. Glaude Jr., *Exodus! Religion, Race, and Nation in Early Nineteenth-Century Black America* (Chicago: Univ. of Chicago Press, 2000).

2. Mark A. Noll, *America's God: From Jonathan Edwards to Abraham Lincoln* (New York: Oxford Univ. Press, 2002), 5.

3. See, for example, Albert J. Raboteau, "The Black Experience in American Evangelicalism: The Meaning of Slavery," in *African-American Religion: Interpretive Essays in History and Culture*, ed. Timothy E. Fulop and Albert J. Raboteau, 89–106 (New York: Routledge, 1997); for millennialism, see Ruth Bloch, *Visionary Republic: Millennial Themes in American Thought, 1756–1800* (New York: Cambridge Univ. Press, 1985), 3, 230.

4. Sources for the scholarly debate about republicanism and liberalism are extensive. See, for example, Robert E. Shalhope, "Republicanism and Early American Historiography," *William and Mary Quarterly* 39 (April 1982): 334–356; Joyce Appleby, ed., "Special Issue: Republicanism in the History and Historiography of the United States," *American Quarterly* 37 (fall 1985): 461–598; Bernard Bailyn, *The Ideological Origins of the American Revolution* (Cambridge, Mass.: Harvard Univ. Press, 1967); Isaac Kramnick, *Republicanism and Bourgeois Radicalism: Political Ideology in Late Eighteenth-Century England and America* (Ithaca, N.Y.: Cornell Univ. Press, 1990); Isaac Kramnick, "The Great National Discussion: The Discourse of Politics in 1787," *William and Mary Quarterly* 45 (January 1988): 3–32; James T. Kloppenberg, "The Virtues of Liberalism: Christianity, Republicanism, and Ethics in Early American Political Discourse," *Journal of American History* 74 (June 1987): 9–33; Joyce Appleby, *Liberalism and Republicanism in the Historical Imagination* (Cambridge, Mass.: Harvard Univ. Press, 1992); Michael Zuckert, *Natural Rights and the New Republicanism* (Princeton, N.J.: Princeton Univ. Press, 1994); Alan Gibson, "Ancients, Moderns and Americans: The Republicanism-Liberalism Debate Revisited," *History of Political Thought* 21 (summer 2000): 261–307; Daniel T. Rodgers, "Republicanism: The Career of a Concept," *Journal of American History* 79 (June 1992): 11–38; Steve Pincus, "Neither Machiavellian Moment nor Possessive Individualism: Commercial Society and the Defenders of the English Commonwealth," *American Historical Review* 103 (June 1998): 705–736; Annie Mitchell, "A Liberal 'Cato,'" *American Journal of Political Science* 48 (July 2004): 588–603; see also Joyce Appleby, "The Social Origins of American Revolutionary Ideology," *Journal of American History* 64 (March 1978): 935–958; Rogers Smith, *Civic Ideals: Conflicting Visions of Citizenship in U.S. History* (New Haven, Conn.: Yale Univ. Press, 1997).

5. Gibson, "Ancients, Moderns and Americans," 275–293.

6. See, for example, Benedict Anderson, *Imagined Communities: Reflections on the Origin and Spread of Nationalism* (1983; revised and extended edition, London: Verso, 1993); Ernst Gellner, *Nations and Nationalism* (Ithaca, N.Y.: Cornell Univ. Press, 1983); Eric J. Hobsbawm, *Nations and Nationalism since 1780: Programme, Myth, Reality* (Cambridge: Cambridge Univ. Press, 1990); Anthony D. Smith, *The Ethnic Origins of Nations* (Oxford: Blackwell, 1986); John Hutchinson and Anthony D. Smith, eds., *Nationalism: Critical Concepts in Political Science*, vol. 1 (New York: Routledge, 2000).

7. Leslie M. Harris, *In the Shadow of Slavery: African Americans in New York City, 1626–1863* (Chicago: Univ. of Chicago Press, 2003), 118–133.

8. Kevin Gaines, *Uplifting the Race: Black Leadership, Politics, and Culture in the Twentieth Century* (Chapel Hill: Univ. of North Carolina Press, 1996), xiv.

9. See, for example, Jennifer L. Goloboy, "The Early American Middle Class," *Journal of the Early Republic* 25 (winter 2005): 537–545; Dallett C. Hemphill, "Middle Class Rising in Revolutionary America: The Evidence from Manners," *Journal of Social History* 30 (winter 1996): 317–344; see especially Stuart Blumin, *The Emergence of the Middle Class: Social Experience in the American City, 1760–1900* (New York: Cambridge Univ. Press, 1989; Mary P. Ryan, *Cradle of the Middle Class: The Family in Oneida County, New York, 1790–1865* (New York: Cambridge Univ. Press, 1981).

CHAPTER 1. BECOMING AFRICAN, BECOMING CHRISTIAN

1. For a thorough discussion of the diverse West and West Central African peoples and cultures enslaved in North America, see Michael A. Gomez, *Exchanging Our Country Marks: The Transformation of African Identities in the Colonial and Antebellum South* (Chapel Hill: Univ. of North Carolina Press, 1998), 17–154.

2. Chloe Spear, *Memoir of Mrs. Chloe Spear, a Native of Africa who was Enslaved in Childhood and Died in Boston, January 3, 1815 . . . aged 65 years, By a Lady of Boston* (Boston, 1832), 1–44.

3. Duncan J. MacLeod, "Toward Caste," in *Slavery and Freedom in the Age of the American Revolution*, ed. Ira Berlin and Ronald Hoffman, 217–220 (Charlottesville: Univ. Press of Virginia, 1983); Ira Berlin, "Time, Space, and the Evolution of Afro-American Society on British Mainland North America," *American Historical Review* 85 (February 1980): 47; Ira Berlin, *Generations of Captivity: A History of African American Slaves* (Cambridge, Mass.: Harvard Univ. Press, 2003), 81–82; Graham R. Hodges, *Root and Branch: African Americans in New York and East Jersey, 1613–1863* (Chapel Hill: Univ. of North Carolina Press, 1999), 9–10, 82–83.

4. Ira Berlin, "Time, Space," 46–49; Ira Berlin, *Many Thousands Gone: The First Two Centuries of Slavery in North America* (Cambridge, Mass.: Harvard Univ. Press, 1998), 182–184; Edgar McManus, *Black Bondage in the North* (Syracuse, N.Y.: Syracuse Univ. Press, 1973), 58–88.

5. Lorenzo Greene, *The Negro in Colonial New England* (1942; reprint, New York: Atheneum, 1968), 167–190; McManus, *Black Bondage in the North*, 91–97.

6. Edgar McManus, *A History of Negro Slavery in New York* (Syracuse, N.Y.: Syracuse Univ. Press, 1966), 95.

7. For a full discussion of northern slave statutes, see McManus, *Black Bondage in the North*, 55–88; McManus, *A History of Negro Slavery in New York*, 95.

8. Greene, *The Negro in Colonial New England*, 144–166; McManus, *Black Bondage in the North*, 108–159; Spear, *Memoir of Mrs. Chloe Spear*, 21–26; Porter, *Early Negro Writing*, 547–548.

9. William Douglass, *Annals of the First African Church in the United States of America Now Styled the African Episcopal Church of St. Thomas* (Philadelphia: King and Baird, Printers, 1862), 119.

10. See McManus, *Black Bondage in the North,* 125–142; McManus, *A History of Negro Slavery in New York,* 121–140; Greene, *The Negro in Colonial New England,* 160–163; Thomas J. Davis, *A Rumor of Revolt: The Great Negro Plot* (New York: Free Press, 1985), ix–x.

11. Duncan MacLeod, "Toward Caste," 221–229; see also Philip R. P. Coelho and Robert A. McGuire, "African and European Bound Labor in the British New World: The Biological Consequences of Economic Choices," *Journal of Economic History* 57 (March 1997): 98–102, for a discussion of the effects of African versus European disease factors impacting the biological environment in the economic choices of northern employers; Arthur Zilversmit, *The First Emancipation: The Abolition of Slavery in the North* (Chicago: Univ. of Chicago Press, 1967), 46–47; McManus, *Black Bondage in the North,* 143–179.

12. Willie Lee Rose, *Slavery and Freedom* (New York: Oxford Univ. Press, 1982), 6; McManus, *Black Bondage in the North,* 154–159.

13. Benjamin Quarles, *The Negro in the American Revolution* (1961; reprint, New York: Norton, 1973), vii–xi, 51–67, 158–181; McManus, *Black Bondage in the North,* 154–159; see also Ellen Gibson Wilson, *The Loyal Blacks* (New York: Putnam's Sons, 1976).

14. Timothy Breene, "Ideology and Nationalism on the Eve of the American Revolution," *Journal of American History* 84 (June 1997): 29, 31–33.

15. Zilversmit, *The First Emancipation,* 55–222; Leon Litwack, *North of Slavery: The Negro in the Free States, 1790–1860* (Chicago: Univ. of Chicago Press, 1961), 11; McManus, *Black Bondage in the North,* 167–168, 172–173, 211, 215.

16. Robert W. Fogel and Stanley Engerman, "Philanthropy at Bargain Prices: Notes on the Economics of Gradual Emancipation," *Journal of Legal Studies* 3 (June 1974): 377–401.

17. Zilversmit, *The First Emancipation,* 200–222; Nell Irvin Painter, *Sojourner Truth: A Life, a Symbol* (New York: Norton, 1996), 24.

18. Porter, *Early Negro Writing,* 551–555; Zilversmit, *The First Emancipation,* 190–191.

19. Sterling Stuckey, *Slave Culture: Nationalist Theory and the Foundations of Black America* (New York: Oxford Univ. Press, 1987), 47–53; see also Michael A. Gomez, "African Identity and Slavery in the Americas," *Radical History Review* 75 (fall 1999): 111–120.

20. Stuckey, *Slave Culture,* 3; Gomez, *Exchanging Our Country Marks,* 154–185.

21. See Stuckey, *Slave Culture,* 47–49; See also Michael P. Johnson, "Denmark Vesey and His Co-Conspirators," *William and Mary Quarterly* 58 (October 2001): 915–971, for an in-depth examination and critique of the historical use of the primary sources for the Denmark Vesey conspiracy. Johnson argues that historians who assert the existence of an actual conspiracy have unwittingly used sources that tell us more about the problem of relying on and misinterpreting the few extant sources than whether a conspiracy actually occurred.

22. Davis, *Rumor of Revolt,* 54–55; See Gomez, *Exchanging Our Country Marks,* 17–153; and Michael Mullin, *Africa in America: Slave Acculturation and Resistance in the American South and the British Caribbean, 1736–1831* (Urbana: Univ. of Illinois Press, 1992), 283–291, for a discussion of provenance of sub-Saharan African slaves in the Americas; Leslie M. Harris, *In the Shadow of Slavery: African Americans in New York City, 1626–1863* (Chicago: Univ. of Chicago Press, 2003), 29, 45–47.

23. Gomez and other scholars argue that evidence asserting that newly arrived Africans of the same ethnicity were immediately separated is weak. In fact, evidence points to the possibility that they were kept together. Gomez, *Exchanging Our Country Marks,* 173; Joseph E. Holloway, "The Origins of African American Culture," in *Africanisms in American Culture,* ed. Joseph E.

Holloway, 20–37 (Bloomington: Indiana Univ. Press, 1990); see also William D. Piersen, *Black Yankees: The Development of an Afro-American Subculture in Eighteenth-Century New England* (Amherst: Univ. of Massachusetts Press, 1988), 8.

24. For a synopsis of the difference between slave societies and societies with slaves, see Berlin, *Generations of Captivity,* 8–11; Piersen, *Black Yankees,* 3–7; Gomez, *Exchanging Our Country Marks,* 27–37.

25. Gomez, *Exchanging Our Country Marks,* 5, 17–37; Piersen, *Black Yankees,* 7.

26. Albert J. Raboteau, *Slave Religion: The "Invisible Institution" in the Antebellum South* (New York: Oxford Univ. Press, 1978), 11–13; Stuckey, *Slave Culture,* 6, 11, 25; Mechal Sobel, *Trabelin' On: The Slave Journey to an Afro-Baptist Faith* (Princeton, N.J.: Princeton Univ. Press, 1988), 5–21. For an in-depth discussion of cultural differences and similarities among West and West Central African people, see Gomez, *Exchanging Our Country Marks,* 38–153; see also Sidney W. Mintz and Richard Price, *An Anthropological Approach to the Afro-American Past* (Philadelphia: Institute for the Study of Human Issues, 1976), 22–23.

27. Gomez, *Exchanging Our Country Marks,* 48; Stuckey, *Slave Culture,* 12, 24.

28. Piersen, *Black Yankees,* 14–15, 43; Gomez, *Exchanging Our Country Marks,* 26–27.

29. Shane White, *Somewhat More Independent: The End of Slavery in New York City, 1770–1810* (Athens: Univ. of Georgia Press, 1991), 3–4.

30. Gomez, *Exchanging Our Country Marks,* 5, 154–155.

31. Quoted in Gary Nash, *Forging Freedom: The Formation of Philadelphia's Black Community, 1720–1840* (Cambridge, Mass.: Harvard Univ. Press, 1988), 13.

32. For examples of burial practices, see Piersen, *Black Yankees,* 40, 74–80, 96–99; Harris, *In the Shadow of Slavery,* 1–2, 41; Stuckey, *Slave Culture,* 25, 39; Nash, *Forging Freedom,* 11, 13, 36, 94, 222; Gomez, *Exchanging Our Country Marks,* 49–51; Robert Farris Thompson, *Flash of the Spirit: African and Afro-American Art and Philosophy* (New York: Vintage, 1984); White, *Somewhat More Independent,* 185–206; Daniel A. Payne, *Recollections of Seventy Years* (Nashville: Publishing House of the A.M.E. Sunday School Union, 1888; reprint, Salem, N.H.: Ayer, 1991), 253–257. For a synopsis of African cultural influence in the northern colonies/states, see James Horton and Lois Horton, *In Hope of Liberty: Culture, Community and Protest among Northern Free Blacks, 1700–1860* (New York: Oxford Univ. Press, 1997), 30–35.

33. Piersen, *Black Yankees,* 117–136; Harris, *In the Shadow of Slavery,* 40–41.

34. Porter, *Early Negro Writing,* 539–540; Piersen, *Black Yankees,* 44; see also Robert E. Desrochers Jr., "'Not Fade Away': The Narrative of Venture Smith, an African American in the Early Republic," *Journal of American History* 84 (June 1997): 40–66, and David Waldstreicher, "The Vexed Story of Human Commodification Told by Benjamin Franklin and Venture Smith," *Journal of the Early Republic* 24 (summer 2004): 268–278.

35. Porter, *Early Negro Writing,* 538–557.

36. For an example of how Native Americans constructed a common ethnic identity from several shrinking ethnic groups, see James Merrell, *The Indians' New World: Catawbas and Their Neighbors from European Contact throughout the Era of Removal* (Chapel Hill: Univ. of North Carolina Press, 1989); see also Patrick Griffen, "The People with No Name: Ulster's Migrants and Identity Formation in Eighteenth-Century Pennsylvania," *William and Mary Quarterly* 58 (July 2001): 587–614.

37. Porter, *Early Negro Writing,* 557.

38. See John Hutchinson and Anthony D. Smith, eds., *Nationalism: Critical Concepts in Political Science,* vol. 1 (New York: Routledge, 2000), and Anthony D. Smith, *The Ethnic Origins of*

Nations (Oxford: Blackwell, 1986), 22–30. My ideas are also inspired broadly by Benedict Anderson, *Imagined Communities: Reflections on the Origin and Spread of Nationalism* (1983; revised and extended edition, London: Verso, 1993), and K. Anthony Appiah, "Race, Culture, Identity: Misunderstood Connections," in *Color Conscious: The Political Morality of Race,* ed. K. Anthony Appiah and Amy Gutmann, 30–105 (Princeton, N.J.: Princeton Univ. Press, 1996), see especially pages 96–97; Charles Taylor, "The Politics of Recognition," in *Multiculturalism and "The Politics of Recognition,"* ed. Charles Taylor and Amy Gutmann, 32–36, 66 (Princeton, N.J.: Princeton Univ. Press, 1992); Charles Taylor, *Sources of the Self: The Making of Modern Identity* (Cambridge, Mass.: Harvard Univ. Press, 1989), 14–19, 25–32, 525 n. 13. Taylor notes in this last reference the significance of names: "A human being has to have a name. . . . Being called into conversation is a precondition of developing human identity."

39. Herbert Aptheker, ed., *A Documentary History of the Negro People in the United States: From Colonial Times through the Civil War* (New York: Citadel Press, 1961), 1:1–2; Porter, *Early Negro Writing,* 557.

40. Aptheker, *Documentary History,* 1:17; Porter, *Early Negro Writing,* 324–329, 345–346, 366, 391; Phillis Wheatley, *The Collected Works of Phillis Wheatley,* The Schomburg Library of Nineteenth-Century Black Women Writers, ed. John C. Shields (New York: Oxford Univ. Press, 1988), 165.

41. My understanding of identity formation is also helped by Stuart Hall's essay "Cultural Identity and Diaspora," in *Identity: Community, Culture, Difference,* ed. Jonathan Rutherford, 222–237 (London: Lawrence and Wishart, 1990); and Griffen, "The People with No Name," 587–614.

42. For recognition of distinct ethnic identities, see Gomez, *Exchanging Our Country Marks,* 19–20.

43. See Porter, *Early Negro Writing,* vii–viii, 315. For an insightful discussion on the use of the term "Negro," see Patrick Rael, *Black Identity and Black Protest in the Antebellum North* (Chapel Hill: Univ. of North Carolina Press, 2002), 82–117.

44. A black woman contributor to the *Liberator* asked, "Why do our friends, as well as our enemies, call us 'negroes?'" The writer considered it "a term of reproach." See Julie Winch, "'You Have Talents—Only Cultivate Them': Philadelphia's Black Female Literary Societies and the Abolitionist Crusade," in *The Abolitionist Sisterhood: Women's Political Culture in Antebellum America,* ed. Jean Fagan Yellin and John C. Van Horne, 103 (Ithaca, N.Y.: Cornell Univ. Press, 1994).

45. Porter, *Early Negro Writing,* 385; for Russell Parrott, see Gary Nash, *Forging Freedom,* 238; William B. Gravely, "The Dialectic of Double-Consciousness in Black American Freedom Celebrations, 1808–1863," *Journal of Negro History* 67 (winter 1982): 307.

46. Porter, *Early Negro Writing,* 35, 368; see also Taylor, *Sources of the Self,* 14–19, for a discussion of the importance of the modern idea of a sense of self-worth, respect for others, and understanding of the meaning of a full life.

47. Gomez, *Exchanging Our Country Marks,* 115, 124–128; Porter, *Early Negro Writing,* 35.

48. Porter, *Early Negro Writing,* 385–386, 368; see also Harris, *In the Shadow of Slavery,* 89–91.

49. Russell Parrott, *The Abolition of the Slave Trade* (Philadelphia, 1814); Porter, *Early Negro Writing,* 385 (see also 345–350, 391–399).

50. Porter, *Early Negro Writing,* 386.

51. Porter, *Early Negro Writing,* 386, 18–20, 35, 367–368.

52. Porter, *Early Negro Writing,* 384–385.

53. See Taylor, "The Politics of Recognition," 34.

54. Gomez, *Exchanging Our Country Marks,* 96–98.

55. Greene, *The Negro in Colonial New England*, 257, 263–267; Aptheker, *Documentary History*, 1:1–2.

56. Raboteau, *Slave Religion*, 98–103. Quote in Greene, *The Negro in Colonial New England*, 264–267; Hodges, *Root and Branch*, 55. For an insightful assessment of mid-Atlantic early black conversions, see the introduction in Graham R. Hodges, ed., *Black Itinerants of the Gospel: The Narratives of John Jea and George White* (Madison, Wisc.: Madison House, 1993), 1–49.

57. John C. Van Horne, ed., *Religious Philanthropy and Colonial Slavery: The American Correspondence of the Associates of Dr. Bray, 1717–1777* (Urbana: Univ. of Illinois Press, 1985), 1–7, 31; Greene, *The Negro in Colonial New England*, 269; Raboteau, *Slave Religion*, 96–126; Nash, *Forging Freedom*, 10.

58. Frank J. Klingberg, *Anglican Humanitarianism in Colonial New York* (Philadelphia: Church Historical Society, 1940), 161–165.

59. Mark Noll, *America's God: From Jonathan Edwards to Abraham Lincoln* (New York: Oxford Univ. Press, 2002), 5, 44; see also Nathan O. Hatch, *The Democratization of American Christianity* (New Haven, Conn.: Yale Univ. Press, 1989), 102–113.

60. Mark Noll, *America's God*, 9, 44, 145; see also Noll, *America's God*, 60–61, 447–451, for a discussion of the uses of republicanism and liberalism and the ways in which contradictions abound in using either term. Republicanism and liberalism are not mutually exclusive terms.

61. Raboteau, *Slave Religion*, 128–129; Sidney Ahlstrom, *A Religious History of the American People* (New Haven, Conn.: Yale Univ. Press, 1972), 284–285; William Stevens Perry, ed., *Historical Collections Relating to the American Colonial Church* (Hartford, Conn., 1870–1878), 3:190–192, 353–355.

62. Sobel, *Trabelin' On*, 19–21.

63. Ahlstrom, *A Religious History*, 170, 292; Sobel, *Trabelin' On*, 91–97.

64. John W. Lewis, *The Life, Labors, and Travels of Elder Charles Bowles of the Free Will Baptist Denomination* (Watertown, N.Y.: Ingalls and Stowell's Steam Press, 1852), 5–7.

65. Lewis, *Life, Labors, and Travels*, 8; Sobel, *Trabelin' On*, 89–91.

66. Lewis, *Life, Labors, and Travels*, 24–26, 30, 33, 37–38, 62, 90–91, 147–148, 209; Sobel, *Trabelin' On*, 79–98.

67. Richard Allen, *The Life Experience and Gospel Labors of the Rt. Rev. Richard Allen . . .* (1833; reprint, Nashville: Abingdon Press, 1960), 15; for an important biography of Allen, see Richard Newman, *Freedom's Prophet: Bishop Richard Allen, the AME Church, and the Black Founding Fathers* (New York: New York Univ. Press, 2008).

68. Jarena Lee, *The Life and Religious Experience of Jarena Lee, a Coloured Lady, Giving an Account of Her Call to Preach the Gospel* (1836), 25–52, Zilpha Elaw, *Memoirs of the Life, Religious Experience, Ministerial Travels, and Labours of Mrs. Elaw* (1846), 53–160, and Julia J. Foote, *A Brand Plucked from the Fire: An Autobiographical Sketch* (1879), 162–234, in *Sisters of the Spirit: Three Black Women's Autobiographies of the Nineteenth Century*, ed. William L. Andrews, 27–38; 53–60; 75–82; 180–193, 200–211 (Bloomington: Indiana Univ. Press, 1986).

69. Elaw, *Memoirs*, 56.

70. Ahlstrom, *A Religious History*, 324–327; Allen, *Life Experience and Gospel Labors*, 15–16; see also Noll, *America's God*, 341.

71. Raboteau, *Slave Religion*, 129–148; Dee Andrews, *The Methodists and Revolutionary America, 1760–1800: The Shaping of an Evangelical Culture* (Princeton, N.J.: Princeton Univ. Press, 2000), 76–92; Sobel, *Trablin' On*, 79–98.

72. Sobel, *Trabelin' On*, 86–88.

73. Albert J. Raboteau, "The Slave Church in the Era of the American Revolution," in *Slavery and Freedom in the Age of the American Revolution*, ed. Ira Berlin and Ronald Hoffman, 194–195, 203 (Charlottesville: Univ. Press of Virginia, 1983).

74. Spear, *Memoir of Mrs. Chloe Spear,* 18–44.

75. Spear, *Memoir of Mrs. Chloe Spear,* 49–50; Gomez, *Exchanging Our Country Marks,* 272–275.

76. Raboteau, "The Slave Church," 194–199; Sobel, *Trabelin' On,* 86. For the integration of liberal principles in evangelical Christianity, to be discussed more fully in the next chapter, see Noll, *America's God.*

77. See Noll, *America's God,* 343; see also Charles F. Irons, *The Origins of Proslavery Christianity* (Chapel Hill: Univ. of North Carolina Press, 2008).

78. For Taylor's discussion of the importance of a frame or horizon, see *Sources of the Self,* 26–27.

79. Allen, *Life Experience and Gospel Labors,* 19.

80. Allen, *Life Experience and Gospel Labors,* 24; for a detailed description of the beginnings of black churches in Philadelphia, see Milton C. Sernett, *Black Religion and American Evangelicalism: White Protestants, Plantation Missions, and the Flowering of Negro Christianity, 1787–1865* (Metuchen, N.J.: Scarecrow, 1975), 117–118, 219–220; Gary Nash, *Forging Freedom,* 96–99; Dee Andrews, "The African Methodists of Philadelphia, 1794–1802," *Pennsylvania Magazine of History and Biography* 108 (October 1984): 471–486.

81. Milton C. Sernett, ed., *Afro-American Religious Historical Documents* (Syracuse, N.Y.: Syracuse Univ. Press, 1986), 150–158; William J. Walls, *The African Methodist Episcopal Zion Church: Reality of the Black Church* (Charlotte, N.C.: African Methodist Zion Publishing House, 1974), 26, 40–44.

82. Jeremiah Asher, *Incidents in the Life of Rev. J. Asher* (1850; reprint, Freeport, N.Y.: Books for Libraries Press, 1971), 27–56.

83. William T. Catto, *A Semi-Centenary Discourse Delivered in the First African Presbyterian Church in Philadelphia, 1857 and History of the First African Presbyterian Church* (Philadelphia: Joseph M. Wilson, 1857), 18–20.

84. Benjamin Rush to Granville Sharp, 1792, Henry E. Huntington Library, file #479380.

85. Porter, *Early Negro Writing,* 337; see also Will B. Gravely, "The Rise of African Churches in America (1786–1822)," in *African-American Religion: Interpretive Essays in History and Culture,* ed. Timothy E. Fulop and Albert J. Raboteau, 135–158 (New York: Routledge, 1997), and Albert J. Raboteau, "The Black Experience in American Evangelicalism," in *African-American Religion: Interpretive Essays in History and Culture,* ed. Timothy E. Fulop and Albert J. Raboteau, 98–106, esp. 101–102 (New York: Routledge, 1997).

86. Porter, *Early Negro Writing,* 336–342.

87. Porter, *Early Negro Writing,* 338.

88. Absalom Jones and Richard Allen, "A Narrative of the Proceedings of the Colored People During the Awful Calamity in Philadelphia in the Year 1793; and a Refutation of Some Censures Thrown upon Them in Some Publications," in Allen, ed., *Life Experience and Gospel Labors,* 69–71; see also Noll, *America's God,* 147–149, 227–228. See Lawrence Levine, *Black Culture and Black Consciousness: Afro-American Folk Thought from Slavery to Freedom* (New York: Oxford Univ. Press, 1977), 3–135, for an in-depth discussion of themes in black Christianity.

89. Porter, *Early Negro Writing,* 340; Spear, *Memoir of Mrs. Chloe Spear,* 51.

90. Allen, *Life Experience and Gospel Labors,* 27.

CHAPTER 2. BECOMING AMERICAN

1. Sources for the scholarly debate about republicanism and liberalism are extensive, illustrating that terminology and precise definition remain problematic. See Alan Gibson, "Ancients, Moderns and Americans: The Republicanism-Liberalism Debate Revisited," *History of Political*

Thought 21 (summer 2000): 261–307; Daniel T. Rodgers, "Republicanism: The Career of a Concept," *Journal of American History* 79 (June 1992): 11–38; Mark A. Noll, *America's God: From Jonathan Edwards to Abraham Lincoln* (New York: Oxford Univ. Press, 2002), 73, 447–451.

2. Noll, *America's God,* 13–19, 73, 82–84, 93.

3. Noll, *America's God,* 88–89.

4. *Collections of the Massachusetts Historical Society, 1792–1941* (7 series of 10 volumes), *Jeremy Belknap Papers,* vol. 3, 5th series (Boston, 1887), 432–433. For an extensive discussion of the petitions, see Rita Roberts, "In Quest of Autonomy: Northern Black Activism between the Revolution and the Civil War" (Ph.D. diss., University of California, Berkeley, 1988), 7–18; see also Thomas J. Davis, "Emancipation Rhetoric, Natural Rights, and Revolutionary New England: A Note on Four Black Petitions in Massachusetts, 1773–1777," *New England Quarterly* 62 (June 1989): 248–263. In order not to confuse the meaning of various writings, I have kept spelling, punctuation, and grammar the same as appeared in the original documents.

5. *Collections of the Massachusetts Historical Society,* 3:433.

6. *Collections of the Massachusetts Historical Society,* 3:432–433; Michael Zuckert, *Natural Rights and the New Republicanism* (Princeton, N.J.: Princeton Univ. Press, 1994), 16–22; see also Steve Dworetz, *The Unvarnished Doctrine: Locke, Liberalism, and the American Revolution* (Durham, N.C.: Duke Univ. Press, 1990).

7. *Collections of the Massachusetts Historical Society,* 3:433.

8. *Collections of the Massachusetts Historical Society,* 3:433.

9. *Collections of the Massachusetts Historical Society,* 3:436; Bernard Bailyn, *The Ideological Origins of the American Revolution* (Cambridge, Mass.: Harvard Univ. Press, 1967), 232–235.

10. Herbert Aptheker, ed., *A Documentary History of the Negro People in the United States: From Colonial Times through the Civil War* (New York: Citadel Press, 1961), 1:6.

11. Aptheker, *Documentary History,* 1:6–7.

12. *Collections of the Massachusetts Historical Society,* 3:436.

13. *Collections of the Massachusetts Historical Society,* 3:437.

14. *New London Gazette,* May 1, 1772.

15. *Collections of the Massachusetts Historical Society,* 3:437.

16. Aptheker, *Documentary History,* 1:6–8.

17. Aptheker, *Documentary History,* 1:6, 8; *Collections of the Massachusetts Historical Society,* 3:387.

18. *Collections of the Massachusetts Historical Society,* 3:434–435; Aptheker, *Documentary History,* 1:6–8. For an argument that the emigrationists' expressions reflected proto-nationalist sentiment, see Floyd Miller, *The Search for a Black Nationality: Black Emigration and Colonization, 1787–1863* (Urbana: Univ. of Illinois Press, 1975), 3–20; see also Gary B. Nash, *Race and Revolution* (Madison, Wisc.: Madison House, 1990), 67. For liberal ideals of happiness, see Jerome Huyler, *Locke in America: The Moral Philosophy of the Founding Era* (Lawrence: Univ. Press of Kansas, 1995), 85–93.

19. Aptheker, *Documentary History,* 1:11; Noll, *America's God,* 93–113.

20. Aptheker, *Documentary History,* 1:14–16; Lamont D. Thomas, *Rise to Be a People: A Biography of Paul Cuffe* (Urbana: Univ. of Illinois Press, 1986), 8–11.

21. Aptheker, *Documentary History,* 1:14–16.

22. For the definitive text on the role of blacks in the Revolutionary War, see Benjamin Quarles, *The Negro in the American Revolution* (1961; reprint, New York: Norton, 1973). Frederick Douglass, quoted in Quarles, *Negro in American Revolution,* viii; see also Lois Horton, "From Class

to Race in Early America: Northern Post-Emancipation Racial Reconstruction," *Journal of the Early Republic* 19 (winter 1999): 636–638.

23. Rita Roberts, "Patriotism and Political Criticism: The Evolution of Political Consciousness in the Mind of a Black Revolutionary Soldier," *Eighteenth-Century Studies* 27 (summer 1994): 569–588; for an in-depth and particularly comprehensive biography of Haynes, see John Saillant, *Black Puritan, Black Republican: The Life and Thought of Lemuel Haynes, 1753–1833* (New York: Oxford Univ. Press, 2003); for a contemporary biography of Haynes, see Timothy Mather Cooley, *Sketches of the Life and Character of the Rev. Lemuel Haynes* (1837; reprint, New York: Negro Universities Press, 1969). To avoid confusion, Haynes's spelling and punctuation in both the ballad and essay have been retained.

24. Ruth Bogin, ed., "'The Battle of Lexington': A Patriotic Ballad by Lemuel Haynes," *William and Mary Quarterly* 42 (October 1985): 501–502.

25. Julie Winch, *A Gentleman of Color: The Life of James Forten* (New York: Oxford Univ. Press, 2002), 36–47; William C. Nell, *The Colored Patriots of the American Revolution, with Sketches of Several Distinguished Colored Persons* (1855; reprint, New York: Arno and the New York Times, 1968), 166–171; Charlotte Forten Grimké, *The Journals of Charlotte Forten Grimké*, The Schomburg Library of Nineteenth-Century Black Women Writers, ed. Brenda Stevenson, 3–4 (New York: Oxford Univ. Press, 1988).

26. Winch, *A Gentleman of Color,* 38.

27. Phillis Wheatley, *The Collected Works of Phillis Wheatley,* The Schomburg Library of Nineteenth-Century Black Women Writers, ed. John C. Shields, 146 (New York: Oxford Univ. Press, 1988); Nell, *Colored Patriots,* 322–323; James O. Horton and Lois Horton, *In Hope of Liberty: Culture, Community and Protest among Northern Free Blacks, 1700–1860* (New York: Oxford Univ. Press, 1997), 55–71.

28. Nell, *Colored Patriots,* 323; Quarles, *The Negro in the American Revolution,* 185.

29. Lemuel Haynes, *The Nature and Importance of TRUE REPUBLICANISM, with a Few Suggestions Favorable to Independence* (Rutland, Vt.: William Fay, Printer, 1801), 22.; see John Saillant, "Lemuel Haynes's Black Republicanism and the American Republican Tradition, 1775–1820," *Journal of the Early Republic* 14 (autumn 1994): 293–324. For a related topic, see John Saillant, "Lemuel Haynes and the Revolutionary Origins of Black Theology, 1776–1801," *Religion and American Culture* 2 (winter 1992): 79–102.

30. Ruth Bogin, "'Liberty Further Extended': A 1776 Antislavery Manuscript by Lemuel Haynes," *William and Mary Quarterly* 40 (January 1983): 94–95.

31. Bogin, "'Liberty Further Extended,'" 94–96.

32. Bogin, "'Liberty Further Extended,'" 96–97.

33. Porter, ed., *Early Negro Writing,* 20–21.

34. Bogin, "'Liberty Further Extended,'" 102.

35. Bogin, "'Liberty Further Extended,'" 101; for a fuller discussion of the theological implications of Haynes's essay, see Saillant, *Black Puritan, Black Republican,* 9–45.

36. Porter, ed., *Early Negro Writing,* 9, 17, 18, 25, 71, 84, 341; Horton and Horton, *In Hope of Liberty,* 25, 112, 126; Acts 10:34–35, 17:26 (KJV); Colossians 3:25 (KJV); Galatians 2:28 (KJV); for confusion about Prince Hall's birth, status, and country of birth, see Joanna Brooks, "Prince Hall, Freemasonry, and Genealogy," *African American Review* 34 (summer 2000): 198.

37. Porter, ed., *Early Negro Writing,* 18, 20–22, 25–27, 345.

38. Porter, ed., *Early Negro Writing,* 9, 345, 356, 359–362, 366, 374.

39. Richard Allen, *The Life Experience and Gospel Labors of the Rt. Rev. Richard Allen . . .* (1833; reprint, Nashville: Abingdon Press, 1960), 48–65. Portions of this chapter were presented at the Organization of American Historians annual meeting in 1994 and benefited from the valuable comments of Emma Lapsansky-Werner, Spencer Crew, and James Horton; see also John Saillant, *Black Puritan, Black Republican,* 108.

40. Allen, *Life Experience and Gospel Labors,* 55.

41. Allen, *Life Experience and Gospel Labors,* 64.

42. Allen, *Life Experience and Gospel Labors,* 60, 68; see also Thomas E. Will, "Liberalism, Republicanism, and Philadelphia's Black Elite in the Early Republic: The Social Thought of Absalom Jones and Richard Allen," *Pennsylvania History* 69 (2002): 558–576.

43. Allen, *Life Experience and Gospel Labors,* 71.

44. Allen, *Life Experience and Gospel Labors,* 71.

45. Porter, ed., *Early Negro Writing,* 19, 25, 100–101; Huyler, *Locke in America,* 231–234.

46. Richard Newman, ed., *Black Preacher to White America: The Collected Writings of Lemuel Haynes, 1774–1833* (Brooklyn: Carlson, 1990), 66–67.

47. Newman, ed., *Black Preacher to White America,* 79.

48. Porter, ed., *Early Negro Writing,* 102.

49. Porter, ed., *Early Negro Writing,* 330–332, see also page 114.

50. Newman, ed., *Black Preacher to White America,* 81–82; for virtue as the critical element in liberalism and the new republic, see James T. Kloppenberg, "The Virtues of Liberalism: Christianity, Republicanism, and Ethics in Early American Political Discourse," *Journal of American History* 74 (June 1987): 16–19; Huyler, *Locke in America,* 232–234, 241; Richard C. Sinopoli, *The Foundations of American Citizenship: Liberalism, the Constitution, and Civic Virtue* (New York: Oxford Univ. Press, 1992).

51. Newman, ed., *Black Preacher to White America,* 167; Porter, ed., *Early Negro Writing,* 359–362.

52. Porter, ed., *Early Negro Writing,* 361–362.

53. Porter, ed., *Early Negro Writing,* 350–351, 98–99.

54. Porter, ed., *Early Negro Writing,* 350, 358–363.

55. Newman, ed., *Black Preacher to White America,* 149–151, 155–157; Noah Worcester, *Abraham and Lot: A Sermon, on the Way of Peace, and the Evils of War: Delivered at Salisbury, in New-Hampshire, on the Day of the National Feast, August 20, 1812* (Concord, N.H.: George Hough, 1812).

56. Porter, ed., *Early Negro Writing,* 5; Irving H. Bartlett, *From Slave to Citizen: The Story of the Negro in Rhode Island* (Providence, R.I.: The Urban League of Greater Providence, 1954); see also Irving Bartlett, "The Free Negro in Providence, Rhode Island," *Negro History Bulletin* 14 (December 1950): 51–67.

57. Dorothy Sterling, ed., *We Are Your Sisters: Black Women in the Nineteenth Century* (New York: Norton, 1984), 104–119; Porter, ed., *Early Negro Writing,* 5–62.

58. Porter, ed., *Early Negro Writing,* 9; Sterling, *We Are Your Sisters,* 108–109.

59. William Douglass, *Annals of the First African Church in the United States of America Now Styled the African Episcopal Church of St. Thomas* (Philadelphia: King and Baird, Printers, 1862), 33–36.

60. Porter, ed., *Early Negro Writing,* 11, 30, 43, 47, 53, 92.

61. For racial discrimination in northern schools, see Leon Litwack, *North of Slavery: The Negro in the Free States, 1790–1860* (Chicago: Univ. of Chicago Press, 1961), 113–142; Porter, ed., *Early Negro Writing,* 79; Aptheker, *A Documentary History,* 1:19–20.

62. Sterling, *We Are Your Sisters,* 109–110; Carleton Mabee, *Black Education in New York State:*

From Colonial to Modern Times (Syracuse, N.Y.: Syracuse Univ. Press, 1979), 49–50; Gerda Lerner, ed., *Black Women in White America: A Documentary History* (New York: Pantheon, 1972; reprint, New York: Vintage, 1992),76; Douglass, *Annals of the First African Church,* 172.

63. Bartlett, *From Slave to Citizen,* 35; Porter, ed., *Early Negro Writing,* 84–86, 92–95.

64. Mabee, *Black Education in New York,* 21–23; Leslie Harris, *In the Shadow of Slavery: African Americans in New York City, 1626–1863* (Chicago: Univ. of Chicago Press, 2003), 134–135; Julian Rammelkamp, "The Providence Negro Community, 1820–1842," *Rhode Island History* 7 (January 1948): 26–27.

65. Douglass, *Annals of the African Church,* 12.

66. J. Albert Cassedy, *The Firemen's Record* (Philadelphia, 1891), 51–53; Raymond J. Hall, *Black Separatism in the United States* (Hanover, N.H., 1978), 23; Porter, ed., *Early Negro Writing,* 53–54.

67. Porter, ed., *Early Negro Writing,* 27, 356, 341, 379; see also pages 35–36, 372, 389.

68. Newman, ed., *Black Preacher to White America,* 86.

69. Miller, *The Search for a Black Nationality,* 7–8; George C. Mason, *Reminiscences of Newport* (Newport, R.I.: C. E. Hammett Jr., 1884), 154–159.

70. Thomas, *Rise to Be a People,* 3–9, 13–19, 22–31; see also Miller, *The Search for a Black Nationality,* 22–25.

71. Winch, *A Gentleman of Color,* 8–17, 63–73, 77–106; see also Ray Allen Billington, "James Forten: Forgotten Abolitionist," *Negro History Bulletin* 13 (November 1949): 31–33; Brooks, "Prince Hall, Freemasonry, and Genealogy," 197–199; Miller, *The Search for a Black Nationality,* 4.

72. Julie Winch, *Philadelphia's Black Elite: Activism, Accommodation, and the Struggle for Autonomy, 1787–1848* (Philadelphia: Temple Univ. Press, 1988), 4–7.

73. Winch, *Philadelphia's Black Elite,* 6; see, for example, Porter, ed., *Early Negro Writing,* 417.

74. Kevin Gaines, *Uplifting the Race: Black Leadership, Politics, and Culture in the Twentieth Century* (Chapel Hill: Univ. of North Carolina Press, 1996), 4–6.

75. Allen, *Life Experience and Gospel Labors,* 73–74; Porter, ed., *Early Negro Writing,* 9–11, 43, 49, 263–264; Douglass, *Annals of the First African Church,* 16; see Gaines, *Uplifting the Race;* see also Harris, *In the Shadow of Slavery,* 119–133.

76. Porter, ed., *Early Negro Writing,* 362, see also pages 322–323, 339, 352–353, 379.

77. Porter, ed., *Early Negro Writing,* 25.

78. Harris, *In the Shadow of Slavery,* 119–122.

79. For a comprehensive assessment of free black status in the North, see Litwack, *North of Slavery.*

80. Litwack, *North of Slavery,* 20–24; P. J. Staudenraus, *The African Colonization Movement, 1816–1865* (New York: Columbia Univ. Press, 1961), 1–8, 12–30, 117–121.

81. William T. Hamilton, *A Word for the African: A Sermon for the Benefit of the American Colonization Society* (Newark, N.J.: W. Tuttle and Co., Printer, 1825), 19–21; Staudenraus, *The African Colonization Movement,* 117.

82. Hamilton, *A Sermon for the Benefit of the American Colonization Society.*

83. William Lloyd Garrison, *Thoughts on African Colonization . . .* (Boston, 1832; reprint, New York: Arno and the New York Times, 1968), 8–9; John Bracey, August Meier, Elliott Rudwick, eds., *Black Nationalism in America* (Indianapolis, Ind.: Bobbs-Merrill, 1970), 45–46; for an in-depth assessment of James Forten's role in early anticolonization activities, see Winch, *A Gentleman of Color,* 177–206.

84. Porter, ed., *Early Negro Writing,* 266.

85. Garrison, *Thoughts on African Colonization,* 8–9.

86. Porter, ed., *Early Negro Writing*, 267.

87. Porter, ed., *Early Negro Writing*, 267; Litwack, *North of Slavery*, 25–26.

88. Porter, ed., *Early Negro Writing*, 266–267.

89. Douglass, *Annals of the First African Church*, 25–29; Miller, *The Search for a Black Nationality*, 6–12.

90. Miller, *The Search for a Black Nationality*, 74–82; Horton and Horton, *In Search of Liberty*, 191–194; Winch, *Philadelphia's Black Elite*, 49–61.

91. Carter G. Woodson, ed., *The Mind of the Negro as Reflected in Letters Written During the Crisis, 1800–1860* (1926; reprint, New York: Russell and Russell, 1969), 2–3.

CHAPTER 3. THEY WANT US SLAVES FOREVER

1. Leon Litwack, *North of Slavery: The Negro in the Free States, 1790–1860* (Chicago: Univ. of Chicago Press, 1961), 75–84, 93–94, 153–155, 115–117.

2. Gilbert Barnes, *The Antislavery Impulse: 1830–1844* (New York: Appleton-Century, 1933), 27; Benjamin Quarles, *Black Abolitionists* (1969; reprint, New York: Oxford Univ. Press, 1975), 10–12.

3. Jessie Carney Smith and Carrel Peterson Horton, comps. and eds., *Historical Statistics of Black America* (New York: Gale Research, 1995), 2:1539–1541; Bureau of the Census, U.S. Department of Commerce, *Negro Population, 1790–1915* (Washington D.C.: Government Printing Office, 1918), 44–45.

4. Howard Holman Bell, ed., *Minutes of the Proceedings of the National Negro Conventions, 1830–1864* (New York: Arno and the New York Times, 1969), 1830 Convention, 10.

5. Quarles, *Black Abolitionists*, 17; William C. Nell, *The Colored Patriots of the American Revolution, with Sketches of Several Distinguished Colored Persons* (1855; reprint, New York: Arno and the New York Times, 1968), 345; Walker, *WALKER'S APPEAL*, 3.

6. *Freedom's Journal*, March 16, 1827.

7. See, for example, *Freedom's Journal*, March 16, 1827.

8. Walker, *WALKER'S APPEAL*, vii–viii, 56–58; *Freedom's Journal*, March 16, 1827; for Walker's article, see *Freedom's Journal*, December 19, 1828; for a recent examination of David Walker, see Peter Hinks, *To Awaken My Afflicted Brethren: David Walker and the Problem of Antebellum Slave Resistance* (University Park: Pennsylvania State Univ. Press, 1997); see also James O. Horton and Lois Horton, *Black Bostonians: Family, Life, and Community Struggles in the Antebellum North* (New York: Holmes and Meier, 1979), 81, 93.

9. Walker, *WALKER'S APPEAL*, 1, 7, 16–18, 28–29, 39; see also Albert J. Raboteau, "The Black Experience in American Evangelicalism: The Meaning of Slavery," in *African-American Religion: Interpretive Essays in History and Culture*, ed. Timothy E. Fulop and Albert J. Raboteau, 96 (New York: Routledge, 1997).

10. Walker, *WALKER'S APPEAL*, 20–23, 28.

11. Walker, *WALKER'S APPEAL*, 20–23, 28.

12. Walker, *WALKER'S APPEAL*, 3.

13. Walker, *WALKER'S APPEAL*, 3, 9–10.

14. Anne C. Loveland, "Evangelicalism and Immediate Emancipation in American Antislavery Thought," *Journal of Southern History* 32(May 1966): 172–175; see also Mark Noll, *America's God: From Jonathan Edwards to Abraham Lincoln* (New York: Oxford Univ. Press, 2002), 296, 307.

15. Walker, *WALKER'S APPEAL*, 18.

16. Walker, *WALKER'S APPEAL*, 35–43.

17. See Timothy E. Fulop, "'The Future Golden Day of the Race': Millennialism and Black

Americans in the Nadir, 1877–1901," in Fulop and Raboteau, eds., *African-American Religion,* 229–231; Ruth Bloch, *Visionary Republic: Millennial Themes in American Thought, 1756–1800* (New York: Cambridge Univ. Press, 1985), 230–231.

18. Walker, *WALKER'S APPEAL,* 2, 11, 18, 21–26, 35–39, 64, 75; Noll, *America's God,* 230–235; for a literary critique of *WALKER'S APPEAL,* see Carla Peterson, *"Doers of the Word": African American Women Speakers and Writers in the North, 1830–1880* (New York: Oxford Univ. Press, 1995; reprint, New Brunswick, N.J.: Rutgers Univ. Press, 1998), 64–65.

19. *Liberator,* December 1, 1832.

20. Maria W. Stewart, *Maria W. Stewart, America's First Black Woman Political Writer: Essays and Speeches,* ed. Marilyn Richardson, 30, 40 (Bloomington: Indiana Univ. Press, 1987). See Richardson's thoughtful introduction for David Walker's influence on Maria Stewart and insight into Stewart's life and contribution to antebellum American political thought.

21. Stewart, *Maria W. Stewart, America's First Black Woman Political Writer,* 53–54; Sue E. Houchins, ed., *Spiritual Narratives,* The Schomburg Library of Nineteenth-Century Black Women Writers (New York: Oxford Univ. Press, 1988), xxix–xliv, 3–10.

22. For formation of the white American middle class, see Mary P. Ryan, *Cradle of the Middle Class: The Family in Oneida County, New York, 1790–1865* (New York: Cambridge Univ. Press, 1981), 12–17, 60–104.

23. Stewart, *Maria W. Stewart, America's First Black Woman Political Writer,* 56–59; see Peterson, *"Doers of the Word,"* 56–73, for an in-depth literary analysis of Maria Stewart's writing and position in antebellum northern society.

24. Stewart, *Maria W. Stewart, America's First Black Woman Political Writer,* 57; James Horton and Lois Horton, "Violence, Protest, and Identity: Black Manhood in Antebellum America," in *Free People of Color: Inside the African American Community,* ed. James O. Horton, 81–90 (Washington, D.C.: Smithsonian Institution Press, 1993).

25. Stewart, *Maria W. Stewart, America's First Black Woman Political Writer,* 38–39, 60.

26. Stewart, *Maria W. Stewart, America's First Black Woman Political Writer,* 29–32, 35.

27. Stewart, *Maria W. Stewart, America's First Black Woman Political Writer,* 45–48.

28. Stewart, *Maria W. Stewart, America's First Black Woman Political Writer,* 68–70.

29. Bell, *Minutes of the Proceedings of the National Negro Conventions,* 1830 Convention, 9–10; Howard H. Bell, *A Survey of the Negro Convention Movement, 1830–1861* (New York: Arno and New York Times, 1969), 10–37.

30. Joel Schor, *Henry Highland Garnet: A Voice of Black Radicalism in the Nineteenth Century* (Westport, Conn.: Greenwood, 1977), 4–14; Carleton Mabee, *Black Education in New York State: From Colonial to Modern Times* (Syracuse N.Y.: Syracuse Univ. Press, 1979), 22.

31. Charlotte Forten Grimké, *The Journals of Charlotte Forten Grimké,* The Schomburg Library of Nineteenth-Century Black Women Writers, ed. Brenda Stevenson, 3–18 (New York: Oxford Univ. Press, 1988); Julie Winch, *A Gentleman of Color: The Life of James Forten* (New York: Oxford Univ. Press, 2002), 256–257; Mabee, *Black Education in New York State,* 22, 65, 95–96; Horton and Horton, *Black Bostonians,* 57–58; see also C. Peter Ripley et al., eds., *The Black Abolitionist Papers* (Chapel Hill: Univ. of North Carolina Press, 1991), 3:360 n.

32. Dorothy Sterling, ed., *We Are Your Sisters: Black Women in the Nineteenth Century* (New York: Norton, 1984), 130–131.

33. Schor, *Henry Highland Garnet,* 10, 16–19; James Horton, "Black Education at Oberlin College," *Journal of Negro Education* 54 (fall 1985): 482–484; Harry C. Silcox, "Nineteenth-Century Philadelphia Black Militant: Octavius Catto," *Pennsylvania History* 44 (January 1977): 54–55;

Mabee, *Black Education in New York*, 21–51, 64–65; Winch, *A Gentleman of Color*, 116–117; see also Martin Delany, *The Condition, Elevation, Emigration and Destiny of the Colored People of the United States Politically Considered* (1852; reprint, Baltimore: Black Classic Press, 1993), 110–133.

34. William Still, *The Underground Railroad: A Record of Facts, Authentic Narratives, Letters, . . .* (1872; reprint, Medford, N.J.: Plexus, 2005), 525; Winch, *A Gentleman of Color*, 116–117; Martin Delany, *The Condition, Elevation, Emigration and Destiny*, 92–110.

35. See for example, Sterling, *We Are Your Sisters*, 126.

36. Bell, *Minutes of the Proceedings of the National Negro Conventions*, 1830 Convention, 6–11, 1831 Convention, 5, 15, 1832 Convention, 36.

37. *Freedom's Journal*, March 16, 1827; *The Rights of All*, May 29, 1829; for the penny press, see Michael Schudson, *Discovering the News: A Social History of American Newspapers* (New York: Basic Books, 1978), and Frank Luther Mott, *American Journalism: A History of Newspapers in the United States through 250 Years, 1690–1940* (New York: Macmillan, 1941).

38. *Freedom's Journal*, March 16, 1827; *Freedom's Journal*, April 4, 1828; *The Rights of All*, May 29, 1829; *Colored American*, March 4, 1837; see also *Colored American*, June 4, 1839. Samuel Cornish's name is not listed as editor and the banner is replaced with a list of the new editors and proprietors.

39. *Freedom's Journal*, March 16, 1827; *The Rights of All*, May 29, 1829; see also Bell, *Minutes of the Proceedings of the National Negro Conventions*, 1834 Convention, 3.

40. Benjamin Quarles, *Black Abolitionists*, 68–69.

41. See chapter 1 above.

42. Bell, *Minutes of the Proceedings of the National Negro Conventions*, 1831 Convention, 10.

43. Bell, *Minutes of the Proceedings of the National Negro Conventions*, 1831 Convention, 4–5, 1835 Convention, 9.

44. Bell, *Minutes of the Proceedings of the National Negro Conventions*, 1831 Convention, 4–5.

45. Herbert Aptheker, ed., *A Documentary History of the Negro People in the United States: From Colonial Times through the Civil War* (New York: Citadel Press, 1961), 1:108–109; Quarles, *Black Abolitionists*, 19–20.

46. *Proceedings of the Pennsylvania Antislavery Convention* (Harrisburg, 1837), 56; Carter G. Woodson, ed., *Negro Orators and Their Orations* (New York: Russell and Russell, 1925), 89.

47. William Lloyd Garrison, *Thoughts on African Colonization . . .* (Boston, 1832; reprint, New York: Arno and the New York Times, 1968), i–ii.

48. Horton and Horton, *Black Bostonians*, 88–89; Quarles, *Black Abolitionists*, 30–32.

49. Horton and Horton, *Black Bostonians*, 61; Jane Pease and William Pease, *They Who Would Be Free: Blacks' Search for Freedom, 1830–1861* (New York: Atheneum, 1974), 14; see Benjamin Quarles, *Black Abolitionists*, for a general treatment of black abolitionism.

50. Quarles, *Black Abolitionists*, 61–67; James O. Horton and Lois Horton, *In Hope of Liberty: Culture, Community and Protest among Northern Free Blacks, 1700–1860* (New York: Oxford Univ. Press, 1997), 227; for U.S. black abolitionists' activity in Great Britain, see Richard Blackett, *Building an Antislavery Wall: Black Americans in the Atlantic Abolition Movement, 1830–1860* (Baton Rouge: Louisiana State Univ. Press, 1983).

51. For the multiple meanings of virtue in this era, see James T. Kloppenberg, "The Virtues of Liberalism: Christianity, Republicanism, and Ethics in Early American Political Discourse," *Journal of American History* 74 (June 1987): 9–33.

52. Frederick Douglass, *Narrative of the Life of Frederick Douglass, an American Slave*, ed. Houston A. Baker Jr., 81–82, 93 (1845; reprint, New York: Viking Penguin Books, 1986); see also William Wells Brown, *From Fugitive Slave to Free Man: The Autobiographies of William Wells*

Brown, ed. William L. Andrews, 34–42, 59, 77 (New York: Penguin Books, 1993); Harriet Jacobs, *Incidents in the Life of a Slave Girl: Written by Herself*, ed. Jean Fagan Yellin (Cambridge, Mass.: Harvard Univ. Press, 1987); *Freedom's Journal*, April 13, 1827.

53. Quoted in Quarles, *Black Abolitionists*, viii.

54. Garrison, *Thoughts on African Colonization*, 78–89; David Ruggles, *An Antidote for a Poisonous Combination* (New York: 1838), 9; David Ruggles, *The Abrogation of the Seventh Commandment by the American Churches* (New York: 1835); Samuel Ringgold Ward, *Autobiography of a Fugitive Negro, His Anti-Slavery Labours in the United States, Canada, and England* (1855; reprint, New York: Arno and the New York Times, 1968), 67; John Blassingame, ed., *The Frederick Douglass Papers*, Series One, vols. 1–5 (New Haven, Conn.: Yale Univ. Press, 1979–1992), 2:182–183; *Freedom's Journal*, March 30, 1827, April 13, 1827, November 30, 1827; *Colored American*, March 4, 1837; Raboteau, "The Black Experience in American Evangelicalism," 98.

55. Ohio Anti-Slavery Convention Proceedings, 22–24 April 1835 (Anti-Slavery Collection, Boston Public Library, File #7588.75).

56. *Colored American*, May 27, 1837; *Freedom's Journal*, April 13, 1827; see also *The Rights of All*, May 29, 1829.

57. Samuel E. Cornish and Theodore S. Wright, *The Colonization Scheme Considered . . .* (Newark, N.J.: Aaron Guest, 1840), 15; see Frederick Douglass, *My Bondage and My Freedom*, ed. William L. Andrews, 9–23 (1855; reprint, Urbana: Univ. of Illinois Press, 1987), for James McCune Smith's introduction; *Colored American*, May 27, 1837.

58. *Colored American*, September 22, 1838; Blassingame, ed., *Frederick Douglass Papers*, 2:3, 9; James Forten Jr., *An Address Delivered before the Ladies' Anti-Slavery Society of Philadelphia, On the Evening of the 14th of April, 1836* (Philadelphia: Merrihew and Gunn, 1836), 3–6; *Anti-Slavery Advocate*, July 1, 1859; *Colored American*, March 4, 1837; *Freedom's Journal*, June 29, 1827.

59. *National Reformer*, January 1839; Blassingame, ed., *Frederick Douglass Papers*, 2:76, 144–145.

60. William Lloyd Garrison, ed., "Sentiments of the People of Color," in *Thoughts on African Colonization . . .* (Boston, 1832; reprint, New York: Arno and the New York Times, 1968), 17, 27, 31.

61. *Colored American*, May 30, 1840.

62. Bell, *Minutes of the Proceedings of the National Negro Conventions*, 1835 Convention, 27–28; *Colored American*, May 27, 1837; John Mercer Langston, *Freedom and Citizenship* (1883; reprint, Miami: Mnemosyne, 1969), 59–60.

63. *Anti-Slavery Advocate*, March 2, 1859, April 2, 1859, October 1, 1859; Douglass, *Narrative*, 153–154.

64. Aptheker, *Documentary History*, 1:108–109; Bell, *Minutes of the Proceedings of the National Negro Conventions*, 1835 Convention, 29–30.

65. Alexander Crummell, "The Condition of the Black and Colored Population of the United States," Report 1848, Alexander Crummell Papers, Schomburg Library, New York Public Library; James McCune Smith, *The Destiny of the People of Color: A Lecture, Delivered before the Philomathean Society and Hamilton Lyceum in January, 1841* (New York: 1843); *Colored American*, June 10, 1837.

66. Litwack, *North of Slavery*, 216; Quarles, *Black Abolitionists*, 47–49.

67. James Brewer Stewart, *Holy Warriors: The Abolitionists and American Slavery* (New York: Hill and Wang, 1976), 142–144; see also *Freedom's Journal*, June 15, 1827.

68. Woodson, *Negro Orators*, 90.

69. Woodson, *Negro Orators*, 91.

70. Stewart, *Holy Warriors*, 89–96.

71. James Forten Jr., *Address before the American Moral Reform Society* (Philadelphia, 1837), 43.

72. Blassingame, ed., *Frederick Douglass Papers,* 3:39–40.

73. *Colored American,* October 7, 1837, May 2, 1840, April 25, 1840, March 21, 1840, November 29, 1839.

CHAPTER 4. WE DO NOT ALL OF US THINK ALIKE

1. James Horton and Lois Horton, *In Hope of Liberty: Culture, Community and Protest among Northern Free Blacks, 1700–1860* (New York: Oxford Univ. Press, 1997), 191; Michael A. Gomez, *Exchanging Our Country Marks: The Transformation of African Identities in the Colonial and Antebellum South* (Chapel Hill: Univ. of North Carolina Press, 1998), 20–26.

2. See chapter 1 for discussion of black leaders' construction and idealization of an African "country."

3. Garrison, "Sentiments of the People of Color," 9.

4. *Freedom's Journal,* November 2, 1827

5. Geroge R. Price and James Brewer Stewart, eds., *To Heal the Scourge of Prejudice: The Life and Writings of Hosea Easton* (Amherst: Univ. of Massachusetts Press, 1999), 58.

6. Garrison, "Sentiments of People of Color," 14, 17, 18–19.

7. Garrison, "Sentiments of People of Color," 24–27.

8. Garrison, "Sentiments of the People of Color," 29, 19, 30.

9. Garrison, "Sentiments of People of Color," 16.

10. Howard Holman Bell, ed., *Minutes of the Proceedings of the National Negro Conventions, 1830–1864* (New York: Arno and New York Times, 1969), 1830 Convention, 10; Garrison, "Sentiments of People of Color," 26.

11. Garrison, "Sentiments of People of Color," 20. For a discussion of black response to Haitian emigration in this period and the Haitian government's interest in black American immigration, see Bruce Dain, *A Hideous Monster of the Mind: American Race Theory in the Early Republic* (Cambridge, Mass.: Harvard Univ. Press, 2002), 81–111.

12. See Dorothy Porter, ed., *Early Negro Writing, 1760–1837* (1971; reprint, Baltimore: Black Classic Press, 1995), vii–xii; *Freedom's Journal,* December 2, 1827; see also Garrison, "Sentiments of People of Color," 9, 10, 15, 21, 24, 36. See Anthony D. Smith, *Ethnic Origins of Nations* (Oxford: Blackwell, 1986), 22–24, for a discussion of the "dimensions of *ethnie.*"

13. Mark Noll, *America's God: From Jonathan Edwards to Abraham Lincoln* (New York: Oxford Univ. Press, 2002), 165–166, 169–170, 174.

14. David Brion Davis, *The Problem of Slavery in Western Culture* (Ithaca, N.Y.: Cornell Univ. Press, 1966), 386–387; Timothy L. Smith, "Righteousness and Hope: Christian Holiness and the Millennial Vision in America, 1800–1900," *American Quarterly* 31 (spring 1979): 21–45.

15. Smith, "Righteousness and Hope," 21.

16. Smith, "Righteousness and Hope," 27.

17. Smith, "Righteousness and Hope," 25–27; James Brewer Stewart, *Holy Warriors: The Abolitionists and American Slavery* (New York: Hill and Wang, 1976), 50–73.

18. Ronald G. Walters, *American Reformers, 1815–1860* (New York: Hill and Wang, 1978), 121–143.

19. Joel Schor, *Henry Highland Garnet: A Voice of Black Radicalism in the Nineteenth Century* (Westport, Conn.: Greenwood, 1977), 100; for a fuller discussion of black temperance organizations, see Donald Yacovone, "The Transformation of the Black Temperance Movement, 1827–1854: An Interpretation," *Journal of the Early American Republic* 8 (autumn 1988): 281–297.

20. Bell, *Minutes of the Proceedings of the National Negro Conventions,* 1831 Convention, 5, 1832 Convention, 36, 1833 Convention, 5, 13, 28, 33.

21. Bell, *Minutes of the Proceedings of the National Negro Conventions,* 1834 Convention, 31, 1835 Convention, 14–15; Sterling Stuckey, *The Ideological Origins of Black Nationalism* (Boston: Beacon, 1972), 252–260.

22. *Colored American,* March 3, 1838; see also Richard P. McCormick, "William Whipper: Moral Reformer," *Pennsylvania History* 43 (January 1976): 31–32.

23. *The Minutes and Proceedings of the First Annual Moral Reform Society* (Philadelphia, 1837), 43; Carlton Mabee, *Black Freedom: The Nonviolent Abolitionists from 1830 through the Civil War* (New York: Macmillan, 1970), 36, 57–58; Walters, *American Reformers,* 105; *National Reformer,* September 1838.

24. Porter, ed., *Early Negro Writing,* 201.

25. Smith, "Righteousness and Hope," 29.

26. Bell, *Minutes of the Proceedings of the National Negro Conventions,* 1834 Convention, 10–13, 1835 Convention, 4–5; *Colored American,* July 11, 1840, September 16, 1837; Leigh R. Whipper Papers, Moorland-Spingarn Research Center, Howard University.

27. See Porter, ed., *Early Negro Writing,* 158–160, 58, 85, 93.

28. *Colored American,* September 15, 1838.

29. Bell, *Minutes of the Proceedings of the National Negro Conventions,* 1835 Convention, 32; *Colored American,* September 15, 1838; Stuckey, *Ideological Origins,* 118–125.

30. *Colored American,* September 15, 1838.

31. *Colored American,* July 18, 1840; Stuckey, *Ideological Origins,* 252–260.

32. *Colored American,* May 2, 1840.

33. As Sterling Stuckey suggests, a close study of Garnet's later comments about separatism and labels of identification strongly indicates that Garnet, a close friend and former New Canaan and Oneida classmate of Thomas Sipkins Sidney, authored the Sidney letters. I have ruled out Stuckey's other candidate, Alexander Crummell, also a close friend of Garnet and Sidney, as the possible writer because his writing style seems inconsistent with the Sidney letters. See Stuckey, *Ideological Origins,* 15–17; Milton C. Sernett, *North Star Country: Upstate New York and the Crusade for African American Freedom* (Syracuse, N.Y.: Syracuse Univ. Press, 2002), 22.

34. Stuckey, *Ideological Origins,* 149–160.

35. Stuckey, *Ideological Origins,* 160.

36. Stuckey, *Ideological Origins,* 160–164.

37. Stuckey, *Ideological Origins,* 162.

38. Henry Highland Garnet, *The Past and Present Condition and the Destiny of the Colored Race* (1848; reprint, Miami: Mnemosyne, 1969), 6–12, 19.

39. *Colored American,* November 9, 1839, July 18, 1840.

40. *The North Star,* February 25, 1848, March 3, 1848, March 10, 1848

41. *The North Star,* March 6, 1848; John Blassingame, ed., *The Frederick Douglass Papers,* Series One, vols. 1–5 (New Haven, Conn.: Yale Univ. Press, 1979–1992), 2:110–111; Waldo Martin, *The Mind of Frederick Douglass* (Chapel Hill: Univ. of North Carolina Press, 1984), 100–102; *Colored American,* September 2, 1837.

42. Charlotte Forten Grimké, *The Journals of Charlotte Forten Grimké,* The Schomburg Library of Nineteenth-Century Black Women Writers, ed. Brenda Stevenson, 17 (New York: Oxford Univ. Press, 1988); Martin, *The Mind of Frederick Douglass,* 101–102; *Proceedings of the Boston School Integration Celebration* (Boston, 1855), 4–5.

43. Philip Foner and George E. Walker, eds., *Proceedings of the Black State Conventions, 1840–1865* (Philadelphia: Temple Univ. Press, 1979), 1:229. I agree with Patrick Rael that arguments asserting that black activists were either integrationists or separatists/nationalists are simplistic and reductionistic. See Patrick Rael in *Black Identity and Black Protest in the Antebellum North* (Chapel Hill: Univ. of North Carolina Press, 2002), 10.

44. Foner and Walker, eds., *Proceedings of the Black State Conventions,* 2:59.

45. *Colored American,* May 23, 1840.

46. Horton and Horton, *In Hope of Liberty,* 218; Linda Marie Perkins, "Quaker Beneficence and Black Control: The Institute for Colored Youth, 1852–1903," in *New Perspectives on Black Educational History,* ed. Vincent P. Franklin and James D. Anderson, 19–23 (Boston: Hall, 1978).

47. Foner and Walker, eds., *Proceedings of the Black State Conventions,* 1:149–151.

48. Foner and Walker, eds., *Proceedings of the Black State Conventions,* 1:151.

49. Daniel Payne, *Recollections of Seventy Years* (Nashville: Publishing House of the A.M.E. Sunday School Union, 1888; reprint, Salem, N.H.: Ayer, 1991), 74–94.

50. Payne, *Recollections,* 252–255; Forten Grimké, *The Journals of Charlotte Forten Grimké,* 153; Albert J. Raboteau, *Slave Religion: The "Invisible Institution" in the Antebellum South* (New York: Oxford Univ. Press, 1978), 59–75. Excavations of seventeenth–nineteenth-century burial sites in New York City and Philadelphia reveal the continuation of West African burial practices. Many northern blacks decorated their graves with personal belongings of the deceased. This West African practice was believed to free the spirits of the deceased. See Mechal Sobel, *Trablin' On: The Slave Journey to an Afro-Baptist Faith* (Princeton, N.J.: Princeton Univ. Press, 1988), 242; Leslie M. Harris, *In the Shadow of Slavery: African Americans in New York City, 1626–1863* (Chicago: Univ. of Chicago Press, 2003), 1–2.

51. For an analysis of twentieth-century complaints about uneducated black clerics, see Barbara D. Savage, *Your Spirits Walk beside Us: The Politics of Black Religion* (Cambridge, Mass.: Harvard Univ. Press, 2008), 20–67.

52. *Colored American,* July 1, 1837, August 12, 1837; Daniel A. Payne, *A History of the African Methodist Episcopal Church* (1891; reprint, New York: Arno and New York Times, 1969), 115, 153.

53. Payne, *A History of the African Methodist Episcopal Church,* 98, 100, 115–117, 133–134, 138, 141, 153–156, 168, 177, 191; *The North Star,* March 10, 1848; see also Foner and Walker, eds., *Proceedings of the Black State Conventions,* 1:228.

54. Payne, *Recollections,* 116–119; Robert A. Warner, "Amos Gerry Beman—1812–1874, A Memoir on a Forgotten Leader," *Journal of Negro History* 22 (April 1937): 217–218.

55. For an astute discussion of "community among ourselves," see Saidiya V. Hartman, *Scenes of Subjection: Terror, Slavery, and Self-Making in Nineteenth-Century America* (New York: Oxford Univ. Press, 1997), 61.

56. *Proceedings of the Boston School Integration Celebration,* 22.

57. Garnet, *Past and Present,* 29.

58. *Colored American,* May 2, 1840; *Liberator,* December 18, 1832; see also Rael, *Black Identity and Black Protest,* 82–117.

59. *Colored American,* March 4, 1837.

60. *Colored American,* November 18, 1837.

61. Foner and Walker, eds., *Proceedings of the Black State Conventions,* 1:11–12.

62. Foner and Walker, eds., *Proceedings of the Black State Conventions,* 1:8.

63. Foner and Walker, eds., *Proceedings of the Black State Conventions,* 1:18.

64. For American citizenship and free black status, see James Kettner, *The Development of*

American Citizenship, 1608–1870 (Chapel Hill: Univ. of North Carolina Press, 1978), 230–232, 311–324; *Colored American*, May 23, 1840; Bell, *Minutes of the Proceedings of the National Negro Conventions*, 1831 Convention, 4–5, 1833 Convention, 34–35, 1834 Convention, 16; Foner and Walker, eds., *Proceedings of the Black State Conventions*, 1:177.

65. Martin, *The Mind of Frederick Douglass*, 23, 31–32, 182; William Edward Farrison, *William Wells Brown: Author and Reformer* (Chicago: Univ. of Chicago Press, 1969), 97; for an analysis of Frederick Douglass's switch from the Constitution as a proslavery to an antislavery document, see James Oakes, *The Radical and the Republican: Frederick Douglass, Abraham Lincoln, and the Triumph of Anti-Slavery Politics* (New York: Norton, 2007).

66. William C. Nell, *The Colored Patriots of the American Revolution, with Sketches of Several Distinguished Colored Persons* (1855; reprint, New York: Arno and the New York Times, 1968), 312, 338–340; Foner and Walker, eds., *Proceedings of the Black State Conventions*, 1:29.

67. Foner and Walker, eds., *Proceedings of the Black State Conventions*, 2:131.

68. Foner and Walker, eds., *Proceedings of the Black State Conventions*, 1:229; *Anglo-African Magazine* (1859), 1:146.

69. *Colored American*, October 17, 1840, February 13, 1841; *National Reformer*, February 1839.

70. *Colored American*, July 15, 1837, June 6, 1840.

71. See James O. Horton, ed., *Free People of Color: Inside the African American Community* (Washington, D.C.: Smithsonian Institution Press, 1993), 80–120, for a detailed description of gender conventions among antebellum northern blacks; *Weekly Advocate*, January 1, 1837, February 11, 1837.

72. Sanford's first name is not recorded.

73. Bell, *Minutes of the Proceedings of the National Negro Conventions*, 1848 Convention, 11–12, 17.

74. Foner and Walker, eds., *Proceedings of the Black State Conventions*, 1:91, 227; C. Peter Ripley et al., eds., *The Black Abolitionist Papers* (Chapel Hill: Univ. of North Carolina Press, 1985), 4:295–297.

75. See, for example, Bell, *Minutes of the Proceedings of the National Negro Conventions*, 1831 Convention, 5, 10; 1847 Convention, 6, 17–21; *Colored American*, October 21, 1837.

76. *Freedom's Journal*, October 13, 1827, November 2, 1827, November 9, 1827, November 16, 1827, November 30, 1827; *Colored American*, November 18, 1837; Foner and Walker, eds., *Proceedings of the Black State Conventions*, 1:5–26; Schor, *Henry Highland Garnet*, 142–143; Walters, *American Reformers*, 115–116.

77. Foner and Walker, eds., *Proceedings of the Black State Conventions*, 1:7.

78. Martin, *The Mind of Frederick Douglass*, 32–40.

79. Lori Ginzberg, *Women and the Work of Benevolence: Morality, Politics, and Class in the 19th-Century United States* (New Haven, Conn.: Yale Univ. Press, 1990), 98–132; see also James B. Stewart, *Abolitionist Politics and the Coming of the Civil War* (Amherst: Univ. of Massachusetts Press, 2008), 13–19.

CHAPTER 5. THEY DESPISE US FOR OUR COLOR

1. Sarah Douglass to William Bassett, December 1837, in *Letters of Theodore Dwight Weld, Angelina Grimké Weld and Sarah Grimké, 1822–1844*, ed. Gilbert H. Barnes and Dwight L. Dumond, 1:829–831 (New York: Appleton-Century, 1934); Dorothy Sterling, ed., *We Are Your Sisters: Black Women in the Nineteenth Century* (New York: Norton, 1984), 116, 126–133.

2. For political, economic, and social repression of northern blacks, see Leon Litwack, *North*

of Slavery: The Negro in the Free States, 1790–1860 (Chicago: Univ. of Chicago Press, 1961); for increased racism in the antebellum era and its meaning, see James Brewer Stewart, "Modernizing 'Difference': The Political Meanings of Color in the Free States, 1776–1840," *Journal of the Early Republic* 19 (winter 1999): 691–712; John Wood Sweet, *Bodies Politic: Negotiating Race in the American North, 1730–1830* (Baltimore: Johns Hopkins Univ. Press, 2003); Eric Lott, *Love and Theft: Blackface Minstrelsy and the American Working Class* (New York: Oxford Univ. Press, 1993); Robert Toll, *Blacking Up: The Minstrel Show in Nineteenth-Century America* (New York: Oxford Univ. Press, 1974); David Roediger, *The Wages of Whiteness: Race and the Making of the American Working Class* (London: Verso, 1991). For racial ideology, see George Fredrickson, *The Black Image in the White Mind: The Debate on Afro-American Character and Destiny, 1817–1914* (New York: Harper and Row, 1971), and George Fredrickson, *Racism: A Short History* (Princeton, N.J.: Princeton Univ. Press, 2002); Bruce Dain, *A Hideous Monster of the Mind: American Race Theory in the Early Republic* (Cambridge, Mass.: Harvard Univ. Press, 2002).

3. Samuel Ringgold Ward, *Autobiography of a Fugitive Negro, His Anti-Slavery Labours in the United States, Canada, and England* (1855; reprint, New York: Arno and the New York Times, 1968), 42; *Colored American*, September 26, 1840, July 8, 1837, June 9, 1838, July 8, 1838; *Weekly Advocate,* January 14, 1837; C. Peter Ripley et al., eds., *The Black Abolitionist Papers* (Chapel Hill: Univ. of North Carolina Press, 1992), 5:91 (hereinafter cited as *BAP*); see also Waldo E. Martin, *The Mind of Frederick Douglass* (Chapel Hill: Univ. of North Carolina Press, 1984), 109–110; John W. Blassingame, ed., *The Frederick Douglass Papers,* Series One, vols. 1–5 (New Haven, Conn.: Yale Univ. Press, 1979–1992), 2:113; James Forten Jr., *An Address Delivered before the Ladies' Anti-Slavery Society of Philadelphia, On the Evening of the 14th of April, 1836* (Philadelphia: Merrihew and Gunn, 1836), 7.

4. Hosea Easton, *A Treatise on the Intellectual Character, and Civil and Political Condition of the Colored People of the U. States . . .* (Boston: Isaac Knapp, 1837), 35–45.

5. Easton, *Treatise,* 35–45; Samuel E. Cornish and Theodore S. Wright, *The Colonization Scheme Considered . . .* (Newark, N.J.: Aaron Guest, 1840), 3–4; Dorothy Porter, ed., *Early Negro Writing, 1760–1837* (1971; reprint, Baltimore: Black Classic Press, 1995), 281–285.

6. Easton, *Treatise,* 37–38, 42–46.

7. Martin R. Delany, *The Condition, Elevation, Emigration and Destiny of the Colored People of the United States Politically Considered* (1852; reprint, Baltimore: Black Classic Press, 1993), 12–13.

8. Frederick Douglass, *The Life and Writings of Frederick Douglass,* ed. Philip S. Foner, 2:295 (New York: International Publishers, 1950).

9. Philip S. Foner and George E. Walker, eds., *Proceedings of the Black State Conventions, 1840–1865* (Philadelphia: Temple Univ. Press, 1979), 1:114–115.

10. *Colored American,* April 15, 1837; Blassingame, ed., *Frederick Douglass Papers,* 2:108–109, 113; Garnet, *Past and Present,* 27–28; *BAP,* 3:430–431; see also Joanne Pope Melish, "The 'Condition' Debate and Racial Discourse in the Antebellum North," *Journal of the Early Republic* 19 (winter 1999): 651–672.

11. *BAP,* 3:247–251; Douglass, *Life and Writings,* 2:129.

12. *The Rights of All,* September 18, 1829.

13. Foner and Walker, eds., *Proceedings of the Black State Conventions,* 2:60.

14. See Emma Jones Lapsansky, "'Since They Got Those Separate Churches': Afro-Americans and Racism in Jacksonian Philadelphia," *American Quarterly* 32 (spring 1980): 54–78.

15. Foner and Walker, eds., *Proceedings of the Black State Conventions,* 1:126–133.

16. Foner and Walker, eds., *Proceedings of the Black State Conventions,* 1:126–132.

17. *Colored American*, June 24, 1837; *BAP*, 3:119–131, 4:242; Foner and Walker, eds., *Proceedings of the Black State Conventions*, 1:126–132.

18. *BAP*, 4:242–244; Douglass, *Life and Writings*, 2:139.

19. I believe Frances Watkins Harper wrote under the pseudonym "Jane Rustic" in the *Anglo-African Magazine*. The language and even more the ideas, sharp wit, and sentiments are the same. Also, Rustic's narrator shares Watkins life story. *Anglo-African Magazine* (1859), 1:160, 340–341; Sarah Douglass to William Bassett, in *Letters of Theodore Dwight Weld*, ed. Barnes and Dumond, 1:830–831; *BAP*, 3:221–222; see also Anne M. Boylan, "Benevolence and Antislavery Activity among African American Women in New York and Boston, 1820–1840," in *The Abolitionist Sisterhood: Women's Political Culture in Antebellum America*, ed. Jean Fagan Yellin and John C. Van Horne, 120 (Ithaca, N.Y.: Cornell Univ. Press, 1994).

20. Easton, *Treatise*, 37–38.

21. *BAP*, 3:225; *Colored American*, June 30, 1838, July 29, 1837, February 6, 1841.

22. *National Reformer*, November 1838; David Walker, *WALKER'S APPEAL . . . TO THE COLOURED CITIZENS OF THE WORLD, BUT IN PARTICULAR, AND VERY EXPRESSLY, TO THOSE OF THE UNITED STATES OF AMERICA*, 3rd ed., ed. Charles M. Wiltse, 9 (1829, reprint of 3rd ed., New York: Hill and Wang, 1965); Litwack, *North of Slavery*, 105–106.

23. *Colored American*, February 6, 1841.

24. *National Reformer*, November 1838.

25. *Colored American*, June 30, 1838; Walker, *WALKER'S APPEAL*, 9.

26. Litwack, *North of Slavery*, 105–106, 139, 142–152.

27. Charlotte Forten Grimké, *The Journals of Charlotte Forten Grimké*, The Schomburg Library of Nineteenth-Century Black Women Writers, ed. Brenda Stevenson, 139–140 (New York: Oxford Univ. Press, 1988).

28. Litwack, *North of Slavery*, 93–94; *BAP*, 4:225, 228.

29. Dain, *A Hideous Monster of the Mind*, 1–8.

30. Porter, ed., *Early Negro Writing*, 283; see also Easton, *Treatise*, 5.

31. Garnet, *Past and Present*, 6–7; Easton, *Treatise*, 5; Acts 17:26 was the *National Reformer*'s flag.

32. James W. C. Pennington, *A Text Book of the Origin and History, &c. &c. of the Colored People* (Hartford: Skinner, 1841), 7–16; Garnet, *Past and Present*, 6–7; Easton, *Treatise*, 8; *Anglo-African Magazine* (1859), 1:248.

33. Garnet, *Past and Present*, 6–7; Easton, *Treatise*, 8; Pennington, *A Text Book of the Origin and History*, 7–16; see also *Freedom's Journal*, February 29, 1828.

34. *Freedom's Journal*, February 29, 1828; *Anglo-African Magazine* (1859), 1:248; Mia Bay, *White Image in Black Mind: African American Ideas about White People, 1830–1925* (New York: Oxford Univ. Press, 2000), 26–30; Dain, *Hideous Monster of the Mind*, 126–128.

35. Fredrickson, *Racism*, 52, 66–68, and Fredrickson, *Black Image in the White Mind*, 2, 12–21, 126.

36. Cited in Bay, *White Image in Black Mind*, 16–17; Garnet, *Past and Present*, 6; Douglass, *Life and Writings*, 2:289–295.

37. Delany, *The Condition, Elevation, Emigration and Destiny*, 11; see also *Freedom's Journal*, April 13, 1827.

38. Douglass, *Life and Writings*, 2:295.

39. Delany, *The Condition, Elevation, Emigration and Destiny*, 18, 82, 209.

40. Richard Allen and Absalom Jones, "A Narrative of the Proceedings of the Awful Calamity . . . ," in Richard Allen, *The Life Experience and Gospel Labors of the Rt. Rev. Richard Allen* (1833; reprint, Nashville: Abingdon Press, 1960), 69. See Dain, *Hideous Monster of the Mind*, for

an analysis of late eighteenth- and early nineteenth-century black writers on the idea of race, especially Phillis Wheatley.

41. Douglass, *Life and Writings*, 2:289–302; Garnet, *Past and Present*, 7–12; Delany, *The Condition, Elevation, Emigration and Destiny*, 129; Pennington, *A Text Book of the Origin and History*, 22–31; *Freedom's Journal*, April 6, 1827; see also Bay, *White Image in the Black Mind*, 16–30; Dain, *Hideous Monster of the Mind*, 13–14, 38–54.

42. Easton, *Treatise*, 8–9; *Freedom's Journal*, April 20, 1827; Garnet, *Past and Present*, 6–7.

43. *Freedom's Journal*, April 6, 1827; Garnet, *Past and Present*, 7–12; Easton, *Treatise*, 8–20; *Anglo-African Magazine* (1859), 1:5–17; 225–238; Bay, *White Image in the Black Mind*, 29–30.

44. *Freedom's Journal*, April 6, 13, 20, 1827; Pennington, *A Text Book of the Origin and History*, 33–38. For a thoughtful analysis of the significance of Egypt and Ethiopia to antebellum black thinkers see Mia Bay, *White Image in the Black Mind*, 24–30; and Bruce Dain, *Hideous Monster of the Mind*, 112–148.

45. Douglass, *Life and Writings*, 2:301.

46. Fredrickson, *Black Image in White Mind*, 74–75; Douglass, *Life and Writing*, 2:296–299.

47. *Anglo-African Magazine* (1859), 1:4–5; *Frederick Douglass' Paper*, June 3, 1853; and May 19, 1854; Frederick Douglass, *My Bondage and My Freedom*, ed. William L. Andrews, 9 (1855; reprint, Urbana: Univ. of Illinois Press, 1987).

48. *Anglo-African Magazine* (1859), 1:5–17, 225–238; Easton, *Treatise*, 8.

49. *The Rights of All*, June 12, 1829.

50. Walker, *WALKER'S APPEAL*, 13–14.

51. Delany, *The Condition, Elevation, Emigration and Destiny*, 53–57; Douglass, *Life and Writings*, 2:303.

52. Delany, *The Condition, Elevation, Emigration and Destiny*, 64–65.

53. Walker, *WALKER'S APPEAL*, 10–12.

54. Easton, *Treatise*, 5–6; Garnet, *Past and Present*, 6–7.

55. Robert Benjamin Lewis, *Light and Truth: Collected From the Bible and Ancient and Modern History Containing the Universal History of the Colored and the Indian Race from the Creation of the World to the Present Time* (1836; reprint, Boston: Committee of Colored Gentlemen, 1844); Bay, *White Image in the Black Mind*, 44–46.

56. *Freedom's Journal*, April 6, 13, 20, 1827, and April 18, 1828; I agree with Bruce Dain and Mia Bay that John Russwurm wrote the "Mutability of Human Affairs" articles. As Dain notes, the language and style are very much Russwurm's. See Bay, *White Image in the Black Mind*, 26–30; Dain, *Hideous Monster*, 123; Douglass, *Life and Writings*, 2:306.

57. *BAP*, 3:350; see also John Stauffer, *The Black Hearts of Men: Radical Abolitionists and the Transformation of Race* (Cambridge, Mass.: Harvard Univ. Press, 2002); Bay, *White Image in the Black Mind*, 58–63; Dain, *Hideous Monster of the Mind*, 237–249; see also Leslie M. Harris, *In the Shadow of Slavery: African Americans in New York City, 1626–1863* (Chicago: Univ. of Chicago Press, 2003), 132, for a discussion of the future reformers who attended the African Free School.

58. *Anglo-African Magazine* (1859), 1:238. See Dain, *Hideous Monster of the Mind*, 245, 261–262, for an in-depth discussion of Smith's scientific sources for his racial theory.

59. James McCune Smith, "Introduction," in Frederick Douglass, *My Bondage and My Freedom*, ed. William L. Andrews, 22–23 (1855; reprint, Urbana: Univ. of Illinois Press, 1987); Bay, *White Image in the Black Mind*, 37–39, 42.

60. *Anglo-African Magazine* (1859), 1:12–15.

61. Walker, *WALKER'S APPEAL*, 16–17; see also Bay, *White Image in the Black Mind*, 32–35.

62. Walker, *WALKER'S APPEAL*, 24.

63. Walker, *WALKER'S APPEAL*, 12–13.

64. Walker, *WALKER'S APPEAL*, 3, 17.

65. Delany, *The Condition, Elevation, Emigration and Destiny*, 37.

66. See Fredrickson, *Racism*, 154, for a discussion of Kwame Anthony Appiah's distinction between racism and racialism.

67. *National Reformer*, January 1839; *Anglo-African Magazine* (1859), 1:1, 227–229; Douglass, *Life and Writings*, 2:303; For Douglass's attitude about phrenology, see Martin, *The Mind of Frederick Douglass*, 172.

68. Porter, ed., *Early Negro Writing*, 284.

69. *The North Star*, May 5, 1848.

70. *Anglo-African Magazine* (1859), 1:226.

71. James Forten Jr., *An Address Delivered before the Ladies' Anti-Slavery Society of Philadelphia*, 8.

72. Cornish and Wright, *The Colonization Scheme Considered*, 6–9; *Colored American*, January 13, 1839.

73. Delany, *The Condition, Elevation, Emigration and Destiny*, 20–22.

74. Garnet, *Past and Present*, 24–26; *BAP*, 3:430–431.

75. Delany, *The Condition, Elevation, Emigration and Destiny*, 87; Martin, *The Mind of Frederick Douglass*, 95.

76. *Anglo-African Magazine* (1859), 1:247–249.

77. Delany, *The Condition, Elevation, Emigration and Destiny*, 87.

78. Thomas Jefferson, *Notes on the State of Virginia*, Query 14, University of Virginia Electronic Text Center, http://etext.virginia.edu/toc/modeng/public/JefVirg.html, 267.

79. See Fredrickson, *Black Image in the White Mind*, 97–129.

80. James Oliver Horton, ed., *Free People of Color: Inside the African American Community* (Washington, D.C.: Smithsonian Institution Press, 1993), 126–142; Litwack, *North of Slavery*, 179–182.

81. Delany, *The Condition, Elevation, Emigration and Destiny*, 87.

82. Garnet, *Past and Present*, 20–21, 24–25.

83. Garnet, *Past and Present*, 20; *BAP*, 4:290–291; James McCune Smith, *The Destiny of the People of Color: A Lecture, Delivered before the Philomathean Society and Hamilton Lyceum in January, 1841* (New York, 1843), 6–11.

84. Ernest Lee Tuveson, *Redeemer Nation: The Idea of America's Millennial Role* (Chicago: Univ. of Chicago Press, 1968).

CHAPTER 6. WE LOVE OUR COUNTRY . . . BUT WE LOVE LIBERTY MORE

1. Ronald G. Walters, *American Reformers, 1815–1860* (New York: Hill and Wang, 1978), 214; Howard Holman Bell, ed., *Minutes of the Proceedings of the National Negro Conventions, 1830–1864* (New York: Arno and New York Times, 1969), 1843 Convention, 3–4. For the quote in the chapter title, see Bell, *Minutes of the Proceedings of the National Negro Conventions*, 1843 Convention, 5.

2. Bell, *Minutes of the Proceedings of the National Negro Conventions*, 1843 Convention, 4–10.

3. Henry Highland Garnet, ed., *Walker's Appeal in Four Articles and An Address to the Slaves of the United States of America* (1848; reprint, Salem, N.H.: Ayer, 1984), 90–93.

4. Garnet, *Walker's Appeal in Four Articles and An Address to the Slaves*, 90–96.

5. Garnet, *Walker's Appeal in Four Articles and An Address to the Slaves*, 96; Carleton Mabee,

Black Freedom: The Nonviolent Abolitionists from 1830 through the Civil War (New York: Macmillan, 1970), 55–56, 63–64, 88, 291–297; see also Lawrence J. Friedman, *Gregarious Saints: Self and Community in American Abolitionism, 1830–1870* (Cambridge, Mass.: Harvard Univ. Press, 1987), 196–208, 218–222.

6. Bell, *Minutes of the Proceedings of the National Negro Conventions,* 1843 Convention, 12–13.

7. Bell, *Minutes of the Proceedings of the National Negro Conventions,* 1843 Convention, 13–14, 17–19, 23–26; Benjamin Quarles, *Black Abolitionists* (1969; reprint, New York: Oxford Univ. Press, 1975), 224–225; C. Peter Ripley et al., eds., *The Black Abolitionist Papers* (Chapel Hill: Univ. of North Carolina Press, 1985), 3:153–154 (hereinafter cited as *BAP*).

8. Bell, *Minutes of the Proceedings of the National Negro Conventions,* 1834 Convention, 21–23; Dorothy Porter, ed., *Early Negro Writing, 1760–1837* (1971; reprint, Baltimore: Black Classic Press, 1995), 626; *Colored American,* February 17, 1838; Foner and Walker, eds., *Proceedings of the Black State Conventions,* 2:46.

9. Philip S. Foner, ed., *The Voice of Black America: Major Speeches by Negroes in the United States, 1797–1971* (New York: Simon and Schuster, 1972), 33–36.

10. Quoted in Waldo Martin, *The Mind of Frederick Douglass* (Chapel Hill: Univ. of North Carolina Press, 1984), 89; see Nathan Huggins, *Slave and Citizen: The Life of Frederick Douglass* (Boston: Little, Brown, 1980), 59–61.

11. Porter, ed., *Early Negro Writing,* 626.

12. Foner, ed., *The Voice of Black America,* 204–205.

13. Garnet, *Walker's Appeal in Four Articles and An Address to the Slaves,* 37, 96. For white attitudes, see George Fredrickson, *The Black Image in the White Mind: The Debate on Afro-American Character and Destiny, 1817–1914* (New York: Harper and Row, 1971), 101–117; Friedman, *Gregarious Saints,* 169–173.

14. Frederick Douglass, *Narrative of the Life of Frederick Douglass, an American Slave,* ed. Houston A. Baker Jr., 101–114 (1845; reprint, New York: Penguin Books, 1986); see also Ronald T. Takaki, *Violence in the Black Imagination: Essays and Documents* (1972; expanded ed., New York: Oxford Univ. Press, 1993), 17–33.

15. Michael Feldberg, *The Turbulent Era: Riot and Disorder in Jacksonian America* (New York: Oxford Univ. Press, 1980), 3–8, 114–116.

16. Quarles, *Black Abolitionists,* 204–205; Joel Schor, *Henry Highland Garnet: A Voice of Black Radicalism in the Nineteenth Century* (Westport, Conn.: Greenwood, 1977), 145–146.

17. Alice Felt Tyler, *Freedom's Ferment: Phases of American Social History from the Colonial Period to the Outbreak of the Civil War* (1944; reprint, New York: Harper and Row, 1962), 411–413.

18. *BAP,* 3:217; Mabee, *Black Freedom,* 64; Herbert Aptheker, ed., *A Documentary History of the Negro People in the United States: From Colonial Times through the Civil War* (New York: Citadel Press, 1961), 1:280; Bell, *Minutes of the Proceedings of the National Negro Conventions,* 1847 National Convention, 13–17; 31–32, 1848 National Convention, 9–11, 13–16.

19. Aptheker, *Documentary History,* 1:288–290; Frederick Douglass, *The Life and Writings of Frederick Douglass,* ed. Philip S. Foner, 1:253–255 (New York: International Publishers, 1950); see also Schor, *Henry Highland Garnet,* 103–107.

20. Howard Jones, *Mutiny on the Amistad: The Saga of a Slave Revolt and Its Impact on American Abolition, Law, and Diplomacy* (New York: Oxford Univ. Press, 1987), 205; Mabee, *Black Freedom,* 55–56; see also John Stauffer, *The Black Hearts of Men: Radical Abolitionists and the Transformation of Race* (Cambridge, Mass.: Harvard Univ. Press, 2002), 8–44.

21. Aptheker, *Documentary History,* 1:290–291; *BAP,* 3:482–483.

22. Mabee, *Black Freedom*, 64; Foner and Walker, eds., *Proceedings of the Black State Conventions*, 1:229.

23. Douglass, *Life and Writings*, 1:398–399.

24. Litwack, *North of Slavery*, 248–249.

25. Foner and Walker, eds., *Proceedings of the Black State Conventions*, 1:45.

26. Aptheker, *Documentary History*, 1:305–306; Foner and Walker, eds., *Proceedings of the Black State Conventions*, 1:72–73; *BAP*, 4:227–229.

27. Quarles, *Black Abolitionists*, 207–209; *Boston Slave Riot, and Trial of Anthony Burns* (Boston: Fetridge, 1854); Foner and Walker, eds., *Proceedings of the Black State Conventions*, 1:135; William Cheek and Aimee Lee Cheek, *John Mercer Langston and the Fight for Black Freedom, 1829–65* (Urbana: Univ. of Illinois Press, 1989), 316–319.

28. Quarles, *Black Abolitionists*, 228–229; Cheek and Cheek, *John Mercer Langston*, 170–174.

29. William J. Watkins, *Our Rights As Men: An Address Delivered in Boston, Before the Legislative Committee on the Militia, February 24, 1853* (Boston: Roberts, 1853), 4–8.

30. Foner and Walker, eds., *Proceedings of the Black State Conventions*, 1:72, 89, 99–100, 2:70; Bell, *Minutes of the Proceedings of the National Negro Conventions*, 1853 Convention, 7, 22–23; 1855 Convention, 30–33; Martin, *The Mind of Frederick Douglass*, 36–40.

31. Martin, *The Mind of Frederick Douglass*, 58–60; Douglass, *Life and Writings*, 1:399–401; Bell, *Minutes of the Proceedings of the National Negro Conventions*, 1853 Convention, 7, 22–25; Foner and Walker, eds., *Proceedings of the Black State Conventions*, 1:133.

32. See Stauffer, *The Black Hearts of Men*, 8–44; *BAP*, 5:65.

33. *BAP*, 5:44.

34. Douglass, *Life and Writings*, 2:533–538; See Tunde Adeleke, "Violence as an Option for Free Blacks in Nineteenth-Century America," *Canadian Review of American Studies* 35 (2005): 87–107.

35. Don E. Fehrenbacher, *Slavery, Law, and Politics: The Dred Scott Case in Historical Perspective* (New York: Oxford Univ. Press, 1981), 183–213.

36. *Freedom's Journal*, January 31, 1829; *The Rights of All*, October 9, 1829; see Howard Holman Bell, *A Survey of the Negro Convention Movement, 1830–1861* (New York: Arno and New York Times, 1969), for an analysis of the national and state emigration conventions in this period.

37. Porter, ed., *Early Negro Writing*, 282–285; *Colored American*, March 14, 1840, April 11, 1840, May 2, 1840, May 9, 1840, October 31, 1840, January 16, 1841, November 7, 1841.

38. Julie Winch, "'You Have Talents—Only Cultivate Them': Philadelphia's Black Female Literary Societies and the Abolitionist Crusade," in *The Abolitionist Sisterhood: Women's Political Culture in Antebellum America*, ed. Jean Fagan Yellin and John C. Van Horne, 112 (Ithaca, N.Y.: Cornell Univ. Press, 1994).

39. *BAP*, 5:63–64; see also David R. Roediger, *The Wages of Whiteness: Race and the Making of the American Working Class* (London: Verso, 1999).

40. Bell, *Minutes of the Proceedings of the National Negro Conventions*, 1847 Convention, 28; *Colored American*, November 18, 1837; Schor, *Henry Highland Garnet*, 100–103; *The North Star*, January 19, 1849, January 26, 1849.

41. Foner and Walker, eds., *Proceedings of the Black State Conventions*, 1:223–226, 275–279, 335.

42. Schor, *Henry Highland Garnet*, 110–125.

43. *BAP*, 4:128–129; Tunde Adeleke, *Without Regard to Race: The Other Martin Robison Delany* (Jackson: Univ. Press of Mississippi, 2003), 40–52; see also Floyd Miller, *The Search for a Black Nationality: Black Emigration and Colonization, 1787–1863* (Urbana: Univ. of Illinois Press, 1975), 116–119.

44. *BAP*, 4:129, 2:149–157; Miller, *The Search for a Black Nationality*, 121–125; Martin R.

Delany, *The Condition, Elevation, Emigration and Destiny of the Colored People of the United States Politically Considered* (1852; reprint, Baltimore: Black Classic Press, 1993), 11–66, 147–208; see Rogers Smith, *Civic Ideals: Conflicting Visions of Citizenship in U.S. History* (New Haven, Conn.: Yale Univ. Press, 1997).

45. Foner and Walker, eds., *Proceedings of the Black State Conventions*, 1:223.

46. Mary Ann Shadd, *A Plea for Emigration: or Notes of Canada West. . .* (Detroit, 1852), iii–29; Jim Bearden and Linda Butler, *Shadd: The Life and Times of Mary Ann Shadd Cary* (Toronto: NC Press, 1977), 59–60; Jane Rhodes, *Mary Ann Shadd Cary: The Black Press and Protest in the Nineteenth Century* (Bloomington: Indiana Univ. Press, 1998), 1–20, 29–50; Mary Ann Shadd Cary Papers, Moorland-Spingarn Research Center, Howard University.

47. Rhodes, *Mary Ann Shadd Cary*, 43–99; *BAP*, 2:192.

48. Rhodes, *Mary Ann Shadd Cary*, 49–50, 80, 117, 133; Miller, *The Search for a Black Nationality*, 105–106, 143–160.

49. Miller, *The Search for a Black Nationality*, 107–110, 161–165; *BAP*, 2:140–141; Bell, *A Survey of the Negro Convention Movement*, 206.

50. Miller, *The Search for a Black Nationality*, 162–198; Schor, *Henry Highland Garnet*, 151–170.

51. For Cary's support of limited African emigration, see Rhodes, *Mary Ann Shadd Cary*, 133; M. R. Delany, "Official Report of the Niger Valley Exploring Party," in *Search for a Place: Black Separatism and Africa, 1860*, ed. Howard H. Bell, 39 (Ann Arbor: Univ. of Michigan Press, 1969); see also Richard Blackett, "Martin R. Delany and Robert Campbell: Black Americans in Search of an African Colony," *Journal of Negro History* 62 (January 1977): 1–25.

52. *Constitution of the African Civilization Society* (New Haven, Conn.: Thomas J. Stafford, Printer, 1861); *BAP*, 5:3–6.

53. Bell, ed., *Search for a Place*, 38.

54. Bell, ed., *Search for a Place*, 102–106, 110.

55. Benjamin Quarles, ed., "Letters from Negro Leaders to Gerrit Smith," *Journal of Negro History* 27 (October 1942): 450–451; Bell, ed., *Search for a Place*, 18, 111–120.

56. Quarles, ed., "Letters from Negro Leaders to Gerrit Smith," 450–451; Robert P. McCormick, "William Whipper: Moral Reformer," *Pennsylvania History* 43 (January 1976): 39–42.

57. Douglass, *Life and Writings*, 2:100–102, 3:85–88; David Blight, *Frederick Douglass' Civil War: Keeping Faith in Jubilee* (Baton Rouge: Louisiana State Univ. Press, 1989), 132–133; Miller, *The Search for a Black Nationality*, 239–240; *BAP*, 5:110, 128.

58. Foner and Walker, eds., *Proceedings of the Black State Conventions*, 1:99–101.

59. *BAP*, 5:71–73.

60. *BAP*, 5:88–96.

61. Foner and Walker, eds., *Proceedings of the Black State Conventions*, 1:101, 308; *BAP*, 5:398–400.

62. *BAP*, 5:114–116.

63. *BAP*, 5:120–127; Foner, ed., *The Voice of Black America*, 256.

64. Douglass, *Life and Writings*, 3:266–270; *BAP*, 5:148–158; James Oakes, *The Radical and the Republican: Frederick Douglass, Abraham Lincoln, and the Triumph of Antislavery Politics* (New York: Norton, 2007), 149–185; see also Foner, ed., *The Voice of Black America*, 259–262; Clarence Walker, *A Rock in a Weary Land: The African Methodist Episcopal Church during the Civil War and Reconstruction* (Baton Rouge: Louisiana State Univ. Press, 1982), 30–43.

65. *AME Christian Recorder*, September 27, 1862.

66. For an example of criticism of the Emancipation Proclamation, see *BAP*, 5:184–186.

67. Foner, ed., *The Voice of Black America,* 277; *BAP,* 5:138–139.

68. See, for example, *AME Christian Recorder,* September 27, 1862, January 1, 1863, January 10, 1863; *BAP,* 5:134; Foner and Walker, eds., *Proceedings of the Black State Conventions,* 1:140, 154, 201, 349; Douglass, *Life and Writings,* 3:382–383, 392–394.

EPILOGUE

1. C. Peter Ripley et al., eds., *The Black Abolitionist Papers* (Chapel Hill: Univ. of North Carolina Press, 1991), 4:42–44; 3:479–480.

2. *Douglass' Monthly,* March 1863.

3. Abraham Lincoln, "Second Inaugural Address" (March 4, 1865), in *Collected Works of Abraham Lincoln,* vol. 8, ed. Roy P. Basler, Marion Dolores Pratt, and Lloyd A. Dunlap, 332–333 (New Brunswick, N.J.: Rutgers Univ. Press, 1953).

4. Barack Obama, "The America We Love," Independence, Missouri, *New York Times,* June 30, 2008.

BIBLIOGRAPHY

PRIMARY SOURCES
Manuscript Collections

Anti-Slavery Collection. Boston Public Library.
Cary, Mary Ann Shadd, Papers. Moorland-Spingarn Research Center. Howard University.
Crummell, Alexander, Papers. Schomburg Library, New York Public Library.
Rush, Benjamin, to Granville Sharp. 1792. Henry E. Huntington Library, San Marino, Calif. File #479380.
Whipper, Leigh R., Papers. Moorland-Spingarn Research Center. Howard University.

Periodicals

AME Christian Recorder. Philadelphia, 1852–1863.
Anglo-African Magazine. New York, 1859–1860.
Anti-Slavery Advocate. Dublin, Ireland, 1852–1863.
Colored American. New York, 1837–1841.
Douglass' Monthly. Rochester, N.Y., 1859–1863.
Freedom's Journal. New York, 1827–1829.
Liberator. Boston, 1831–1865.
National Reformer. Philadelphia, 1838–1839.
New London Gazette. New London, Conn., 1823–1844.
The North Star,. Rochester, N.Y., 1847–1851.
The Provincial Freeman. Toronto, Canada West, 1853–1857.
The Rights of All. New York, 1829.
Weekly Advocate. New York, 1837.
Weekly Anglo-African. New York, 1859–1863.

Other Primary Sources

Allen, Richard. *The Life Experience and Gospel Labors of the Rt. Rev. Richard Allen. . . .* 1833. Reprint, Nashville: Abingdon Press, 1960.

Andrews, William L., ed. *From Fugitive Slave to Free Man: The Autobiographies of William Wells Brown*. New York: Penguin Books, 1993.

———, ed. *Sisters of the Spirit: Three Black Women's Autobiographies of the Nineteenth Century*. Bloomington: Indiana Univ, Press, 1986.

Aptheker, Herbert, ed. *A Documentary History of the Negro People in the United States: From Colonial Times through the Civil War*. 7 vols. New York: Citadel Press, 1961–1968.

Asher, Jeremiah. *Incidents in the Life of Rev. J. Asher*. 1850. Reprint, Freeport, N.Y.: Books for Libraries Press, 1971.

Barnes, Gilbert H., and Dwight L. Dumond, eds. *Letters of Theodore Dwight Weld, Angelina Grimké Weld and Sarah Grimké, 1822–1844*. New York: Appleton-Century, 1934.

Bell, Howard Holman, ed. *Minutes of the Proceedings of the National Negro Conventions, 1830–1864*. New York: Arno and the New York Times, 1969.

Blassingame, John, ed. *The Frederick Douglass Papers*. Series One, vols. 1–5. New Haven, Conn.: Yale Univ. Press, 1979–1992.

Bogin, Ruth, ed. "'The Battle of Lexington': A Patriotic Ballad by Lemuel Haynes." *William and Mary Quarterly* 42 (October 1985): 499–506.

———, ed. "'Liberty Further Extended': A 1776 Antislavery Manuscript by Lemuel Haynes." *William and Mary Quarterly* 40 (January 1983): 85–105.

Boston Slave Riot, and Trial of Anthony Burns. Boston: Fetridge, 1854.

Bureau of the Census. U.S. Department of Commerce. *Negro Population, 1790–1915*. Washington, D.C.: Government Printing Office, 1918.

Cassedy, J. Albert. *The Firemen's Record*. Philadelphia, 1891.

Catto, William T. *A Semi-Centenary Discourse Delivered in the First African Presbyterian Church in Philadelphia, 1857 and History of the First African Presbyterian Church*. Philadelphia: Joseph M. Wilson, 1857.

Collections of the Massachusetts Historical Society, 1792–1941. 7 series of 10 volumes. *Jeremy Belknap Papers*. 5th series, vol. 3. Boston, 1887.

Constitution of the African Civilization Society. New Haven, Conn.: Thomas J. Stafford, Printer, 1861.

Cooley, Timothy Mather. *Sketches of the Life and Character of the Rev. Lemuel Haynes*. 1837. Reprint, New York: Negro Universities Press, 1969.

Cornish, Samuel E., and Theodore S. Wright. *The Colonization Scheme Considered. . . .* Newark, N.J.: Aaron Guest, 1840.

Dann, Martin E., ed. *The Black Press, 1827–1890: The Quest for National Identity*. New York: Putnam's Sons, 1971.

Delany, Martin. *The Condition, Elevation, Emigration and Destiny of the Colored People of the United States Politically Considered*. 1852. Reprint, Baltimore: Black Classic Press, 1993.

Douglass, Frederick. *The Life and Writings of Frederick Douglass*. 4 vols. Edited by Philip S. Foner. New York: International Publishers, 1950–1955.

———. *My Bondage and My Freedom*. Edited by William L. Andrews. 1855. Reprint, Urbana: Univ. of Illinois Press, 1987.

———. *Narrative of the Life of Frederick Douglass, an American Slave*. Edited by Houston A. Baker Jr. 1845. Reprint, New York: Penguin Books, 1986.

Douglass, William. *Annals of the First African Church in the United States of America Now Styled the African Episcopal Church of St. Thomas.* Philadelphia: King and Baird, Printers, 1862.

Easton, Hosea. *A Treatise on the Intellectual Character, and Civil and Political Condition of the Colored People of the U. States. . . .* Boston: Isaac Knapp, 1837.

Foner, Philip S., ed. *The Voice of Black America: Major Speeches by Negroes in the United States, 1797–1971.* New York: Simon and Schuster, 1972.

Foner, Philip S., and George E. Walker, eds. *Proceedings of the Black State Conventions, 1840–1865.* 2 vols. Philadelphia: Temple Univ. Press, 1979.

Forten, James, Jr. *Address before the American Moral Reform Society.* Philadelphia, 1837.

———. *An Address Delivered before the Ladies' Anti-Slavery Society of Philadelphia, On the Evening of the 14th of April, 1836.* Philadelphia: Merrihew and Gunn, 1836.

Forten Grimké, Charlotte. *The Journals of Charlotte Forten Grimké.* The Schomburg Library of Nineteenth-Century Black Women Writers. Edited by Brenda Stevenson. New York: Oxford Univ. Press, 1988.

Garnet, Henry Highland. *The Past and Present Condition and the Destiny of the Colored Race.* 1848. Reprint, Miami: Mnemosyne, 1969.

———, ed. *Walker's Appeal in Four Articles and An Address to the Slaves of the United States of America.* 1848. Reprint, Salem, N.H.: Ayer, 1984.

Garrison, William Lloyd, ed. "Sentiments of the People of Color." In *Thoughts on African Colonization.* Boston, 1832. Reprint, New York: Arno and the New York Times, 1968.

———. *Thoughts on African Colonization. . . .* Boston, 1832. Reprint, New York: Arno and the New York Times, 1968.

Hamilton, William T. *A Word for the African: A Sermon for the Benefit of the American Colonization Society.* Newark, N.J.: W. Tuttle and Co., Printer, 1825.

Haynes, Lemuel. *DISSIMULATION ILLUSTRATED: A Sermon Delivered at Brandon, Vermont, February 22, 1813 Before the Washington Benevolent Society.* Rutland, Vt.: Fay and Davison, Printers, 1814.

———. *The Influence of Civil Government on Religion: A Sermon Delivered at Rutland, West Parish, September 4, 1798. At the Annual Freeman's Meeting.* Rutland, Vt.: John Walker, 1798.

———. *The Nature and Importance of TRUE REPUBLICANISM, with a Few Suggestions Favorable to Independence.* Rutland, Vt.: William Fay, Printer, 1801.

Hodges, Graham R., ed. *Black Itinerants of the Gospel: The Narratives of John Jea and George White.* Madison, Wisc.: Madison House, 1993.

Houchins, Sue E., ed. *Spiritual Narratives.* The Schomburg Library of Nineteenth-Century Black Women Writers. New York: Oxford Univ. Press, 1988.

Jacobs, Harriet. *Incidents in the Life of a Slave Girl: Written by Herself.* Edited by Jean Fagan Yellin. Cambridge, Mass.: Harvard Univ. Press, 1987.

Jefferson, Thomas. *Notes on the State of Virginia.* 1781. Electronic Text Center, University of Virginia Library, http://etext.virginia.edu/toc/modeng/public/JefVirg.html.

Jones, Absalom, and Richard Allen. "A Narrative of the Proceedings of the Colored People During the Awful Calamity in Philadelphia in the Year 1793; and a Refutation of Some Censures Thrown upon Them in Some Publications." In *Life Experience and Gospel Labors of the Rt. Rev. Richard Allen,* by Richard Allen. 1833. Reprint, Nashville: Abingdon Press, 1960.

Langston, John Mercer. *Freedom and Citizenship.* 1883. Reprint, Miami: Mnemosyne, 1969.

Lerner, Gerda, ed. *Black Women in White America: A Documentary History.* New York: Pantheon, 1972. Reprint, New York: Vintage, 1992.

Lewis, John W. *The Life, Labors, and Travels of Elder Charles Bowles of the Free Will Baptist Denomination.* Watertown, N.Y.: Ingalls and Stowell's Steam Press, 1852.

Lewis, Robert Benjamin. *Light and Truth: Collected From the Bible and Ancient and Modern History Containing the Universal History of the Colored and the Indian Race from the Creation of the World to the Present Time.* 1836. Reprint, Boston: Committee of Colored Gentlemen, 1844.

Lincoln, Abraham. *Collected Works of Abraham Lincoln.* Vol. 8. Edited by Roy P. Basler, Marion Dolores Pratt, and Lloyd A. Dunlap. New Brunswick, N.J.: Rutgers Univ. Press, 1953.

Mason, George C. *Reminiscences of Newport.* Newport, R.I.: C. E. Hammett Jr., 1884.

The Minutes and Proceedings of the First Annual Moral Reform Society. Philadelphia, 1837.

Nell, William C. *The Colored Patriots of the American Revolution, with Sketches of Several Distinguished Colored Persons.* 1855. Reprint, New York: Arno and the New York Times, 1968.

Newman, Richard, ed. *Black Preacher to White America: The Collected Writings of Lemuel Haynes, 1774–1833.* Brooklyn: Carlson, 1990.

Obama, Barack. "The America We Love." Independence, Missouri. *New York Times,* June 30, 2008. http://www.nytimes.com/2008/06/30/us/politics/30text-obama.html (accessed November 12, 2009).

Parrott, Russell. *The Abolition of the Slave Trade.* Philadelphia, 1814.

Payne, Daniel A. *A History of the African Methodist Episcopal Church.* 1891. Reprint, New York: Arno and the New York Times, 1969.

———. *Recollections of Seventy Years.* Nashville: Publishing House of the A.M.E. Sunday School Union, 1888. Reprint, Salem, N.H.: Ayer, 1991.

Pennington, James W. C. *A Text Book of the Origin and History, &c. &c. of the Colored People.* Hartford: Skinner, 1841.

Perry, William Stevens, ed., *Historical Collections Relating to the American Colonial Church.* 5 vols. Hartford, Conn., 1870–1878.

Porter, Dorothy, ed. *Early Negro Writing, 1760–1837.* 1971. Reprint, Baltimore: Black Classic Press, 1995.

Price, George R., and James Brewer Stewart, eds. *To Heal the Scourge of Prejudice: The Life and Writings of Hosea Easton.* Amherst: Univ. of Massachusetts Press, 1999.

Proceedings of the Boston School Integration Celebration. Boston, 1855.

Proceedings of the Pennsylvania Antislavery Convention. Harrisburg, 1837.

Quarles, Benjamin, ed. "Letters from Negro Leaders to Gerrit Smith." *Journal of Negro History* 27 (October 1942): 432–453.

Ripley, C. Peter, Roy Finkenbine, Michael Hembree, and Donald Yacovone, eds. *The Black Abolitionist Papers.* 5 vols. Chapel Hill: Univ. of North Carolina Press, 1985–1992.

Ruggles, David. *The Abrogation of the Seventh Commandment by the American Churches.* New York, 1835.

———. *An Antidote for a Poisonous Combination.* New York, 1838.

Sernett, Milton C., ed. *Afro-American Religious Historical Documents.* Syracuse, N.Y.: Syracuse Univ. Press, 1986.

Shadd, Mary Ann. *A Plea for Emigration: or Notes of Canada West. . . .* Detroit, 1852.

Smith, James McCune. *The Destiny of the People of Color: A Lecture, Delivered before the Philomathean Society and Hamilton Lyceum in January, 1841* (New York, 1843).

Spear, Chloe. *Memoir of Mrs. Chloe Spear, a Native of Africa who was Enslaved in Childhood and Died in Boston, January 3, 1815 . . . aged 65 years, By a Lady of Boston.* Boston, 1832.

Sterling, Dorothy, ed. *We Are Your Sisters: Black Women in the Nineteenth Century.* New York: Norton, 1984.

Stewart, Maria W. *Maria W. Stewart, America's First Black Woman Political Writer: Essays and Speeches.* Edited by Marilyn Richardson. Bloomington: Indiana Univ. Press, 1987.

Still, William. *The Underground Railroad: A Record of Facts, Authentic Narratives, Letters. . . . 1872.* Reprint, Medford, N.J.: Plexus, 2005.

Van Horne, John C., ed. *Religious Philanthropy and Colonial Slavery: The American Correspondence of the Associates of Dr. Bray, 1717–1777.* Urbana: Univ. of Illinois Press, 1985.

Walker, David. *WALKER'S APPEAL . . . TO THE COLOURED CITIZENS OF THE WORLD, BUT IN PARTICULAR, AND VERY EXPRESSLY, TO THOSE OF THE UNITED STATES OF AMERICA.* Edited by Charles M. Wiltse. 1829. Reprint of 3rd ed., New York: Hill and Wang, 1965.

Ward, Samuel Ringgold. *Autobiography of a Fugitive Negro, His Anti-Slavery Labours in the United States, Canada, and England.* 1855. Reprint, New York: Arno and the New York Times, 1968.

Watkins, William J. *Our Rights As Men: An Address Delivered in Boston, Before the Legislative Committee on the Militia, February 24, 1853.* Boston: Roberts, 1853.

Wheatley, Phillis. *The Collected Works of Phillis Wheatley.* The Schomburg Library of Nineteenth-Century Black Women Writers. Edited by John C. Shields. New York: Oxford Univ. Press, 1988.

Woodson, Carter G., ed. *The Mind of the Negro as Reflected in Letters Written During the Crisis, 1800–1860.* 1926. Reprint, New York: Russell and Russell, 1969.

———. *Negro Orators and Their Orations.* New York: Russell and Russell, 1925.

Worester, Noah. *Abraham and Lot: A Sermon, on the Way of Peace, and the Evils of War: Delivered at Salisbury, in New-Hampshire, on the Day of the National Feast, August 20, 1812.* Concord, N.H.: George Hough, 1812.

SECONDARY SOURCES

Adeleke, Tunde. "Violence as an Option for Free Blacks in Nineteenth-Century America." *Canadian Review of American Studies* 35 (2005): 87–107.

———. *Without Regard to Race: The Other Martin Robison Delany.* Jackson: Univ. Press of Mississippi, 2003.

Ahlstrom, Sidney. *A Religious History of the American People*. New Haven, Conn.: Yale Univ. Press, 1972.

Anderson, Benedict. *Imagined Communities: Reflections on the Origin and Spread of Nationalism*. 1983. Revised and extended edition, London: Verso, 1993.

Andrews, Dee. "The African Methodists of Philadelphia, 1794–1802." *Pennsylvania Magazine of History and Biography* 108 (October 1984): 471–486.

———. *The Methodist and Revolutionary America, 1760–1800: The Shaping of an Evangelical Culture*. Princeton, N.J.: Princeton Univ. Press, 2000.

Appiah, K. Anthony. *The Ethics of Identity*. Princeton, N.J.: Princeton Univ. Press, 2005.

———. "Race, Culture, Identity: Misunderstood Connections." In *Color Conscious: The Political Morality of Race*, edited by K. Anthony Appiah and Amy Gutmann, 30–105. Princeton, N.J.: Princeton Univ. Press, 1996.

Appleby, Joyce. *Liberalism and Republicanism in the Historical Imagination*. Cambridge, Mass.: Harvard Univ. Press, 1992.

———. "The Social Origins of American Revolutionary Ideology." *Journal of American History* 64 (March 1978): 935–938.

———, ed. "Special Issue: Republicanism in the History and Historiography of the United States." *American Quarterly* 37 (fall 1985): 461–598.

Arnke, Georgia. *After Identity: Rethinking Race, Sex, and Gender*. New York: Cambridge Univ. Press, 2007.

Bailyn, Bernard. *The Ideological Origins of the American Revolution*. Cambridge, Mass.: Harvard Univ. Press, 1967.

Barnes, Gilbert. *The Antislavery Impulse: 1830–1844*. New York: Appleton-Century, 1933.

Bartlett, Irving H. "The Free Negro in Providence, Rhode Island." *Negro History Bulletin* 14 (December 1950): 51–67.

———. *From Slave to Citizen: The Story of the Negro in Rhode Island*. Providence, R.I.: The Urban League of Greater Providence, 1954.

Bay, Mia. *White Image in the Black Mind: African American Ideas about White People, 1830–1925*. New York: Oxford Univ. Press, 2000.

Bearden, Jim, and Linda Butler. *Shadd: The Life and Times of Mary Ann Shadd Cary*. Toronto: NC Press, 1977.

Bell, Howard Holman, ed. *Search for a Place: Black Separatism and Africa, 1860*. Ann Arbor: Univ. of Michigan Press, 1969.

———. *A Survey of the Negro Convention Movement, 1830–1866*. New York: Arno and the New York Times, 1969.

Berlin, Ira. *Generations of Captivity: A History of African American Slaves*. Cambridge, Mass.: Harvard Univ. Press, 2003.

———. *Many Thousands Gone: The First Two Centuries of Slavery in North America*. Cambridge, Mass.: Harvard Univ. Press, 1998.

———. "Time, Space, and the Evolution of Afro-American Society on British Mainland North America." *American Historical Review* 85 (February 1980): 44–78.

Billington, Ray Allen. "James Forten: Forgotten Abolitionist." *Negro History Bulletin* 13 (November 1949): 31–36, 45.

Blackett, Richard. *Building an Antislavery Wall: Black Americans in the Atlantic Abolition Movement, 1830–1860.* Baton Rouge: Louisiana State Univ. Press, 1983.

———. "Martin R. Delany and Robert Campbell: Black Americans in Search of an African Colony." *Journal of Negro History* 62 (January 1977): 1–25.

Blight, David. *Frederick Douglass' Civil War: Keeping Faith in Jubilee.* Baton Rouge: Louisiana State Univ. Press, 1989.

———. *Race and Reunion: The Civil War in American Memory.* Cambridge, Mass.: Harvard Univ. Press, 2001.

Bloch, Ruth. *Visionary Republic: Millennial Themes in American Thought, 1756–1800.* New York: Cambridge Univ. Press, 1985.

Blumin, Stuart. *The Emergence of the Middle Class: Social Experience in the American City, 1760–1900.* New York: Cambridge Univ. Press, 1989.

Boylan, Anne M. "Benevolence and Antislavery Activity among African American Women in New York and Boston, 1820–1840." In *The Abolitionist Sisterhood: Women's Political Culture in Antebellum America,* edited by Jean Fagan Yellin and John C. Van Horne, 119–137. Ithaca, N.Y.: Cornell Univ. Press, 1994.

Bracey, John, August Meier, and Elliott Rudwick, eds. *Black Nationalism in America.* Indianapolis, Ind.: Bobbs-Merrill, 1970.

Breene, Timothy. "Ideology and Nationalism on the Eve of the American Revolution." *Journal of American History* 84 (June 1997): 13–39.

Brooks, Joanna. "Prince Hall, Freemasonry, and Genealogy." *African American Review* 34 (summer 2000): 197–260.

Cheek, William, and Aimee Lee Cheek. *John Mercer Langston and the Fight for Black Freedom, 1829–65.* Urbana: Univ. of Illinois Press, 1989.

Coelho, Philip R. P., and Robert A. McGuire. "African and European Bound Labor in the British New World: The Biological Consequences of Economic Choices." *Journal of Economic History* 57 (March 1997): 83–115.

Dain, Bruce. *A Hideous Monster of the Mind: American Race Theory in the Early Republic.* Cambridge, Mass.: Harvard Univ. Press, 2002.

Davis, David Brion. *The Problem of Slavery in Western Culture.* Ithaca, N.Y.: Cornell Univ. Press, 1966.

Davis, Thomas J. "Emancipation Rhetoric, Natural Rights, and Revolutionary New England: A Note on Four Black Petitions in Massachusetts, 1773–1777." *New England Quarterly* 62 (June 1989): 248–263.

———. *A Rumor of Revolt: The Great Negro Plot.* New York: Free Press, 1985.

Desrochers, Robert E., Jr. "Not Fade Away: The Narrative of Venture Smith, an African American in the Early Republic." *Journal of American History* 84 (June 1997): 40–66.

DuBois, W.E.B. *The Philadelphia Negro: A Social Study.* 1899. Reprint, Philadelphia: Univ. of Pennsylvania Press, 1996.

Dunbar, Erica Armstrong. *A Fragile Freedom: African American Women and Emancipation in the Antebellum City.* New Haven, Conn.: Yale Univ. Press, 2008.

Dworetz, Steve. *The Unvarnished Doctrine: Locke, Liberalism, and the American Revolution.* Durham, N.C.: Duke Univ. Press, 1990.

Farrison, William Edward. *William Wells Brown: Author and Reformer*. Chicago: Univ. of Chicago Press, 1969.

Fehrenbacher, Don E. *Slavery, Law, and Politics: The Dred Scott Case in Historical Perspective*. New York: Oxford Univ. Press, 1981.

Feldberg, Michael. *The Turbulent Era: Riot and Disorder in Jacksonian America*. New York: Oxford Univ. Press, 1980.

Fogel, Robert W., and Stanley Engerman. "Philanthropy at Bargain Prices: Notes on the Economics of Gradual Emancipation." *Journal of Legal Studies* 3 (June 1974): 377–401.

Fredrickson, George. *The Black Image in the White Mind: The Debate on Afro-American Character and Destiny, 1817–1914*. New York: Harper and Row, 1971.

———. *Racism: A Short History*. Princeton, N.J.: Princeton Univ. Press, 2002.

Friedman, Lawrence J. *Gregarious Saints: Self and Community in American Abolitionism, 1830–1870*. Cambridge, Mass.: Harvard Univ. Press, 1987.

Fulop, Timothy E. "'The Future Golden Day of the Race': Millennialism and Black Americans in the Nadir, 1877–1901." In *African-American Religion: Interpretive Essays in History and Culture*, edited by Timothy E. Fulop and Albert Raboteau, 227–254. New York: Routledge, 1997.

Fulop, Timothy E., and Albert J. Raboteau, eds. *African-American Religion: Interpretive Essays in History and Culture*. New York: Routledge, 1997.

Gaines, Kevin. *Uplifting the Race: Black Leadership, Politics, and Culture in the Twentieth Century*. Chapel Hill: Univ. of North Carolina Press, 1996.

Gellner, Ernst. *Nations and Nationalism*. Ithaca, N.Y.: Cornell Univ. Press, 1983.

Gibson, Alan. "Ancients, Moderns and Americans: The Republicanism-Liberalism Debate Revisited." *History of Political Thought* 21 (summer 2000): 261–307.

Ginzberg, Lori. *Women and the Work of Benevolence: Morality, Politics, and Class in the 19th-Century United States*. New Haven, Conn.: Yale Univ. Press, 1990.

Glaude, Eddie S., Jr. *Exodus! Religion, Race, and Nation in Early Nineteenth-Century Black America*. Chicago: Univ. of Chicago Press, 2000.

Goloboy, Jennifer L. "The Early American Middle Class." *Journal of the Early Republic* 25 (winter 2005): 537–545.

Gomez, Michael A. "African Identity and Slavery in the Americas." *Radical History Review* 75 (fall 1999): 111–120.

———. *Exchanging Our Country Marks: The Transformation of African Identities in the Colonial and Antebellum South*. Chapel Hill: Univ. of North Carolina Press, 1998.

Gravely, Will B. "The Rise of African Churches in America (1786–1802)." In *African-American Religion: Interpretive Essays in History and Culture*, edited by Timothy E. Fulop and Albert J. Raboteau, 131–151. New York: Routledge, 1997.

———. "The Dialectic of Double-Consciousness in Black American Freedom Celebrations, 1808–1863," *Journal of Negro History* 67 (winter 1982): 302–317.

Greene, Lorenzo. *The Negro in Colonial New England*. 1942. Reprint, New York: Atheneum, 1968.

Griffen, Patrick. "The People with No Name: Ulster's Migrants and Identity Formation in Eighteenth-Century Pennsylvania." *William and Mary Quarterly* 58 (July 2001): 587–614.

Hacking, Ian. *The Social Construction of What?* Cambridge, Mass.: Harvard Univ. Press, 1999.

Hall, Raymond J. *Black Separatism in the United States.* Hanover, N.H., 1978.

Hall, Stuart. "Cultural Identity and Diaspora." In *Identity: Community, Culture, Difference,* edited by Jonathan Rutherford, 222–237. London: Lawrence and Wishart, 1990.

Harris, Leslie M. *In the Shadow of Slavery: African Americans in New York City, 1626–1863.* Chicago: Univ. of Chicago Press, 2003.

Hartman, Saidiya V. *Scenes of Subjection: Terror, Slavery, and Self-Making in Nineteenth-Century America.* New York: Oxford Univ. Press, 1997.

Hatch, Nathan O. *The Democratization of American Christianity.* New Haven, Conn.: Yale Univ. Press, 1989.

Hemphill, Dallett C. "Middle Class Rising in Revolutionary America: The Evidence from Manners." *Journal of Social History* 30 (winter 1996): 317–344.

Hinks, Peter. *To Awaken My Afflicted Brethren: David Walker and the Problem of Antebellum Slave Resistance.* University Park: Pennsylvania State Univ. Press, 1997.

Hobsbawm, Eric J. *Nations and Nationalism since 1780: Programme, Myth, Reality.* Cambridge: Cambridge Univ. Press, 1990.

Hodges, Graham R. *Root and Branch: African Americans in New York and East Jersey, 1613–1863.* Chapel Hill: Univ. of North Carolina Press, 1999.

———. *Slavery and Freedom in the Rural North: African Americans in Monmouth County, New Jersey, 1685–1865.* Madison, Wisc.: Madison House, 1997.

Holloway, Joseph E. "The Origins of African American Culture." In *Africanisms in American Culture,* edited by Joseph E. Holloway, 18–38. Bloomington: Indiana Univ. Press, 1990.

Horton, James O. "Black Education at Oberlin College." *Journal of Negro Education* 54 (fall 1985): 477–499.

———, ed. *Free People of Color: Inside the African American Community.* Washington, D.C.: Smithsonian Institution Press, 1993.

Horton, James O., and Lois Horton. *Black Bostonians: Family, Life, and Community Struggles in the Antebellum North.* New York: Holmes and Meier, 1979.

———. *In Hope of Liberty: Culture, Community and Protest among Northern Free Blacks, 1700–1860.* New York: Oxford Univ. Press, 1997.

Horton, Lois. "From Class to Race in Early America: Northern Post-Emancipation Racial Reconstruction." *Journal of the Early Republic* 19 (winter 1999): 629–649.

Huggins, Nathan. *Slave and Citizen: The Life of Frederick Douglass.* Boston: Little, Brown, 1980.

Hutchinson, John, and Anthony D. Smith, eds. *Nationalism: Critical Concepts in Political Science.* Vol. 1. New York: Routledge, 2000.

Huyler, Jerome. *Locke in America: The Moral Philosophy of the Founding Era.* Lawrence: Univ. Press of Kansas, 1995.

Irons, Charles F. *The Origins of Proslavery Christianity.* Chapel Hill: Univ. of North Carolina Press, 2008.

Johnson, Michael P. "Denmark Vesey and His Co-Conspirators." *William and Mary Quarterly* 58 (October 2001): 915–976.

Jones, Howard. *Mutiny on the Amistad: The Saga of a Slave Revolt and Its Impact on American Abolition, Law, and Diplomacy.* New York: Oxford Univ. Press, 1987.

Kettner, James. *The Development of American Citizenship, 1608–1870.* Chapel Hill: Univ. of North Carolina Press, 1978.

Klingberg, Frank J. *Anglican Humanitarianism in Colonial New York.* Philadelphia: Church Historical Society, 1940.

Kloppenberg, James T. "The Virtues of Liberalism: Christianity, Republicanism, and Ethics in Early American Political Discourse." *Journal of American History* 74 (June 1987): 9–33.

Kramnick, Isaac. "The Great National Discussion: The Discourse of Politics in 1787." *William and Mary Quarterly* 45 (January 1988): 3–32.

———. *Republicanism and Bourgeois Radicalism: Political Ideology in Late Eighteenth-Century England and America.* Ithaca, N.Y.: Cornell Univ. Press, 1990.

Lapsansky, Emma Jones. "'Since They Got Those Separate Churches': Afro-Americans and Racism in Jacksonian Philadelphia." *American Quarterly* 32 (spring 1980): 54–78.

Levine, Lawrence. *Black Culture and Black Consciousness: Afro-American Folk Thought from Slavery to Freedom.* New York: Oxford Univ. Press, 1977.

Litwack, Leon. *North of Slavery: The Negro in the Free States, 1790–1860.* Chicago: Univ. of Chicago Press, 1961.

Lott, Eric. *Love and Theft: Blackface Minstrelsy and the American Working Class.* New York: Oxford Univ. Press, 1993.

Loveland, Anne C. "Evangelicalism and Immediate Emancipation in American Anti-slavery Thought." *Journal of Southern History* 32 (May 1966): 172–178.

Mabee, Carleton. *Black Education in New York State: From Colonial to Modern Times.* Syracuse, N.Y.: Syracuse Univ. Press, 1979.

———. *Black Freedom: The Nonviolent Abolitionists from 1830 through the Civil War.* New York: Macmillan, 1970.

MacLeod, Duncan J. "Toward Caste." In *Slavery and Freedom in the Age of the American Revolution,* edited by Ira Berlin and Ronald Hoffman, 217–236. Charlottesville: Univ. Press of Virginia, 1983.

Martin, Waldo. *The Mind of Frederick Douglass.* Chapel Hill: Univ. of North Carolina Press, 1984.

McCormick, Richard P. "William Whipper: Moral Reformer." *Pennsylvania History* 43 (January 1976): 23–46.

McManus, Edgar. *Black Bondage in the North.* Syracuse, N.Y.: Syracuse Univ. Press, 1973.

———. *A History of Negro Slavery in New York.* Syracuse, N.Y.: Syracuse Univ. Press, 1966.

Melish, Joanne Pope. "The 'Condition' Debate and Racial Discourse in the Antebellum North." *Journal of the Early Republic* 19 (winter 1999): 651–672.

———. *Disowning Slavery: Gradual Emancipation and Race in New England, 1780–1860.* Ithaca, N.Y.: Cornell Univ. Press, 1998.

Merrell, James. *The Indians' New World: Catawbas and Their Neighbors from European Contact throughout the Era of Removal*. Chapel Hill: Univ. of North Carolina Press, 1989.

Miller, Floyd. *The Search for a Black Nationality: Black Emigration and Colonization, 1787–1863*. Urbana: Univ. of Illinois Press, 1975.

Mintz, Sidney W., and Richard Price. *An Anthropological Approach to the Afro-American Past*. Philadelphia: Institute for the Study of Human Issues, 1976.

Mitchell, Annie. "A Liberal 'Cato.'" *American Journal of Political Science* 48 (July 2004): 588–603.

Mott, Frank Luther. *American Journalism: A History of Newspapers in the United States through 250 Years, 1690–1940*. New York: Macmillan, 1941.

Mullin, Michael. *Africa in America: Slave Acculturation and Resistance in the American South and the British Caribbean, 1736–1831*. Urbana: Univ. of Illinois Press, 1992.

Nash, Gary B. *Forging Freedom: The Formation of Philadelphia's Black Community, 1720–1840*. Cambridge, Mass.: Harvard Univ. Press, 1988.

———. *Race and Revolution*. Madison, Wisc.: Madison House, 1990.

Newman, Richard. *Freedom's Prophet: Bishop Richard Allen, the AME Church, and the Black Founding Fathers*. New York: New York Univ. Press, 2008.

———. *The Transformation of American Abolitionism: Fighting Slavery in the Early Republic*. Chapel Hill: Univ. of North Carolina Press, 2002.

Noll, Mark. *America's God: From Jonathan Edwards to Abraham Lincoln*. New York: Oxford Univ. Press, 2002.

Oakes, James. *The Radical and the Republican: Frederick Douglass, Abraham Lincoln, and the Triumph of Anti-Slavery Politics*. New York: Norton, 2007.

Painter, Nell Irvin. *Sojourner Truth: A Life, a Symbol*. New York: Norton, 1996.

Pease, Jane, and William Pease. *They Who Would Be Free: Blacks' Search for Freedom, 1830–1861*. New York: Atheneum, 1974.

Perkins, Linda Marie. "Quaker Beneficence and Black Control: The Institute for Colored Youth, 1852–1903." In *New Perspectives on Black Educational History*, edited by Vincent Franklin and James D. Anderson, 19–43. Boston: Hall, 1978.

Peterson, Carla. *"Doers of the Word": African American Women Speakers and Writers in the North, 1830–1880*. New York: Oxford Univ. Press, 1995. Reprint, New Brunswick, N.J.: Rutgers Univ. Press, 1998.

Piersen, William D. *Black Yankees: The Development of an Afro-American Subculture in Eighteenth-Century New England*. Amherst: Univ. of Massachusetts Press, 1988.

Pincus, Steve. "Neither Machiavellian Moment nor Possessive Individualism: Commercial Society and the Defenders of the English Commonwealth." *American Historical Review* 103 (June 1998): 705–736.

Quarles, Benjamin. *Black Abolitionists*. 1969. Reprint, New York: Oxford Univ. Press, 1975.

———. *The Negro in the American Revolution*. 1961. Reprint, New York: Norton, 1973.

Raboteau, Albert J. "The Black Experience in American Evangelicalism: The Meaning of Slavery." In *African-American Religion: Interpretive Essays in History and Culture*, edited by Timothy E. Fulop and Albert J. Raboteau, 89–106. New York: Routledge, 1997.

———. "The Slave Church in the Era of the American Revolution." In *Slavery and Freedom in the Age of the American Revolution*, edited by Ira Berlin and Ronald Hoffman, 193–213. Charlottesville: Univ. Press of Virginia, 1983.

———. *Slave Religion: The "Invisible Institution" in the Antebellum South.* New York: Oxford Univ. Press, 1978.

Rael, Patrick. *Black Identity and Black Protest in the Antebellum North.* Chapel Hill: Univ. of North Carolina Press, 2002.

Rammelkamp, Julian. "The Providence Negro Community, 1820–1842." *Rhode Island History* 7 (January 1948): 20–33.

Rhodes, Jane. *Mary Ann Shadd Cary: The Black Press and Protest in the Nineteenth Century.* Bloomington: Indiana Univ. Press, 1998.

Roberts, Rita. "In Quest of Autonomy: Northern Black Activism between the Revolution and the Civil War." Ph.D. diss., University of California, Berkeley, 1988.

———. "Patriotism and Political Criticism: The Evolution of Political Consciousness in the Mind of a Black Revolutionary Soldier." *Eighteenth-Century Studies* 27 (summer 1994): 569–588.

Rodgers, Daniel T. "Republicanism: The Career of a Concept." *Journal of American History* 79 (June 1992): 11–38.

Roediger, David. *The Wages of Whiteness: Race and the Making of the American Working Class.* London: Verso, 1991.

Rose, Willie Lee. *Slavery and Freedom.* New York: Oxford Univ. Press, 1982.

Ryan, Mary P. *Cradle of the Middle Class: The Family in Oneida County, New York, 1790–1865.* New York: Cambridge Univ. Press, 1981.

Saillant, John. *Black Puritan, Black Republican: The Life and Thought of Lemuel Haynes, 1753–1833.* New York: Oxford Univ. Press, 2003.

———. "Lemuel Haynes and the Revolutionary Origins of Black Theology, 1776–1801." *Religion and American Culture* 2 (winter 1992): 79–102.

———. "Lemuel Haynes's Black Republicanism and the American Republican Tradition, 1775–1820." *Journal of the Early Republic* 14 (autumn 1994): 293–324.

Savage, Barbara D. *Your Spirits Walk beside Us: The Politics of Black Religion.* Cambridge, Mass.: Harvard Univ. Press, 2008.

Schor, Joel. *Henry Highland Garnet: A Voice of Black Radicalism in the Nineteenth Century.* Westport, Conn.: Greenwood, 1977.

Schudson, Michael. *Discovering the News: A Social History of American Newspapers.* New York: Basic Books, 1978.

Sernett, Milton C. *Black Religion and American Evangelicalism: White Protestants, Plantation Missions, and the Flowering of Negro Christianity, 1787–1865.* Metuchen, N.J.: Scarecrow, 1975.

———. *North Star Country: Upstate New York and the Crusade for African American Freedom.* Syracuse, N.Y.: Syracuse Univ. Press, 2002.

Shalhope, Robert E. "Republicanism and Early American Historiography." *William and Mary Quarterly* 39 (April 1982): 334–356.

Silcox, Harry C. "Nineteenth-Century Philadelphia Black Militant: Octavius Catto." *Pennsylvania History* 44 (January 1977): 53–76.

Sinopoli, Richard C. *The Foundations of American Citizenship: Liberalism, the Constitution, and Civic Virtue.* New York: Oxford Univ. Press, 1992.

Smith, Anthony D. *The Ethnic Origins of Nations.* Oxford: Blackwell, 1986.

Smith, Jesse Carney, and Carrel Peterson Horton, comps. and eds. *Historical Statistics of Black America.* New York: Gale Research, 1995.

Smith, Rogers. *Civic Ideals: Conflicting Visions of Citizenship in U.S. History.* New Haven, Conn.: Yale Univ. Press, 1997.

Smith, Timothy L. "Righteousness and Hope: Christian Holiness and the Millennial Vision in America, 1800–1900." *American Quarterly* 31 (spring 1979): 21–45.

Sobel, Mechal. *Trabelin' On: The Slave Journey to an Afro-Baptist Faith.* Princeton, N.J.: Princeton Univ. Press, 1988.

Staudenraus, P. J. *The African Colonization Movement, 1816–1865.* New York: Columbia Univ. Press, 1961

Stauffer, John. *The Black Hearts of Men: Radical Abolitionists and the Transformation of Race.* Cambridge, Mass.: Harvard Univ. Press, 2002.

Stewart, James Brewer. *Abolitionist Politics and the Coming of the Civil War.* Amherst: Univ. of Massachusetts Press, 2008.

———. *Holy Warriors: The Abolitionists and American Slavery.* New York: Hill and Wang, 1976.

———. "Modernizing 'Difference': The Political Meanings of Color in the Free States, 1776–1840." *Journal of the Early Republic* 19 (winter 1999): 691–712.

Stuckey, Sterling. *The Ideological Origins of Black Nationalism.* Boston: Beacon, 1972.

———. *Slave Culture: Nationalist Theory and the Foundations of Black America.* New York: Oxford Univ. Press, 1987.

Sweet, John Wood. *Bodies Politic: Negotiating Race in the American North, 1730–1830.* Baltimore: Johns Hopkins Univ. Press, 2003.

Takaki, Ronald T. *Violence in the Black Imagination: Essays and Documents.* 1972. Expanded ed. New York: Oxford Univ. Press, 1993.

Taylor, Charles. "The Politics of Recognition." In *Multiculturalism and "The Politics of Recognition,"* edited by Charles Taylor and Amy Gutmann, 25–73. Princeton, N.J.: Princeton Univ. Press, 1992.

———. *Sources of the Self: The Making of Modern Identity.* Cambridge, Mass.: Harvard Univ. Press, 1989.

Thomas, Lamont D. *Rise to Be a People: A Biography of Paul Cuffe.* Urbana: Univ. of Illinois Press, 1986.

Thompson, Robert Farris. *Flash of the Spirit: African and Afro-American Art and Philosophy.* New York: Vintage, 1984.

Toll, Robert. *Blacking Up: The Minstrel Show in Nineteenth-Century America.* New York: Oxford Univ. Press, 1974.

Tuveson, Ernest Lee. *Redeemer Nation: The Idea of America's Millennial Role.* Chicago: Univ. of Chicago Press, 1968.

Tyler, Alice Felt. *Freedom's Ferment: Phases of American Social History from the Colonial Period to the Outbreak of the Civil War.* 1944. Reprint, New York: Harper and Row, 1962.

Waldstreicher, David. "The Vexed Story of Human Commodification Told by Benjamin Franklin and Venture Smith." *Journal of the Early Republic* 24 (summer 2004): 268–278.

Walker, Clarence. *A Rock in a Weary Land: The African Methodist Episcopal Church during the Civil War and Reconstruction.* Baton Rouge: Louisiana State Univ. Press, 1982.

Walls, William J. *The African Methodist Episcopal Zion Church: Reality of the Black Church.* Charlotte, N.C.: African Methodist Zion Publishing House, 1974.

Walters, Ronald G. *American Reformers, 1815–1860.* New York: Hill and Wang, 1978.

Warner, Robert A. "Amos Gerry Beman—1812–1874, A Memoir on a Forgotten Leader." *Journal of Negro History* 22 (April 1937): 200–221.

Wilder, Craig S. *In the Company of Black Men: The African Influence on African American Culture in New York City.* New York: New York Univ. Press, 2001.

White, Shane. *Somewhat More Independent: The End of Slavery in New York City, 1770–1810.* Athens: Univ. of Georgia Press, 1991.

Will, Thomas E. "Liberalism, Republicanism, and Philadelphia's Black Elite in the Early Republic: The Social Thought of Absalom Jones and Richard Allen." *Pennsylvania History* 69 (2002): 558–576.

Wilson, Ellen Gibson. *The Loyal Blacks.* New York: Putnam's Sons, 1976.

Winch, Julie. *A Gentleman of Color: The Life of James Forten.* New York: Oxford Univ. Press, 2002.

———. *Philadelphia's Black Elite: Activism, Accommodation, and the Struggle for Autonomy, 1787–1848.* Philadelphia: Temple Univ. Press, 1988.

———. "'You Have Talents—Only Cultivate Them': Philadelphia's Black Female Literary Societies and the Abolitionist Crusade." In *The Abolitionist Sisterhood: Women's Political Culture in Antebellum America,* edited by Jean Fagan Yellin and John C. Van Horne, 101–117. Ithaca, N.Y.: Cornell Univ. Press, 1994.

Yacovone, Donald. "The Transformation of the Black Temperance Movement, 1827–1854: An Interpretation." *Journal of the Early American Republic* 8 (autumn 1988): 281–297.

Yellin, Jean Fagan, and John C. Van Horne, eds. *The Abolitionist Sisterhood: Women's Political Culture in Antebellum America.* Ithaca, N.Y.: Cornell Univ. Press, 1994.

Zilversmit, Arthur. *The First Emancipation: The Abolition of Slavery in the North.* Chicago: Univ. of Chicago Press, 1967.

Zuckert, Michael. *Natural Rights and the New Republicanism.* Princeton, N.J.: Princeton Univ. Press, 1994.

INDEX

Abolitionist movement: and black reformers of early nineteenth century, 4, 11, 75–88, 92–102, 128–30; black women in, 84, 89, 94, 98, 131, 132, 140; and capitalism, 98; critique of slavery by, 78–84, 94–99; differences within, 100–102; and education of black children, 63; and equal rights, 99–102, 133; and evangelicalism, 95–96; and *Freedom's Journal*, 77; fugitive slaves in, 89, 94, 96; and gradual abolition, 20; immediatism in, 83, 93, 96–97, 108; as integrated movement, 4, 94, 114, 123; and Liberty party, 128–29, 168; and mutual relief societies, 75–76; for northern slaves, 19–20; political approach to, in mid-nineteenth century, 167–73; and political parties, 128–29; and republicanism, 94–95, 99; and second-generation activists, 89; and separate black meetings, 114–15, 123; and slave narratives, 94–95; speakers on antislavery circuit, 94, 99, 186; and support for slave insurrections, 129–30, 168–80, 183; and virtue of abolitionists, 58–59; and Walker's *APPEAL*, 78–84, 93, 176, 178, 179, 202; white church and clergy criticized by, 81–82, 98; whites' involvement in, 54, 83, 93–94, 96, 99–101, 109, 114, 133, 172, 176–78; and women's rights, 101. *See also* Antislavery campaign

The Abrogation of the Seventh Commandment by the American Churches (Ruggles), 96

ACS. *See* American Colonization Society (ACS)

Adams, John, 18, 19

Africa: advanced civilizations in sub-Saharan Africa, 152; and African identity of northern blacks, 13–14, 21–32, 38–39, 84, 103, 104, 112, 187; burial practices in, 23, 24, 25, 222n50; cultural differences and similarities of slaves from, 23–24; dance and music in, 23, 25, 37; ethnic ancestry of slaves from, 22, 23, 25, 28, 29; *Freedom's Journal* on, 76–77; and holidays in colonial America, 25–26; intercultural exchange in, 23; interregional trade in, 23–24; missionaries in, 69, 77, 104–6, 191–93; rejection of African identity of American blacks in nineteenth century, 103–7, 112; religious beliefs and rituals from, 23, 24, 119–20; Ring Shout ceremony in, 24, 119; Shadd on, 189; and slave trade, 22, 28, 29, 30, 31, 52–53, 135; smallpox inoculation in, 25; women's status in West African societies, 31. *See also* Emigration

African Americans. *See* Black women; Blacks; Slavery; Slaves

African Civilization Society, 191, 192

African Methodist Episcopal (A.M.E.) church, 40, 77, 90, 119, 120–22

African Methodist Episcopal Zion church, 40

Agriculture. *See* Farming

Alcohol consumption. *See* Temperance movement

Aldridge, Ira, 159

Allen, Richard: on American identity of blacks, 106; on blacks' duty to act with sobriety, honesty, and industry, 68; and collective identity for Africans, 31; conversion of, to Christianity, 35–36; and emigration of blacks to Africa, 71; on hard work and sobriety, 67; leadership of generally, 200; and Methodism, 36, 39; Newman's study of, 2; opposition to colonization by, 104, 106; in Philadelphia, 39; and political agenda of black evangelicalism, 43; preaching by, 37, 39; property ownership by, 67; and reform movement, 90; self-purchase of freedom for, 39; and separate black churches, 39–40; on whites' claims of